THEOLOGY IN THE ENGLISH POETS.

THEOLOGY

IN THE

ENGLISH POETS.

COWPER—COLERIDGE—WORDSWORTH,
AND BURNS.

BY THE

REV. STOPFORD A. BROOKE, M. A.,

CHAPLAIN IN ORDINARY TO HER MAJESTY THE QUEEN; MINISTER OF ST. JAMES'S
CHAPEL, YORK STREET, ST. JAMES'S.

NEW YORK:

D. APPLETON AND COMPANY,
549 AND 551 BROADWAY.
1875.

PREFACE.

THE Lectures contained in this Volume were delivered on Sunday afternoons in St. James's Chapel, during the season of 1872. Others, on Blake, Shelley, Keats and Byron, delivered in 1873, will be published, I hope, before the close of this year. The thing was an experiment. I began it in May 1871, when I asked the Rev. J. M. Capes to deliver a course of lectures for me, which should not take the form of sermons, but, on the contrary, should avoid it. He chose as his subject the Inner Life of the Romish Church, and afterwards the Relation of Music to Religion. When he had finished his lectures on these subjects, which were as well attended as they eminently deserved to be, I began another course on Theology in the English Poets, which I have continued to the present time. Since I began to carry out the experiment in 1871, the lectures on week-days in St.

Paul's have been established, and in St. James's Church, Piccadilly, discourses have been preached on a few Sunday afternoons on such subjects as the Drama and the Press, by eminent clergymen.   I believe if a similar effort could be made in many of the London churches in the Sunday afternoons, that much good might be done.   It would give variety to clerical work on Sunday, and much knowledge that now remains only as latent force among the clergy might be made dynamic, if I may borrow a term from science.   If, rectors of large churches would ask clergymen who know any subject of the day well to lecture on its religious aspect in the afternoon, and give them half the offertory, if needful, for their trouble, they would please themselves, enlighten their congregations, and fill their churches.   And they would assist the cause of religion among that large number of persons who do not go to church, and who think that Christianity has nothing to do with Politics, Art, Literature or Science.

When I made this experiment, I had long desired to bring the pulpit on Sunday to bear on subjects other than those commonly called religious, and to rub out the sharp lines drawn by that false distinction of sacred and profane.   If what I believed were true, and God in Christ had sanctified all human life; if every sphere of Man's thought and action was in idea, and ought to be in fact, a channel through which God thought and God acted—then there was no subject which did not in the end run up into Theology, which might not in the end be made religious. I wished then to claim as belonging to the province of the Christian ministry, political, historical, scientific, and artistic work, in their connexion with Theology; and to an extent greater than I had hoped for, the effort, so far as I have carried it, has succeeded. The blame of many accustomed to hear nothing but sermons from the pulpit has been wholly outweighed in my mind by the fact of the attendance of many persons who were before uninterested in religious subjects at all. And then, neither the blame nor the praise of the present is any proof of the goodness or badness of a thing.

The Poets themselves formed the only text book I have used, but in the two first lectures, when treating of the growth of the Poetry of Man and of Nature, I have had much help from an admirable Essay of Mr. F. Palgrave's, which appeared in the " Quarterly Review " of July, 1862.

STOPFORD A. BROOKE.

MANCHESTER SQUARE,
   LONDON, *April*, 1874.

CONTENTS.

———————

THEOLOGY IN
THE ENGLISH POETS.

LECTURE I.

FROM POPE TO COWPER.

THE Lectures which I begin to-day, and which I hope to be able to carry on Sunday after Sunday in the afternoons, are on the Theology which may be found in the English Poets. Spoken from this place, they will not enter into poetical criticism, or attempt to estimate the poet; for that would carry me too far from the main subject, within the limits of which I shall endeavour always to remain. The subject is delightful, and it is not difficult to define its special interest.

The Poets of England ever since Cowper have been more and more theological, till we reach such men as Tennyson or Browning, whose poetry is overcrowded with theology. But the theology of the poets is different from that of Churches and Sects, in this especially, that it is not formulated into propositions, but is the natural growth of their own hearts. They are, by their very nature, strongly individual; they grow more by their own special genius than by the influence of the life of the world around them, and they are, therefore, sure to have a theology—that is, a Doctrine of God in his relation to Man, Nature, and their own soul—which will be independent of conventional religious thought. They will be, as poets, free from those claims of dogma which influence ordinary men from their youth up, and from the religious tendencies of surrounding opinion. Their theology will therefore want the logical order which prevails in confessions and articles: and as each will give expression to it in vivid accordance with his natural character, it will be a different thing in each.

The great interest, then, of looking into this subject lies in the freedom and individuality of the thoughts on a subject in which men are so seldom free or individual. We see theology, as it were, in the rough; as, at its beginnings, it must have grown up in the minds of earnest and imaginative men around certain revealed or intuitive truths, such as the Being of God or the need of redemption.

At the same time I shall confine the inquiry to their poetry. I shall not seek in their letters or in their every-day talk for their theology. For in their ordinary intercourse with men they were subject to the same influences as other men, and if religious, held a distinct creed or conformed to a special sect; and if irreligious, expressed the strongest denial of theological opinions. It is plain that in ordinary life their intellect would work consciously on the subject, and their prejudices come into play. But in their poetry, their imagination worked unconsciously on the subject. Their theology was not produced as a matter of intellectual co-ordination of truths, but as a matter of truths which were true because they were felt; and the fact is, that in this realm of emotion where prejudice dies, the thoughts and feelings of their poetry on the subject of God and Man are often wholly different from those expressed in their everyday life. Cowper's theology in his poetry soars beyond the narrow sect to which he belonged into an infinitely wider universe. Shelley, when the fire of emotion or imagination was burning in him, is very different from the violent denier of God and of Christianity whom we meet in his daily intercourse with men. He does carry his atheism and hatred of religion into his verse, but these are the least unconscious portions of his poetry. When he is floating on his wings, he knows not whither, his atheism becomes pantheism, and his hatred of Christianity is lost in enthusiastic but unconscious statement of Christian conceptions.

Therefore I put aside the letters and conversations of the Poets as sources for these Lectures, except so far as they illustrate the treatment of theological subjects in their poetry.

The theological element in English poetry becomes strong in Cowper; but before lecturing on its development in him, it will be necessary to trace its growth up to his time, along the lines on which English poetry mainly ran. This will be the work of the first two lectures, and in carrying it out I shall lay down the mode in which the main subject will be treated.

The devotional element in our English Poetry which belonged to Donne, Herbert, Vaughan, and some of the Puritan Poets, died away in the critical school which began with Dryden and ended with Pope. The "Religio Laici" of Dryden is partly a reproduction of the scholastic theology, partly an attack on the Deists, and it does not contain one single touch of personal feeling towards God. The "Essay on Man" is the preservation in exquisite steel-work of the speculations of Leibnitz and Bolingbroke. It is true the devoutness which belonged to Pope's nature modified the coldness of his philosophy, and there are lines in the Essay on Man which in their temperate but lofty speech concerning charity, are healthier than the whole of Cowper's Hymns, while the "Universal Prayer" is of that noble tolerance and personal humility which, whether it be called deistical or not, belongs to the best religion all over the world.

It has not been sufficiently said that Pope was sincerely devout in heart, just as it has been ignorantly assumed by many that the century in which he lived was irreligious. His age may seem so in contrast with the two centuries that preceded it, in which religious subjects took so overdue a part, and theological feeling ran into bitter uncharitableness. But it was most useful for the whole future of English religion and theology, that with the newly-awakened interest in science, philosophic inquiry and commerce, religion also should learn to extend its influence over other realms; and, in the re-action from intolerance which a wider intellectual life taught it, learn to do more justice to all opinions, and to teach and practise a wider charity. We have not so learned Christ as to call that irreligious. The work of the Latitudinarian School was distinctly a work of charity, and they and the scholars of the age of evidences are not

to be accused of want of religious feeling, because it seemed
to them that to submit their faith to the challenge of free
inquiry, and to establish a kindly tolerance for the sake of
more united work for God, was better and more needful
for the time than the zeal for doctrine which condemns
one's neighbour, or the passionate expression of devotional
feeling which tends to isolate oneself from one's
neighbour. It is still more absurd to call the century
irreligious, when we remember that in its very midst—
not so much in opposition to this sober religion as in
reaction from its lower tone in the less educated clergymen, and in the indignant desire to make a religion for
the common people who were certainly neglected—the
revived religious life of the personal soul took its rise with
the preaching of Wesley.

With this movement, however, the critical school of Poets
had nothing to do. They had written much before it arose;
they belonged not to the country and the people, but to the
city and the cultivated classes, nor did they, any more than
the theologians, speak much of their religious feeling,
or indeed possess much. But it is a very different thing
to say that they had no devotion, and the change, of which
I shall speak, does not assume that there was no personal
religion, but that there was no predominance of it, and
that therefore it was not expressed. Now and then, to
our surprise it breaks out, and it does so in the "Universal Prayer." Beginning with the ordinary and
systematic view of God as universal Ruler, but graced
with the wider charity of a Poet, it passes in the end into
personal devotion. No one can read the following lines
without hearing in them something of the same melody

which afterwards was varied through every key by
Cowper.

> If I am right, Thy grace impart
>   Still in the right to stay ;
> If I am wrong, oh teach my heart
>   To find that better way.
> Save me alike from foolish Pride,
>   Or impious discontent
> At aught Thy Wisdom has denied,
>   Or aught Thy goodness lent.
> Teach me to feel another's woe,
>   To hide the fault I see ;
> That mercy I to others show,
>   That mercy show to me.
> Mean though I am, not wholly so,
>   Since quickened by Thy Breath ;
> Oh lead me wheresoe'er I go,
>   Through this day's life and death.

Nevertheless, this devoutness is of a wholly different
quality from that which we find in Cowper. It is man
bending before an infinite God whom he cannot understand; it is not man rejoicing in being redeemed and
living with God as a child with its father. It is without deep emotion, without that sense of personal union
or personal absence from God which comes of a vivid
realization of Christ as the master and redeemer of the
soul. It is a religion which the absence of Christ made
cold, and it so little tinges the poetry that one can scarcely
say that the poetry was religious at all.

At the same time we must not imagine with those who
lay down the rule that the Poets always represent their
age, that there was little or no personal feeling of devotion
at this time in England, because its poetry was not
in that way devout. That poetry was of the city, represent-

ing the disputes of the sharp wits who argued on theology as they argued on Whig or Tory politics : but outside the city, where intellectual life was not vivid and discussion scarcely known, there was a world of quaint and homely piety of which we get no inkling in the Poets. Many a grave Puritan household, hidden in its orchards, handed down the tradition of the deep devotion of their forefathers; many a quiet parsonage held in it men who had succeeded to the spirit of Herbert, who ministered to English homes where dwelt, behind the village green and among their clipt yews and grassy plots women who devoted their lives to God, and men who prayed with all the spirit of Wilson.

It was this religious life in the country which in the growth of the religious element in our poetry first took form in verse. But how did it happen that English poetry got face to face with this devouter tone, with this simpler religion? One reason may be that the deistical struggle, having reached its height for a time, began to need some repose before its new outbreak. Both sides had in fact exhausted all they had then to say on the subject, and men, wearied with looking after God through the labyrinth of the intellect, now turned to see if they had any chance of finding Him in their hearts, and in that region naturally passed from an intellectual to an emotional religion which at once sought relief in poetry. Another reason was that a slow change had begun to work in our poetry even before the death of Pope and the change may be described as a migration from the town to the country. Poets began to look at Nature, not as it was around the villa at Twickenham, but as it was in its own solitudes. Thomson took

men to the moors and placed them in the woods;
Gray went to the country churchyard, Collins to the hill-
top in the evening, Goldsmith to the village and its rustic
life. At last we reach Cowper in whose verse the town
is as wholly disliked as the country was by Pope, and
Crabbe in whom the whole interest centres round the
morals and manners and annals of the agricultural
poor.

In this wonderful passage of change, poetry found
religion in the country and took it up into itself. That
devotional element entered our poetry which in one form
rose to its height in Cowper; but which, in different
forms, each created by the individuality of the Poets, has
continued with a few exceptions to influence it to the present day.

Green, in his *Spleen*, 1737, a gay little poem too much
neglected, marks a transitional period in this change. He
retires to the country to seek contentment and quietude,
but the influence of the city lingers round him, and he
takes his trip to town to amuse his life, to purchase books,
and hear the news,—

> To see old friends, brush off the clown,
> And quicken taste at coming down.

He is tired of the theological contests between Nonconformists and the Church, between the opinions of
the enthusiast and those of the cooler inquirer; and he
resolves, in the peace of his retirement, to win his own way
to a religion of his own. It is almost the first touch we
get at this time of that individual work on theological
subjects which we find so strongly developed in the Poets

of our century. He is largely influenced by Pope and
the prevailing Deism, but he works out his own belief, and
makes his own speculations ; and though he is not
Christian, he expresses his belief in a personal relation
between himself and God. It is more personal than
Pope would have made it, it is infinitely less than Cowper
would have made it, and the absence of Christ makes
it of an altogether different quality. But the transitional
element in it makes it interesting enough to quote. After
saying that his verse cannot dare to try and express God,
nor paint His features, " veiled by light," he goes on—

> My soul the vain attempt forego :
> Thyself, the fitter subject, know.
> He wisely shuns the bold extreme,
> Who soon lays by the unequal theme,
> Nor runs, with wisdom's sirens caught,
> On quicksands swallowing shipwrecked thought :
> But, conscious of his distance, gives
> Mute praise, and humble negatives.
> In One, no object of our sight,
> Immutable and infinite,
> Who can't be cruel or unjust,
> Calm and resigned, I fix my trust :
> To him my past and present state
> I owe, and must my future fate.
> A stranger, into life I'm come,
> Dying may be our going home ;
> Transported here by angry fate,
> The convicts of a prior state.
> Hence I no anxious thoughts bestow
> On matters I can never know ;
> Through life's foul way, like vagrant, passed,
> He'll grant a settlement at last,
> And with sweet ease the wearied crown,
> By leave to lay his being down.
>
> *   *   *   *   *   *   *

He for His creatures must decree
More happiness than misery,
Or be supposed to create,
Curious to try, what 'tis to hate :
And do an act which rage infers,
'Cause lameness halts, or blindness errs.

There is more of the speculative audacity of the century in that than there is of piety; there is a fine moral certainty that God, however unknown, must be just and loving, but the point in it on which I dwell is its individuality.   It is not a systematic philosophy of religion like Pope's, it is a personally wrought out religion, and it owed that to his country life.   For in such a life, men, removed from the conventional thought of the literary circles in London, had room for individual development, if they had received some previous culture. This was especially true of religious feeling, and a little before the Essay on Man was written, a true devotional element entered into our poetry in the hymns of Watts, and entered it outside of the town.   Watts lived an easy, retired life, in a great country house, from 1712 to 1748.   There is in his hymns that pleasant devotion to God which arises from piety and comfort, from placid enjoyment of the beauty of the world, from a distant con-templation of the sufferings of the poor beyond the gates of the park, and from the gratitude to God which both these enjoyments are likely to create.   Many of them strike a note of very fine praise, others of a didactic charity; and some are touched with a quaint and simple joy.   Few hymns are better and brighter than that which begins—

> I sing the Almighty Power of God,
> That made the mountains rise ;
> That spread abroad the flowing seas,
> And built the lofty skies.

But still, we have in them no special tendency in doctrine, and no passionate or personal feeling of devotion.

It is the quiet, sober, moral religion of England on which we touch ; but even so, it is a wholly different atmosphere from that which Pope breathed, and I doubt if he could have drawn a single breath in it. It is impossible to fancy Pope " abroad in the meadows to see the young lambs," still less to fancy him linking religious feeling to such a sight. The kind of devotion, and the scenery that stirred it, were both out of his sphere. Half a century passes by and the change has deepened ; the seed Watts sowed has sprung into a mighty tree ; the quiet and sober religion of his hymns has become the impassioned and storm-tossed religion of the hymns of Cowper. The praise which filled the heart of Watts when he looked abroad on Nature has become the agonised prayer of Cowper as he looked into the depths of his own soul.

What was the cause of this change, what new influence from without had come upon English poetry ? It was the great religious movement, led by the Wesleys, joined afterwards by the fiery force of Whitfield, which descended through Newton to the hymns and poetry of Cowper. It was a preaching which, beginning in the year 1739, seven years after the first books of the Essay on Man appeared, woke up, and into fierce extremes, the religious heart of England. The vast crowds which on moor or hillside, in the deserted quarries of Devon and Cornwall, listened

to Wesley, excited by their own numbers, almost maddened
by his passionate preaching and prayer, lifted into Heaven
and shaken over Hell in turns as the sermon went on,
crying aloud, writhing on the ground, tears streaming
down their cheeks, could not find in the hymns of Watts
or the metrical Psalms any expression of their wild experience; and the inexpressible emotion of their hearts
demanded voice for itself in poetry and in music, the
two languages of emotion.   Both the Wesleys, but chiefly
Charles, had already, in 1738, seen and prepared for the
want, and a new class of devotional poetry arose.   It was
impassioned, personal and doctrinal; it was impassioned,
for its subject was the history of the heart in its long
struggle with sin, in its wrestling with God, in the
horror of its absence from Him, in the unspeakable joy of
its presence with Him, in its degradation, its redemption,
and its glory, above all in its personal relation to Christ,
and the world of feelings which arose from that relation;
nor was there a single chord of religious feeling left
unsounded, nor any that was not strung to tension.   It
was also made especially personal.   The first person was
continually used, so that each who sung or read the
hymn spoke of himself and felt Christ in contact with
himself.   And it was doctrinal, for whether it sprang
from the party of Wesley or that of Whitfield, or from
their subdivisions, it was built on clear lines of theological thought; and the opposition between the parties,
who knew well the power of verse as a teacher and fixer
of doctrine, caused the lines to be drawn with studious
clearness.

Three things then belonged to it—passion, the personal

element, and expression of doctrine. Neither of the first two were by their nature apart from poetry, and the fact is that so much are they of the essence of poetry, that most of these hymns are by force of them, poetical. Passion had been long asleep in English poetry, ever since the time of Elizabeth, and though I do not say that this religious movement made the passion of the coming poetry, yet it was one of its elements; and it is quite plain that its emotional element was not out of harmony with a school which in a few years, in Wordsworth, Shelley, Byron, and Keats, was destined to express almost every phase of emotion. Neither was its insistance on personal feeling out of tune with the work of a class of men like the Poets who "in themselves possess their own desire." In fact both these elements are characteristic of the poetry which was now about to arise in England. They both took root in Cowper, but they were sown and watered by religion: He struck the first note of the passionate poetry, but the passion in him was in connexion with religion. He struck the first note of that personal poetry which was afterwards carried so far in the Prelude of Wordsworth, the Alastor of Shelley, the Childe Harold of Byron, but he struck it in connexion with religion. Other poets led their passions and their personal history into other realms, but Cowper kept them within the sphere of his relation to God. Other poets derived their passion from different sources—from Nature, from Beauty, from the ideas of political rights and freedom, but Cowper derived it from the daily wrestling of his soul with God. And both the passionate and the personal element came down to Cowper from without, from the great

Methodist movement. For the friend of Cowper was Newton, and Newton was the child of Whitfield.

Both these elements run through the whole of Newton's well-known book, the " Cardiphonia," and (expanded over the whole range of the relations of the soul to Christ) constitute what was then called experimental religion. As such they appear in the "Olney Hymns," written jointly by Newton and Cowper. Of Newton's share in them, with the exception of the beautiful hymn—" How sweet the name of Jesus sounds," I know nothing ; but if they are anything like the " Cardiphonia," they must be characterized by a robust and insensitive piety, and an ardent display, somewhat too public, both of his own sinfulness and of his love of Christ. Those which are written by Cowper are passionate indeed, but it is passion modified by the Poet's tender and reserved individuality ; are personal indeed, but it is egotism decently veiled, and where it is outspoken it is so sudden, so spontaneous— the hymn seeming to burst out of his heart with a cry— that it is redeemed from the charge of deliberate exposure of the sanctuary of the soul. Nothing can be finer, for example, than the swift rush, as if feeling could no longer be repressed, with which this hymn begins—

> Hark ! my soul, it is the Lord;
> 'Tis thy Saviour, hear His word ;
> Jesus speaks, and speaks to thee,
> Say, poor sinner, lovest thou me

The same elements in connexion with religion run through the whole of his poetry, and they deepen into tragedy at the last. But on that I will not touch at present. I only ask you now (for I am but sketching the growth of the religious element in our Poetry, not as yet distinctly touching on Cowper) to think of the new world into which we have entered. Compare the " Universal Prayer "—

> Father of all, in every age,
> In every clime adored,
> By saint, by savage, or by sage,
> Jehovah, Jove or Lord.

with " O, for a closer walk with God," or with " There is a fountain fill'd with blood," and it is not that they are different, it is that owing to the overmastering presence of Christ, as the Saviour of the personal soul, there is scarcely any point of comparison. Compare the two following quotations, the first from the " Essay on Man," the second from the "Task,"—the lines of Pope, impersonal, apart, touched with scorn, thinking of God as Creator alone, with the lines of Cowper, so personal, so self-compassionate, so intense in their realization of Christ, that though no devotion is expressed, they yet thrill with devotion. We step from the one to the other as from a frozen to a tropic isle of religion.

> Placed on this isthmus of a middle state,
> A Being darkly wise, and rudely great :
> With too much knowledge for the sceptic side,
> With too much weakness for the Stoic's pride,
> He hangs between ; in doubt to act, or rest ;
> In doubt to deem himself a God, or beast ;
> In doubt his mind or body to prefer ;
> Born but to die, and reas'ning but to err ;
> Alike in ignorance, his reason such,
> Whether he thinks too little or too much :
> Chaos of Thought and Passion, all confused ;
> Still by himself abused, or disabused ;

2

> Created half to rise, and half to fall ;
> Great lord of all things, yet a prey to all :
> Sole judge of truth, in endless error hurl'd ;
> The glory, jest, and riddle of the world.

There is no passion and there is no personal feeling. Now listen to this in which both these elements are intense :—

> I was a stricken deer that left the herd
> Long since—with many an arrow deep infixed
> My panting side was charged, when I withdrew
> To seek a tranquil death in distant shades.
> There was I found by one, who had Himself
> Been hurt by the archers.   In His side He bore
> And in His hands and feet, the cruel scars.
> With gentle force soliciting the darts
> He drew them forth and healed, and bade me live.

The other element which came from the Methodist movement to Cowper was the doctrinal, and coming to him early in life it was afterwards beaten into his heart by Newton. It took with him the special form of Calvinism, and we shall see what a terrible power it had over him.   But at present, we ask what there could be in Calvinism, whether derived from Whitfield or from the Puritans, which could find a home in Poetry?   Its mere doctrinal scheme, set out with logical severity, its debtor and creditor account, its hard outlines supplied little food to the imagination.   But there was one doctrine among others which did supply food, and that of a terrible kind, to the imagination.   It was the doctrine that God had created some men for destruction, that they were born into the world the victims of a stupendous fate. They might struggle, they might desire to love God, they might cry passionately for redemption, but there was no hope. Over them always hung the thunder-cloud and out of it sooner or later, would issue the lightning of their eternal doom. This mastery of some by a divine and unpitying fate, and their long struggle against it is distinctly poetic; and wherever it has taken form and in whatever manner, it has created poetry. The same sort of idea, only in a less revolting form, was at the root of Greek Tragedy, which represented the freedom of Man struggling with destiny, but preserving or attaining to moral force through the struggle. And the tragic element was deepened when, in spite of the moral victory, the victor yet received the blow of Fate. Something of the same element we find in the dramas of Shakespeare, as, for example, Romeo and Juliet, where from the very beginning of the play, we feel that all the passionate force of young love is doomed to be broken by the iron hand of irresistible circumstance. But the religious form it took in Calvinism did not enter our poetry as a personal element till the time of Cowper and Burns. It has deeply influenced it ever since. And the manner in which it worked was twofold. One was when the poet accepted it and gave tragic importance to his life by it, either by yielding to it in heartbroken humility, as Cowper; or by yielding to it in pride, since it marked him from mankind, as Byron did. And in both these men the emotions it roused were creative of poetry.

The other mode in which it bore upon the poetic power in men was in the hot hatred, the fierce emotion of anger which it stirred in hearts full of love to men, either in those who like Burns, disbelieved in it as having any-thing to do with Christianity, or in those who like

Shelley, believed that it was Christianity and poured out all the passion of their heart against it. Introduced by Cowper as a personal question into our later poetry, no one can doubt the influence it has had ; in fact, its introduction into it has led to the whole question of the relation of the soul to God becoming a distinct element in English poetry up to the present day.

Again I ask you, on this doctrinal side of the question, to look back to the critical school and to compare its theological poetry with that of Cowper. In the fourth act of Dryden's " State of Innocence," Gabriel and Raphael and Adam discuss all the arguments which can be urged on the subject of Fate and Freewill with the greatest precision and clearness. But the matter is treated wholly from the outside, as an abstract question which interested the Poet intellectually. To Cowper the question was one which tortured his heart ; it was a personal matter on which hung his whole life ; and it made all the difference to him between reason or madness. In this matter also the whole poetic atmosphere is changed, we are again in a different world.

I have now traced, and in brief outline only, the growth of the devotional element in our poetry from Dryden to Cowper. With it statements about the theological element have necessarily been mingled, but in accordance with the plan of my lectures, and indeed in accordance with the actual facts, I have spoken of the theological element as it appeared when modified by the distinct personality of the Poet. That is one of the lines on which these lectures are to run; the theology of each Poet as created by his special individuality.

There were two other lines of thought on which I resolved to place these lectures; the theology imported by each poet into the poetry of Man, and the poetry of Nature. For a poetry which had to do with all the questions which belong to man as a whole, and to the growth, origin, and destiny of the individual man:—and a poetry which had to do especially and separately with Nature, with the whole of the outward world and all its parts, with the emotions it stirred and the thoughts that we gave to it, took clear form for the first time towards the close of the eighteenth century, and has never ceased to grow and to add branch to branch, up to the present time. It may be truly said to date from the publication of the "Task" of Cowper in 1785, of the Village of Crabbe in 1783, of the first Poems of Burns in 1786. But nothing is born all in a moment in this world, and the poetry which dealt specially with Man, as well as that which dealt specially with Nature, though they first became clearly defined in Cowper had been slowly growing into form before him. The different stages of the growth of each I must be permitted to sketch with as much conciseness as possible. I will do that for the poetry of Man to-day, in the rest of this Lecture. In the following I shall do the same work for the poetry of Nature, and then take up the Poets themselves, and show how in each the poetry of Man, the poetry of Nature, as well as their personal poetry, became tinged by theology. In each Poet then we shall trace the theology in his human, natural, and personal poetry.

Our object now is to trace the growth of the poetry of Man up to the time of Cowper, when theology distinctly entered into it.

In Dryden, Pope, Swift, Prior, Roscommon and the rest, we find the searching and critical spirit of the eighteenth century looking on man as an intellectual and social being, and their poetry reflects with clearness the leading thoughts about Man of that masculine and vigorous time.   They seek from the intellectual point of view for an explanation of the problems which beset us ; they go on to ask how such circumstances as riches and poverty, the follies of society and its oddities of taste, bear upon his life ; they describe the variety of characters in men and women.   Even the new scientific discoveries of the time, its credulity and scepticism are touched on in this poetry, and an attempt is made in the " Essay on Man " to reduce to a system the dim questionings with regard to the spiritual nature which science and scepticism had awakened.

Pope said that the proper study of mankind was Man. But he approached that study from the side of the intellect alone.   It was by the criticism of the understanding, not by the emotion of the heart that he worked on his subject. The result was cold speculation and brilliant satire, and in neither of those tempers is any one fit to write fairly or nobly about the whole of Human Nature; though he is fitted to write about that which Man does, or Man has, up to a certain point.   The surface of the " study of mankind " is touched it may be in all its points, but the writer does not penetrate into its depths.   It is just the difference between Ben Jonson and Shake-

speare : the one not seriously caring for his characters,
but only how he may develope them; the other
loving, pitying, being personally indignant with his
characters : so that in the one we study not men but the
humours of men ; in the other we study men, nay mankind. The one creates images of men and dresses them
and makes them play their part by strings upon his stage :
the other creates living men, and bids them act, and sits
by watching them with passion. There is the same kind
of difference between Pope's study of man and that study
of him to which Wordsworth, Shelley, and Byron have
accustomed us.

Again we find no large study of mankind as a whole in
Pope. It is classes of men whom we meet, not the conception of the race. The idea of the Universal Man, of
one common mankind, rising above all distinctions of
clan, caste, race, and nation, did not exist in Pope's time ;
we owe it to the Revolution. There were dreams of it,
suggestions, hints, but of the clear, concise, world-sub-
duing conception there is little or no trace; no real poetry
of Man in the true sense of the word existed. Whereas,
since Wordsworth's time, it breathes in every English
Poem. In both the particular and universal view the
change is immense.

The same kind of study of Man lasted during Pope's
life and after his death in 1744. It lives in Johnson's London, 1738, and in his Vanity of Human Wishes,
1749, as observant and indignant satire ; it lives in that
Poem of Akenside's which continued the speculations of
Hutcheson and Shaftesbury. It was the spirit of Pope
enduring after Pope was gone, and even less than Pope

did Akenside bestow human emotion on his speculations. But even before the death of Pope a change had begun. Pope's study of man did not carry him beyond the city; he has no interest in the rustic, in the uneducated, in the relation of man to Nature apart from society, in the past history of man, even of Englishmen. But, in 1726, Thomson makes us touch the farmhouse and the labourer, the traveller lost in the snow, the far-off lives of men of other nations where Winter rules over half the year. We have got out of England, as we have in Dyer's Ruins of Rome in 1740. In Warton's Poems, though his own personality over-shadows everything, we again find ourselves among country people, the milkmaid singing and the woodman at his work. In the exquisitely pencilled " Elegy " of Gray we are brought face to face with the ploughman, the rude forefathers of the hamlet, the village Hampden, the solitary who, far from cities and society—

> Along the cool sequestered vale of life
> Has kept the noiseless tenor of his way.

Again, the speculative study of Man, his origin, duties, and destiny, from the point of view of the inquiring intellect, has now passed away, and there is a tender, but some-what sentimental treatment of Man, as the subject of the musing moralist, as the victim of the passions and changes and ills of life, and as listening to the soothing or warning voice with which Nature speaks to him in his enjoyment or his pain.

There is also a distinct delight shown in the history of Man in the Past, a thing almost impossible to the previous school in which the Present was so powerful that it filled all the view. Both the " Bard " and the "Progress of Poesy," illustrate this new element. The poetry of the two Wartons, about the same date, continually goes over the past glories of the English nation, and Thomas Warton's History of English Poetry was but the beginning of that vivid delight in what our fore-fathers did, to which Chatterton afterwards gave a fresher life, and which runs through all the minor Poets of the time. This new interest in the men of the past—though it is necessary to observe that it did not travel beyond the men of our country, so as to become an interest in mankind—was afterwards stimulated by the influence of the elder Pitt, whose whole life and work exalted England in her own eyes.

The interest in Man was defective then in that it did not embrace mankind. It had also lost, in losing Pope's interest in social life, and in the intellectual and speculative side of human questions, and in its transference from the town to the country, elements which were afterwards to be revived. But though it lost something for the time, it gained new elements, and in a few years after the death of Pope we have seen that we are in a new poetic world upon the subject. Still the interest even in Man in the country, in a simpler, kinder, more rugged, human life, was not the living, close, direct thing it afterwards became. It is the distant, rather dainty interest nursed by college life, which scholars, like Warton, or like Gray looking out on the world from the window of Peterhouse, would be likely to take—a quiet contemplative interest such as he describes in lines, which, written in 1742, embody the spirit in which he looked on Man,—

Where'er the oak's thick branches stretch
  A broader, browner shade,
Where'er the rude and moss-grown beech
  O'ercanopies the glade,
Beside some water's rushy brink
With me the Muse shall sit and think
  (At ease reclined in rustic state)
How vain the ardour of the Crowd,
How low, how little are the Proud,
  How indigent the Great !
Still is the toiling hand of Care :
  The panting herds repose ;
Yet hark ! how through the peopled air
  The busy murmur glows !
The insect youth are on the wing,
Eager to taste the honied spring
  And float amid the liquid noon ;
Some lightly o'er the current skim,
Some show their gaily-gilded trim
  Quick-glancing to the sun.
To Contemplation's sober eye
  Such is the race of Man :
And they that creep, and they that fly
  Shall end where they began.
Alike the Busy and the Gay
But flutter through Life's little day,
  In Fortune's varying colours drest :
Brushed by the hand of rough Mischance,
Or chilled by Age, their airy dance
  They leave, in dust to rest.

Changed as that is from the spirit of Pope, it is a still greater change to turn from its spirit to the stern severity of Crabbe's painting of the human life of the country in the " Parish Register."

If we pass on from Gray a little further to Goldsmith's " Traveller " in 1764 and to his " Village " in 1770, we find that the village life is more homely, more truly sketched, but that its ruder realities are hidden. It is the same sort of interest which Gainsborough took in his rustic children and his cottages, the interest of the artist more than of the man. But in the " Traveller " a new element is added to the poetry of Man—interest in other peoples than the English people ; the horizon of mankind has widened, and this enlargement of our poetic interest in Man beyond the bounds of England which began in Goldsmith, rapidly developed in Cowper, and in the next age grew so intense in Wordsworth that in order to save a great idea necessary as he thought for the progress of the race, he wished in lines which thrill with excitement, that the fleets and armies of England might be beaten by the foreigner. It is perhaps needless to say here that one of the causes of this wider sympathy with man was the growth of prosperity and wealth under the peaceful administration of Walpole. Men had money to travel, and peace and new openings for commerce made it easier to see the world.

In the meantime, the interest in the poor deepened. Adam Smith, 1776, and afterwards others, set on foot a series of inquiries which forced men to look sharply into the relations of capital to labour, of landowners to tenants, of the poor to the rich ; and these, combining with the sentiment which had been growing up for country life and its indwellers, entered as a power into men's hearts, and naturally struck with emotional force upon the Poets; and a few minor poems of the day served as heralds to the intimate treatment of the life of the poor by Crabbe and Cowper. Along with these, as a continuous subject, and indeed always a poetic subject in England, were poems that touched on or glorified Liberty. The change of which

I speak enters into them in the way they altered from
vague declamations about English liberty to deliberate
attacks, for the sake of human liberty, on slavery and
oppression—either imposed by England on subject races,
or by nations beyond our doors on their own subjects.
We shall find this element in the change fully set forth by
Cowper.

We have now arrived at Cowper.   After 1770, a
pause in poetic production took place, and not till more
than twenty years afterwards did the new school spring
to light along with the dawn of freedom.   The interval
is filled with Cowper and Crabbe and Burns.   Burns,
who stands somewhat apart from the influences of the
day, belongs to so different a poetic descent from that
of the English Poets that I shall leave him aside for
separate consideration ; but on Cowper and Crabbe the
influences which led men to investigate the wrongs and
pains of the poor, to extend their human sympathies, to
be indignant with oppression, to see the Man in every
one, however miserable like the cottager, however degraded
like the slave—fell with immense force, and became
creative of a new poetry of Man.   The poetry of Man in
relation to intellect and fine society, the poetry of satire
and speculation, the sentimental poetry of Man, the
light and graceful treatment of the subject of the pastoral
man by Goldsmith—all have vanished ; and in Crabbe,
in his Village, 1783, and in the Parish Register, 1807, we
are brought face to face with the sternest portraiture
of the crimes, the miseries, the starvation of the
labourer.   We see the same passions moving him as
moved the fine gentlemen of Pope, and the scholars

who exchanged letters with Gray, and the wits who met Goldsmith at Johnson's club; only the passions are coarser and the sorrows uglier. We find in his tales, not only the darker but the nobler side of this humble life, its sacrifices, its struggles, its purity in temptation; and the effect of it all in deepening and widening human sympathy cannot be overestimated. We are shown the cottages of the poor, the life of the ploughman, the bargeman, and the fisher; they are sketched, filled in with an unrelenting hand. We are led into the dreadful prisons which disgraced that time, but which Howard had bettered already. We are brought over the wretched hospitals, and find ourselves in the poorhouse, where the neglected, the vain, and the extravagant were rudely housed till death. Nothing is omitted, and as we turn back fifty years, and read the Essay on Man, we rub our eyes and ask, In what new world are we?

This is the history of the change in the Poetry of Man from 1730 to 1790; and its literary and historical interest is considerable. Enough has been said, for our purpose, about this human element in Crabbe. It needs but a slight touch, for it was not tinged in him by any special religious colour. His theology was not individual but conventional, though it was profoundly felt. But when the new poetry of Man was directly connected with the individual emotions of a religious mind like Cowper's on the subjects of theology—and doctrinal as he was, his heart ran continually beyond doctrine—it becomes of special interest to us, and of still more special interest when we find that his religion was one of the causes of its much wider development. When therefore I have sketched in my next lecture the growth of the poetry of Nature to the same point as I have brought to-day the poetry of Man, I shall begin the lectures on the separate Poets with Cowper.

LECTURE II.

THE Poetry of Nature which I have already defined, and which is a distinct thing in our poetry after 1790, did not come into being without previous warning, and the object of this lecture is to sketch its growth from the time of Pope to the time of Wordsworth. In the previous lecture I sketched the growth of the poetry of Man, and of the doctrinal and theological elements in our poetry, and sketched them separately for the sake of greater clearness; but in this lecture I shall throw the theological and poetical subjects together, and while I trace the growth of the poetry of Nature, trace along with it, step by step, the theology that accompanied it, or the elements in it which resisted the presence of a theology.

The poetry which speaks directly of Nature for its own sake is not to be found in England till the time of Cowper when it distinctly began, is not developed till Wordsworth when it rapidly reached its full growth. Chaucer's landscape is for the most part conventional, though what there is of it is touched with the dewy brightness and affection of the Poet. But he saw but little, and nothing solely for its own sake. The Elizabethan Poets introduce bits of landscape, but these are chiefly as

a background for the setting off of their own feelings or
for the display of their characters ; and though the natural
poetry of Shakespeare has his quality of perfectness, it
has little personal love of Nature.   It is not till we get to
Milton, to the "Allegro" and "Penseroso," that we find
any pure natural description, any deliberate choice of
natural beauty as a thing to be studied for its own sake.
When we arrive at the Critical School, Nature is wholly
put out of the field.   It is looked at, when it is at all
touched, from the windows of the suburbs ; the country
is despised and life in it considered inconceivably dull.
Pope condoles with those who are driven from the city,
who dream in the rural shade of triumphs in the town
and wake to find the vision fled, left in "lone woods
or empty walls."   The descriptions in his pastorals have
no resemblance to Nature, and when he steps aside to
praise natural beauty, it is when it has been subjected to
the critical hand of Art.   It was characteristic of the
time that Nature had to undergo the same sort of polish
as verse.   Wild Nature was as bad as wild poetry, and
the art of the landscape gardener must be employed to
check her extravagance and lessen her horrors.   We will
try Pope, however, when he describes a piece of pure landscape that he had seen,—Windsor Forest, in the pastorals :—

> There, interspers'd in lawns and op'ning glades
> Thin trees arise that shun each other's shades.
> Here in full light the russet plains extend :
> There wrapt in clouds the bluish hills ascend.
> Ev'n the wild heath displays her purple dyes,
> And midst the desert fruitful hills arise,
> That crowned with tufted trees and springing corn,
> Like verdant isles the sable waste adorn.

That is concoction, not composition; it is full of stock phrases, and it is plain that Pope made it up in his study with no recollected pleasure of the scene, with even a recollected distress at the distance he was then from town, which expresses itself in such absurd terms as the desert and the sable waste. Indeed, one can scarcely imagine the physical discomfort, the confusion of mind, the boredom which Pope, and Belinda and her court would have suffered if they had been placed side by side with Wordsworth,—

> when from the naked top
> Of some bold headland, he beheld the sun
> Rise up and bathe the world in light !

or asked, with Byron—

> Where mortal foot hath ne'er or rarely been,
> To climb the trackless mountain all unseen,
> With the wild flock that never seek a fold.
> Alone o'er steeps and foaming falls to lean.

But if we can imagine it for a moment, we have some idea of the change in the temper of society with regard to Nature, some cause for wonder at the new world into which, since the days when Pope wrote, we have been brought by the Poets.

The Nature then of which Pope thought was a wholly different thing from that which we conceive; and the theology which he connected with it was just as different. The Nature of which Wordsworth conceived, the living things of earth, and air, and water, that spoke to him like friends and moved by their " own sweet will," was separate from Man, and God spoke through it to Man. In Pope's idea it was mingled up as a part of the system of the universe

with Man, and both had the same kind of life from the
immanent presence of God.   In fact, the Nature of which
Pope spoke was nothing more than that order of the
universe which the recent scientific activity had begun to
impress on cultivated men; and in that order, and not
in the disorder of revealed Religions with their super-
natural interferences, God, the Great Unknown, so far as
Man could presume to scan Him, was most clearly to be
seen.   Here is his view in well-known lines, which seem
but are not Pantheistic, for Pope, as in the line, " The
workman from his work distinct was known," takes care
always to separate the first cause from the things caused.

> All are but parts of one stupendous whole,
> Whose body Nature is, and God the soul ;
> That changed through all, and yet in all the same ;
> Great in the earth, as in th' ethereal frame ;
> Warms in the sun, refreshes in the breeze,
> Glows in the stars, and blossoms in the trees,
> Lives through all life, extends through all extent,
> Spreads undivided, operates unspent :
> Breathes in our soul, informs our mortal part ;
> As full, as perfect, in a hair as heart ;
> As full, as perfect in vile man that mourns
> As the rapt seraph, that adores and burns :
> To him no high, no low, no great, no small—
> He fills, he bounds, connects and equals all.

That is not the Nature we love or we know; we give a
wholly different meaning to the term ; and we approach
Nature in a different way.   Pope, looking on it as a great
system, considered it from his study with all the means
of the observing and inquiring intellect, and never
thought of its beauty as a source of pleasure.   We look
on it as the storehouse of some of our deepest pleasures ;

we consider it with a love which may be called passionate, and we study it by all the means with which emotion furnishes us. Owing to this—and especially to its being seen as separate from us—we are forced, when we come to think of God in connection with it, to have a theology of Nature wholly distinct from this of Pope's, and we shall see how in Wordsworth the whole of the Natural Theology of the eighteenth century disappears. It is this change we shall trace to-day.

It was during the life-time of Pope that the change began; it was when the English heart had been almost exiled from the woods and hills, that the door into the Paradise in which we have wandered with Coleridge, Wordsworth, Shelley, and Keats, and a hundred other lovers of the wild world of earth and air and sea, was opened for our entrance. In 1726, nearly twenty years before the death of Pope, James Thomson published his "Winter," and in 1730, the whole of the "Seasons" was given to the world. The greater part of it must have been, so far as its feeling went, incomprehensible to Pope. That "recollected love," which Thomson said he embodied in his descriptions of Nature, could never have been felt by a single one of the followers of the Critical School.

It is true that the taint of the artificial spirit lingered in his poetry, but for all that it was a new world to the English people. The woods, the rivers, the moors, the cornfields, the mountain floods, the summer skies, the tempests, all the broad aspects of Nature were seen and detailed with some real care and affection. One sees that he is often painting directly from the scene; that sometimes his monotonous, and turgid style is forgotten that

the beauty and peace of the outward world bring him so
much emotion that his verse becomes spontaneous and
tender.   But for the most part he wants the simplicity of
description which passionate love of Nature produces, and,
above all, the sweetness and pathetic truth that comes of
self-consciousness being lost in the life of Nature.   We
stand only on the threshold of the new world when we
read Thomson.   He has none of that solitary emotion for
Nature herself which complains and creates and trembles
with its own excitement in Shelley; none of that intense
quiet of enjoyment which broods like sunlight over
Wordsworth's soul when he steps into a nook in the
woods, and treads lightly lest he should disturb its living
spirit.

For there is as much difference between the feeling of
Thomson about Nature and the conventional coldness of
his descriptions, and the feeling of a poet like Shelley,
as there was between Thomson and Pope.   It is worth
while to compare them at the same work.   Here is
Thomson treating an autumn noon,—

> For now the day
> O'er heaven and earth diffused, grows warm and high,
> Infinite splendour ! wide investing all.
> How still the breeze ! save what the filmy threads
> Of dew evaporate brushes from the plain.
> How clear the cloudless sky, how deeply tinged
> With a peculiar blue !   The ethereal arch
> How swelled immense, amid whose azure throned
> The radiant sun how gay—how calm below
> The gilded earth !

Contrast the note of that—how heavy, elaborate and yet
how true in parts, how unemotional—with this, and think
how wonderful the change,—

Noon descends around me now :
'Tis the noon of Autumn's glow,
When a soft and purple mist
Like a vaporous amethyst,
Or an air-dissolvéd star
Mingling light and fragrance, far
From the curved horizon's bound
To the point of heaven's profound,
Fills the overflowing sky :
And the plains that silent lie
Underneath : the leaves unsodden
Where the infant Frost has trodden
With his morning-wingéd feet
Whose bright print is gleaming yet ;
And the red and golden vines
Piercing with their trellised lines
The rough, dark-skirted wilderness ;
The dun and bladed grass no less
Pointing from this hoary tower
In the windless air ; the flower
Glimmering at my feet ; the line
Of the olive-sandalled Apennine
In the south dimly islanded ;
And the Alps, whose snows are spread
High between the clouds and sun ;
And of living things each one ;
And my spirit, which so long
Darkened this swift stream of song,—
Interpenetrated lie
By the glory of the sky ;
Be it love, light, harmony,
Odour, or the soul of all
Which from heaven like dew doth fall,
Or the mind which feeds this verse
Peopling the lone universe.

It is not a development of the former, it is a different thing altogether. In Thomson, the poet stands apart and apostrophises Nature ; in Shelley, the poet is absorbed into Nature, and his voice is the voice of Nature herself. Whatever theology Shelley had about Nature would naturally, owing to this interpenetration of himself and her, become Pantheistic; or would be content, since delight was so great, not to know and not to care whether it were love from without, or his own mind from within, that made or peopled the universe ; but Thomson's theology of Nature, because he was not interpenetrated by her, would recognize a separate First Cause. His nearness to Pope would also lead him to share in the systematic view of the universe, but this would be deeply modified in him by his close study of natural beauty. He sees the world no longer only as a great order under a great Governor. He sees it as full of varied landscapes of infinite beauty, and each of these as the work of God—as revelations of His character. He hovers round, though he does not clearly touch, the thought of Nature as a living personal image of God. He has begun that separation of Nature from Man which led afterwards to the half pantheistic theology of Nature that Wordsworth worked out, to the wholly pantheistic theology of Shelley.

The impulse given by Thomson to the study of Nature went on increasing. That migration of the poets from the town to the country, of which I spoke, began : men visited the more accessible parts of England and recorded their impressions ; Dyer's " Grongar Hill " is the record of a landscape in South Wales; his " Fleece," and Somerville's "Chase," are both descriptive poems, but they are too slight to contain any theology of Nature. Foreign travel next enlarged the sphere of love of Nature. Everyone knows the letters of Gray, and remembers the lucid simplicity and directness, mingled with the fastidious sentiment of a scholar, of his description of such scenes as the Chartreuse. That is a well-known description, but those in his journal of a "Tour in the North" have been neglected, and they are especially interesting since they go over much of the country in which Wordsworth dwelt, and of which he wrote. They are also the first conscious effort—and in this he is a worthy forerunner of Wordsworth—to describe natural scenery with the writer's eye upon the scene described, and to describe it in simple and direct phrase, in distinction to the fine writing that was then practised. And Gray did this intentionally in the light prose journal he kept, and threw by for a time the refined carefulness and the insistance on human emotion which he thought necessary in poetic description of Nature. In his prose then, though not in his poetry, we have Nature loved for her own sake.*

* I insert here two of these descriptions ; they may perhaps induce some to read Gray's letters, and few letters in the English language are so good :—" I walked out under the conduct of my landlord to Borrodale. The grass was covered with a hoar frost, which soon melted and exhaled in a thin bluish smoke. Crossed the meadows obliquely, catching a diversity of views among the hills over the lake and islands, and changing prospect at every ten paces ; left Cockshut and Castlehill (which we formerly mounted) behind me, and drew near the foot of Wallacrag, whose bare and rocky brow cut perpendicularly down above 400 feet, as I guess, awfully overlooks the way ; our path here tends to the left, and the ground gently rising, and covered with a glade of scattering trees and bushes on the very margin of the water, opens both ways the most delicious view that my eyes ever beheld. Behind you are the magnificent heights of Walla-crag ; opposite lie the thick hanging woods of Lord Egremont, and Newland valley, with green and smiling fields embosomed in the dark cliffs ; to the left, the jaws of Borrodale, with that turbulent chaos of mountain behind mountain, rolled in confusion ; beneath you, and stretching far away to the right, the shining purity of the lake, just ruffled by the breeze enough to show it is alive, reflecting woods, rocks, fields, and inverted tops of mountains, with the

It was different, as I say, in his poetry. The exquisite choice and studious simplicity of the natural description in such poems as the " Elegy," and the " Ode to Eton College" is the result of Art, more than of the pure imagination; and Gray weighed every word, especially every adjective, till he reached what I suppose to be his ideal—that every line was to suggest a sentiment and a landscape.   We feel, then, too much the art and too little the emotion in his work; but then work like this introduced an ideal of style and expression into our poetical language about Nature—a demand for perfection—which it has never since lost, but which it never,

white buildings of Keswick, Crosthwaite Church, and Skiddaw for a back-ground at a distance."

" Mr. Gray to Dr. Wharton.

"Past by the little chapel of Wiborn, out of which the Sunday congregation were then issuing.   Past a beck near Dunmailrouse, and entered Westmoreland a second time, now begin to see Helm-crag, distinguished from its rugged neighbours, not so much by its height, as by the strange, broken outline of its top, like some gigantic building demolished, and the stones that composed it flung across each other in wild confusion.   Just beyond it opens one of the sweetest landscapes that art ever attempted to imitate.   The bosom of the mountains spreading here into a broad bason, discovers in the midst Grassmere-Water; its margin is hollowed into small bays with bold eminences, some of them rocks, some of soft turf, that half conceal and vary the figure of the little lake they command.   From the shore a low promontory pushes itself far into the water, and on it stands a white village with the parish church rising in the midst of it; hanging enclosures, corn-fields, and meadows green as an emerald, with their trees, hedges, and cattle, fill up the whole space from the edge of the water.   Just opposite to you is a large farm-house at the bottom of a steep, smooth lawn, embosomed in old woods, which climb half-way up the mountain side, and discover above them a broken line of crags, that crown the scene.   Not a single red-tile, no flaring gentleman's house or garden walls, break in upon the repose of this little unsuspected paradise; but all is peace, rusticity, and happy poverty in its neatest and most becoming attire."

except in Milton, possessed before. After lines like these, for example, in which every word tells,—

> There pipes the woodlark, and the songthrush there
> Scatters his loose notes in the waste of air,

it was quite impossible to go back wilfully to the careless profusion of epithets, and the hazarded meanings of the Elizabethan writers. Gray established a standard of careful accuracy in natural description which has never left our poetry, and in the great writers of our century nothing is more delightful than the mingling of imagination and emotion with a close and minute truthfulness in their work on Nature.

We find the same exquisite choice and care in Collins. His " Ode to Evening " is as finished and concise in description as it is finished and subtle in sentiment. The key of feeling in which it is written is not for one moment transposed. The landscape and the emotion of the Poet interpenetrate one another, so that a pleasure made up of both blended into one impression is given to the reader. Evening, "maid composed," is to teach him some softened strain,—

> Whose numbers, stealing through thy darkening vale
> May not unseemly with its stillness suit.

Every epithet is chosen and weighed by an art which, first submitting itself to the work of observation, and then letting emotion work on the materials, at last creates such a distant landscape as this,—

> Or if chill, blustering winds or driving rain
> Prevent my willing feet, be mine the hut
>   That from the mountain's side,
>   Views wilds and swelling floods,

3

And hamlets brown, and dim-discovered spires;
And hears their simple bell ; and marks o'er all
        Thy dewy fingers draw
        The gradual dusky veil.

But in neither Gray nor Collins is Nature, I do not say
first, but on an equality with Man, in interest. Nothing
is distinctly written for her and her alone. On the contrary, Man is always the centre, the landscape clusters
round him ; it is used as a means of pleasure for him, or
as echoing his feelings, or as an illustration of moral
lessons useful to him. It is never the first thing in the
poetry. And Gray put it himself in this position. For,
in writing to Beattie about the Minstrel, he says, "As
to description, I have always thought that it made the
most graceful ornament of poetry, but never ought to
make the subject." I need scarcely say how different it
is in the poetry of Wordsworth, in which man and his
emotions are frequently left out altogether. And yet it is
worth saying, for it was this predominance of man in the
poetry of which we speak, that prevented in it any distinct theology of Nature. We know that both Gray and
Collins were religious men, but there is not a trace in
their poetry of any religious feeling connected with
Nature.

The next step in this poetry of Nature is a curious
one. Both Gray and Collins in the midst of natural
scenery speak of Man, and not of themselves. But the
Wartons and Logan, and others of that time, when they
retire to the woods or hills, speak of themselves alone.
They see only their own feelings in Nature, and use her
as the mirror to reflect their melancholy and morbid

moods. They are without any joy or gratitude for her brightness and life. Seeking only sympathy for their spleen, they prefer darksome shades, and gloomy valleys, and autumn in its decay, and, above all, night. Nor can they bear company; they fly from the face of man to the solitudes of Nature, and find there not misery, as Pope would have found, or rapture, as Wordsworth would have found, but a sentimental and faded pleasure.

" Oh tell," cries Warton,—

> How rapturous the joy, to melt
> To melody's assuasive voice; to bend
> The uncertain step along the midnight mead
> And pour your sorrows to the pitying moon ;
> By many a slow trill from the bird of woe
> Oft interrupted ; in embowering woods,
> By darksome brook to muse, and there forget
> The solemn dulness of the tedious world.

How remote from Pope ! but in the following description of the delights of the woodman's life, note the genuine enthusiasm for beauty and the fresher feeling which, with all their sentiment, these poets did not want.

> When morning's twilight-tinctured beam
> Strikes their low thatch with slanting gleam,
> They rove abroad in ether blue
> To dip the scythe in fragrant dew ;
> The sheaf to bind, the beech to fell
> That nodding shades a craggy dell.
> Midst gloomy glades in warbles clear
> Wild Nature's sweetest notes they hear ;
> Or green untrodden banks they view
> The hyacinth's neglected hue ;
> Each native charm their steps explore
> Of Solitude's sequestered store.

We find then the Poets bringing to Nature that per-

sonal element which we traced in the devotional poetry:
and though they only saw themselves in Nature, a kind of
personal affection for her could not but begin to grow in
poetry. They were led to look more directly at Nature,
though it was only to find additional food for their own
pensiveness; they were led to look at the smaller beau-
ties of Nature, to count the primroses on a woodland
bank, to mark the changing lights on a mountain pool.
And for the first time the pleasure of being alone with
Nature in her solitudes now became a distinct element in
modern poetry. It was freed from its sentimentality by
Wordsworth and others; it was freed also from its habit
of self-consciousness. The new Poets felt the frank joy
of Nature, and could not burden it with faded sentiment;
they felt ravished by her beauty and could not think of
themselves. Logan or Warton walking by a brook would
have compared it with the sorrows and solitude of their
hearts: Wordsworth writes as if from another world than
theirs—hearing no echo of himself or of human pain in
the rapture of life that he feels around him by the brook-
side,—

> The spirit of enjoyment and desire
> And hopes and wishes, from all living things
> Went circling, like a multitude of sounds—
> *   *   *   *
> up the brook
> I roamed, in the confusion of my heart,
> Alive to all things, and forgetting all.

Lost, you see, in the gaiety and life of Nature!

It is no wonder where self intruded so much into
natural contemplation as with these Poets, that one finds
no religion linked to their love of Nature. It is no

wonder that, when self, as in Wordsworth, is lost, one finds religion.

The next step, in the order of growth in the poetry of Nature, is made by Goldsmith. We possess from him clear descriptions of natural scenery, uninfluenced by human feeling, untroubled by moralizing thought. The landscapes in the "Traveller" are pure pictures; but they are wholly uncoloured with emotion. Not for a moment does he feel such love to a place for its own sake as Wordsworth expresses forty years after the "Traveller" was published, about a glade of water and one green field,—

> And if a man should plant his cottage near,
> Should sleep beneath the shelter of its trees,
> And blend its waters with his daily meal,
> He would so love it, that in his death hour
> Its image would survive among his thoughts.

Nor is another touch in the same Poem—

> This spot was made by Nature for herself—

less remarkable as a proof of the great change of thought and feeling about Nature between Goldsmith and Wordsworth. Goldsmith coldly delineates the landscape, and never dreams that it may have a life of its own, or share in the life of a spirit. Wordsworth thinks of the whole of Nature as a living person, and of a landscape as dwelt in, even chosen as a special retreat, by Nature, through a special love of it. It is all the distance between a dead and a living universe, and with the conception of a living universe our true poetic theology of Nature begins. But we could not get to that theology till we had conceived

Nature as having a life distinct from ours, and Goldsmith
made one step forward to that, when he freed the landscape in his descriptions from the burden of human
feeling which Gray, Collins, Beattie, and Warton had
imposed on it.

The next step, and an immense one, was made by
Burns, Crabbe, and Cowper.

Leaving Burns aside for separate treatment, I pass
on to the two others in whose work we have for the
first time Nature distinctly studied and loved for her
own sake.   The moralizing of Gray on the landscape,
the transference of emotion to it by Burns, the sentimental note of Warton, have passed away, and we see
Nature as a whole, and separated from Man.

Crabbe's poetry of Nature is as direct in description as
his poetry of Man.   He was a botanist and mineralogist,
and his close study of flowers and stones made him look
accurately into all things.   He paints the very blades
of grass on the common, and the trail of the shell-fish
on the sand.   It is the introduction into our poetry of
that minute observation, and delight in minute things
in Nature, which is so remarkable in the subsequent
poets, which led Coleridge to paint in words the dancing
of the sand at the bottom of a tiny spring, and Wordsworth the daisy's shadow on the naked stone, and
Shelley the almost invisible globes of vapour which the
sun sucks from a forest pool.   The difference is that
Crabbe writes without the imagination which confers life
on the things seen, while the later poets, believing that
all Nature was alive, conceived a living spirit in the sand,
the daisy, and the vapour.   And this distinction, as we

shall see, has its force in relation to the poetical theology of Nature.

Cowper's natural painting is not like Crabbe's, pre-Raphaelite. He paints broad landscapes, and his range is as extensive as the scenery he lived among, and often goes beyond it, neither does he disdain minuteness. He also loved Nature for her own sake, and if Crabbe rode, as we are told, sixty miles in twenty-four hours for the sake of catching one glimpse of the sea, Cowper speaks of the love of Nature as an inextinguishable thirst in man, and bringing his religion to bear on it, declares that this love was infused by God into Man at the creation.

Therefore now, for the first time in English Poetry, we have got three things—Nature studied as a whole, Nature loved for her own sake, and therefore Nature conceived as a distinct subject for poetical treatment.

And when this was done, a distinct Theology of Nature, in our sense of the word, became for the first time possible. Pope had, as we have seen, his own Natural Theology. It was of God's relation to the great whole conceived of as a system which appealed to the intellect and its admiration: and this great whole involved Man and Nature together. When the Poets who came after him little by little divided Nature from Man for separate consideration, and described and dwelt on separate portions of her beauty, they lost the idea of Nature as a whole, and that had to be recovered before a theology of Nature was possible. When it was recovered, as it was by Wordsworth, it was a different conception from that of Pope. Man had been taken out of it. It is plain that as long as Nature was only loved for the feelings it awoke in Man, or for the lessons it gave him, he could not help mingling it up with himself, and there could be no theology of it which was not also a theology of Man. But when it began to be loved for its own sake as separate from us, the poets began to ask, how is God related to it? what is it in Nature which we love? what is the One Spirit in this mighty whole which speaks to us in another voice than that which we hear in our heart?

Again, as long as isolated landscapes and things in Nature were alone described, no conception of the whole was formed. When it was, the Poet naturally asked, what is the source of this Oneness of life, in whom is this whole contained? And out of the effort to reply to these questions the distinct theology of Nature in our poetry took its rise.

Moreover, the new attitude of man towards the whole of Nature tended in the poets to make the new theology religious. It was not the attitude of those who reasoned like Pope on what they saw, it was the attitude of those who loved, and were content alone to love. And the love ended in worship. Some, like Shelley, not believing in revealed religion, not even being Deists, created an all-pervading Spirit in the world, and would not call it God, nor give it personality, but called it Love and Life, and in the love and worship that they gave it found their religion, and had the emotions of religion. It was not the great Order of Pope which awoke their intellectual admiration, it was the animating Love in Nature which stirred their heart. Others, like Wordsworth, believing in God, saw Him in the loveliness and tenderness and quiet that they loved, and worshipped not the Author of a great system whom they dared not scan, but a Divine Spirit in the Universe—not necessarily personal there, though personal in them—and said, " This Presence which disturbs me with the joy of elevated thoughts, this Wisdom and Beauty, is revealing itself to me. I can listen, I can understand its voice. It is in Nature the same voice, though in a different language, which belongs to God my Father in my heart, and the work it is doing on me is a work of education. Not by reason but by feeling, not by admiration but by love, I make its lessons mine. Therefore I shall give myself wholly, when I am with Nature, to absolute self-forgetful love of her." In that way the theology of Nature became religious, and that reacted in turn on the poetical contemplation of Nature, and made it more loving and more intense.

We shall find all this in Wordsworth, but we only find its beginning in Crabbe and Cowper. They had lost, in dividing Man from Nature, Pope's thought of a life immanent in the whole order of things. And in their theology of Nature they were driven to think of it as only " dull matter " in Cowper's phrase, but matter subject to laws which God had ordained. When they looked then at natural things from the Poet's point of feeling, they saw their beauty as the result of this order, and referred the whole to God who directed it from without. Nature was a machine which God had set in motion, but it moved without any living consciousness of its own motion.

The last step, therefore, in the poetic theology of Nature had not then been made. The Poets had not reached the stage in which they were forced, not only by

their own feelings, but also by the needs of their art, to
conceive of the universe beyond themselves as living.
Crabbe made no advance towards it; his was the mechanical theory alone of God and the universe. But Cowper,
though he held the same theory for the most part, made
one step towards the higher view, and he made it through
his religion.   His intense personality forced him, when
under poetic emotion, to lay aside the mechanical theory,
and we find passages where he ceases to interpose
laws between Nature and God.   He transferred from
his theological creed the doctrine of the personal super-
intendence of God over every human life to the realm
of Nature, and bringing God directly into contact with
it, declared that He maintained its course by an unremitting act.   How else could matter seem as if it were
alive,—

> unless impelled
> To ceaseless service by a ceaseless force,
> And under pressure of some conscious cause.
> The Lord of all, Himself through all diffused,
> Sustains and is the Life of all that lives.
> Nature is but the name of an effect
> Whose cause is God.

But his special personal theology which abode in worship
of Christ, carried him still further; and he makes Christ
Himself as the Eternal Word, as the acting Thought of
God—the ruler of the universe, and the author of its
forms.

> One spirit, His
> Who wore the plaited thorns with bleeding brows,
> Rules universal Nature.   Not a flower
> But shows some touch in freckle, streak, or stain,
> Of His unrivalled pencil.   He inspires
> Their balmy odours, and imparts their hues,

And bathes their eyes with nectar, and includes
In grains as countless as the seaside sands
The forms with which he sprinkles all the earth.

We have now made, you observe, a step further. Nature, it is true, is not yet alive, but a spirit of life is now in it, separate from it, but working in it. So near, in fact, have we got to the conception of Nature as alive, that Cowper is betrayed unconsciously into phrases which mingle God up with the universe and make it living. The lines above, which speak of the diffusion of God through all, are repeated in idea in this other phrase:

There lives and works
A soul in all things, and that soul is God.

This is a contradiction of his position of a God wholly distinct from the universe, but it marks the transition to the last step in the poetic idea of Nature. It is the conception of Nature as a living Being to whom affection was due, who could of herself awake feeling and thought in Man, whom we could love as we love our fellow-men, who lived her own life and had conscious pleasure in it—it is this conception which unconsciously in Cowper began to tremble into being. It sprang into full being in Wordsworth, and then, when Nature was conceived of as alive, its theology took a new form, or rather several forms each modified by the personal theology or philosophy of the Poet—in the poetry of England.

I shall trace that through Wordsworth and Shelley; we shall see how it influenced or did not influence the poetry of Byron and Keats; I shall mark the transitional position of Coleridge with regard to it; but before I enter upon it, I must discuss, not only how far Cowper carried the poetry of Man and how he made it theological, but also how far his theology influenced his personal poetry. That will form the subject of my next Lecture.

LECTURE III.

COWPER.

I TRACED in my first lecture the growth of the Poetry of Man from the critical school to Cowper. In Cowper's hands, it took a much wider development. I only laid down the larger lines of its growth, omitting for the sake of clearness a number of branch lines, such as that of the new interest taken in the romantic past, which, touched by Macpherson in his " Ossian," and by Chatterton in his forgeries, was afterwards fully worked out in narrative poetry by Sir Walter Scott : such as the ballad, which chose a short narrative of human passion and related it with simplicity and intensity—or the shorter lyric, which in its treatment of a passing phase of meditative or violent passion of the heart, and in its strict limitation of itself within that phase, so as to preserve what is called lyrical unity, is strictly analogous to the hymn in its treatment of a sudden and transient phase of the life of spiritual feeling.

These and others I pass by—though one sees how largely they entered the work of the poets on Man— because theology of any kind would not be likely to intrude into them.

I remain close then to the large lines I have spoken

of; and my object in the first part of this lecture is, to show how largely Cowper extended the poetry of Man, and how it was influenced, and in him indeed drenched with theology.

I approach the subject by asking where we find him writing, and the question has its meaning. We find him retired in the heart of a very quiet country. The slow eddying Ouse flowed close to his dwelling through its willow-haunted meadows; it accompanied his walks, and its quiet movement seems to flow through his poetry. Day after day, Yardley Wood and the park of the Throckmortons saw the silent poet-face moving amidst their trees. But little society disturbed that sequestered life; few were the men and fewer the women whom he met; he companied with sheep and birds, with his hares and his spaniel, till he grew to know them as his friends; and one would say that in such a life the poetry of Man was not likely to flourish, nor was a wide view of mankind possible. Was it probable that this lawyer's clerk, who had made a hopeless failure of his public life, should say more of human nature and strike deeper into the world of men than the brilliant Londoner, Pope, or the courtly scholar, Gray—that the voice which spoke of Man from the solitude of the country should say more than the voice which spoke of him from the crowded society of the city?

In one point certainly this rural retirement spoiled the largeness of Cowper's view. He saw cities and their evils through the exaggeration of distance, and in that glare of morality in which sin is so magnified that the good which balances it is lost. His doctrinal views had also power over him and he saw the curse which rested on man and nothing else, when he looked upon the city. It was different when he turned his eyes upon the village and the country poor. Seeing clearly their evil he also saw their good, and it is with some naïveté that he imputes more than half the evil in the country to the influence of those who drift thither from the town. But whether in the country or the town, Cowper's religion led him to trace all moral guilt and folly to the world's rejection of Christ.

But the point I wish to draw your attention to is, that unlike the town poet of the past to whom the dwellers in the country are nothing, we have now the country poet deeply interested in the life of towns as well as in the life around him. It is no longer classes of men which awake sympathy, nor special societies; it is no longer the passionate or the moral or the intellectual side of human nature, each alone, on which the poet dwells,—it is the whole of mankind, it is the whole of human nature.

The truth is, the first swell of the great wave which put Man in the foremost place and interest, Man independent of rank and caste and convention and education, Man in his simple elements, was now flowing over Europe. Poets are quick to feel, and it reached the quiet Cowper in his hermitage, as it reached the lowland lad who,

> in his glory and his joy,
> Followed his plough along the mountain side,

and for the first time, as one smells the brine before one sees the ocean, we scent in English poetry, too distinctly to be explained away, the air of those ideas of which the French Revolution was the most local and the most

violent outburst.   For the first time an attempt is made
in poetry to cover the whole range of Man, to think of
Man as one people ; to spread poetical interest over all
who wear a human face.   And it was done, as is commonly the case when the impulse is received from an idea
which has not yet taken any political form, quite unconsciously.   Cowper talked as naturally of *all men* as Pope
did of one of two classes of men : he asks how he and any
man that lives could be strangers to each other ; he conceives of his poetic work as for the service of mankind ;
and such an aim was now for the first time possible.   A
universal idea of Man had passed from political Philo-
sophers to the people, and the undefined emotion it stirred
in the people was felt and thrown into form by the poets.

But the revolutionary idea of the unity of Man was in
Cowper's mind grounded on a theological one, on God as
the common Maker of Man.   He speaks of " the link of
brotherhood, by which one common Maker bound him to
the Kind."   And his work for men was to make them out
of sin and death into life with God, for they are

Bone of my bone, and kindred souls to mine.

To this religious element of an universal brotherhood in
God is to be traced the large range of his human view.   He
looked abroad and saw all men related to God, it mattered
not of what nation, caste, or colour.   As such they had equal
rights and equal duties in a spiritual country of which all
were citizens ; for as he writes, the limiting power of his
doctrinal theology departs and the individual theology of
the poet who sympathizes with all men, takes the upper
hand.   East, west, north, and south, his interest flew.

In his satires he touches, not with savage bitterness, but with a gentleness which healed while it lashed, on nearly every phase of human life in England ; on the Universities and the Schools, the Hospitals and the Prisons; on cities and villages; on the statesman, the clergyman, the lawyer, the soldier, the man of science, the critic, the writer for the press, the pleasure - seeker, the hunter, the musician, the epicure, the card-player, the ploughman, the cottager, and fifty others. Their good side, their follies, their vices, are sketched and ridiculed and praised. The range of his interest was as wide as human life, and as he sketched, he saw as the one ideal and the one remedy for all—the Cross of Christ. Whatever we may think of his religion or the manner of it, there is no doubt but that it indefinitely extended his poetic sympathy, and that in this extension of sympathy we find ourselves in another world altogether than that of Dryden, Pope, or Gray. It is no longer intellectual interest in man, or sentimental interest; it is vivid, personal, passionate.

It went beyond classes of men, it was an interest in his nation; but he derived his patriotism and drew the passion with which he informed it from the connection of his country with God. It was God who was the King of England, and was educating the nation; and this conception bound all citizens together into mutual love of one another and the whole. On this ground he made his impassioned appeal to his countrymen to throw off their vices and follies and to be worthy of their high vocation ; would they not, he asked, be true to Him who had wrought so gloriously among them ? This is the note

of many a passage in the Task, of the whole of his
Poem of Expostulation; and it is not a note of merely
lyric interest in England's glory on the seas, like Thomson's Rule Britannia, nor one of intellectual passion,
like the references to her noble periods of history in the
Bard—it is a note that thrills with emotion for England
as God's nation, and having a work to do for Man.
We already breathe the air of the patriotic poetry of
Wordsworth.

Nor does this interest in man remain fixed in England.
God had children, bone of the Poet's bone, and flesh of
his flesh in other lands.   From the banks of the Ouse his
heart carried him to Greenland, to Italy, to France, to the
islands of the Pacific, to the shores of Africa and South
America.   In these distant lands were his brothers, and
he transferred the inalienable rights of Man from the free
and civilized European to the slave and the savage; there
was no man, he thought, who ought not to feel himself
allied to all the race.

The noblest right of Man was liberty, and this in
Cowper's thought was the gift of God to Man.   Whoever
took it away did the most accursed of all sins.   His poetical
theology saw God as the deliverer and avenger of the
oppressed.   He traces the ruin of Spain to the wrath of
God for its crimes against its subject races.   He places
the cause of the slave in the hands of God.

In Cowper the poetry of human wrong begins, that
long, long cry against oppression and evil done by man
to man, against the political, moral, or priestly tyrant,
which rings louder and louder through Burns, Coleridge,
Wordsworth, Shelley, and Byron, ever impassioned, ever

longing, ever prophetic,—never, in the darkest time, quite despairing.

The wide range given to it by Cowper, the personal passion in it, the glance it took forward to a brighter time, its theological element of God as the source of freedom and the avenger of tyranny, are all elements distinctly new to our poetry, above all new in their tremendous power of awakening and maintaining the humane emotions which must create a human poetry. Cowper carried this poetry of human wrong into the prisons with Howard, and into the cottages and lives of the poor ; he denounced the landowners who abandoned them, and the merchants who " built factories with blood." Passing on, inspired by this cause, he poured out his indignation and his scorn on kings and nobles who used the common-weal for their own purposes. " Patience itself," he cries, " is meanness in a slave." That there should be men base enough to bear the caprice of despots, and to have freedom only on sufferance was the very folly of infamy in his mind. Then he turns to sketch the English King, and his sketch makes the preceding still more forcible.

> We love
> The King who loves the law, respects his bounds,
> And reigns content within them ; him we serve
> Freely and with delight, who leaves us free :
> But recollecting still that he is man,
> We trust him not too far. King though he be,
> And King in England too, he may be weak
> And vain enough to be ambitious still,
> May exercise amiss his proper powers,
> Or covet more than freemen choose to grant :
> Beyond that mark is treason.

We may hear in all this nothing more than the old Whig

doctrines in which the Cowpers had been brought up ;
but there is a newer element in it which insensibly entered
into Cowper, the cry of the coming revolution.   We feel
that plainly when he suddenly places us in front of the
Bastile,—

> Ye horrid towers, the abode of broken hearts,
> Ye dungeons and ye caverns of despair,
> That monarchs have supplied from age to age
> With music such as suits their sovereign ears,
> The sighs and groans of miserable men !
> There's not an English heart that would not leap
> To hear that ye were fallen at last.

And high an English heart did leap, when a few years
afterwards Wordsworth heard that they were fallen, and
recorded his triumphant joy by the voice of the Solitary
in the Excursion.   Nor is it less new in English poetry
to find a Poet putting aside blind patriotism and
rejoicing

> to know
> That even our enemies, so oft employed
> In forging chains for us, themselves were free.

For he who loves freedom does not limit his zeal for it to
his own country—its cause, he says, is the cause of Man,
for it is the cause of God.

But here Cowper could not stop.   He saw a higher
liberty than any on earth, a liberty without which political
liberty was in vain, with which even the slave felt free,
the liberty of heart derived from Heaven :

> Bought with His blood who gave it to mankind.

The whole passage is a noble one, and as emotional as
that which precedes it : in both together, the passion of

religion and the passion of political freedom are fused into one, and they run up into the highest expression then given in the English language of the poetry of human liberty. It had been touched before : Glover, in his "Leonidas ; " Akenside, in a now forgotten poem ; Burke, in prose which we may almost call poetic, and which itself went forth to influence the poets ; Darwin, in "The Botanic Garden," had condemned slavery on the ground more or less of the unity of Man; but by none was so bold, so impassioned, so complete an expression given of the rights of Man as Man as by the retired lawyer's-clerk at Olney. He struck the first note of the revolutionary poetry. He struck it in connection with God, and with us it has never lost that connection.

But even further Cowper carried the poetry of Man. International Union rose before him like a dream; he thought of a higher earth in which wars and hatreds should cease and each nation enjoy the other's good. It was a dream, partly caused by the results of the peaceful and commercial administration of Walpole, but it was like many other dreams, in the air. Cowper grounded it on the natural bond of brotherhood among men, a bond which their common fellowship in sorrow ought to draw closer. Social intercourse, " benevolence and peace and mutual aid," commerce and art were designed, he thought, "To associate all the branches of mankind."

Nor did Cowper forget the work of the natural philosopher, and though driven by his notion of the evil of pride of intellect he set philosophy too much in opposition to religion, yet even here his predominant idea of the union

of all men into one mankind comes in to unite the work
of science with that of art and commerce. " He too,"
speaking of the natural philosopher,

> has a connecting power, and draws
> Man to the centre of the common cause.

All these passages of which I speak were written in 1782,
and no one can deny the novelty of their idea in English
poetry nor the great expansion which that idea gave to
its subjects. For, treated from Cowper's point of view,
from the emotional conception of Man as a great whole,
this thought of an international union, and of its means,
free trade and the rest, becomes a subject capable of
poetical treatment, and it remains such to the present day,
Wordsworth took it up, Shelley idealized it in his aërial
sketches of a world of Love; and Tennyson in well-known
lines embodies the same idea.

Then comes to close this long poetry of Man, Cowper's
vision of the restoration of all things, in which he brings
for the last time God into Man, not now as the Judge,
but as the Redeemer of the Race, " to visit earth in
mercy, to descend, propitious in his chariot paved with
love." All climes are made beautiful in an eternal spring,
" all creatures worship man, and all mankind one Lord,
one Father." Error has no place, nor evil; "all is
harmony and love; for heavenward all things tend;" and
all nations bound together have their centre in Sion where
God reigns.

It was a vision which now for the first time came into
English Poetry. Here and there it may be found before
this time, but it was limited by the want of a universal
idea of Man. But, now, when the great conception

of mankind as One, one in rights and powers and
destiny—of mankind as one universal Brotherhood, was
to be proclaimed in the political and social realms,
and to bring with it the slow overthrow of all exclusive systems of society—the idea of a universal regeneration of the race became for the first time possible.
In Cowper's mind it was limited by his exclusive theology,
but that does not appear in this poetical passage where he
rises on the wings of emotion above his theology. In the
after poets it becomes a noble element in their song. For
whenever it arose, the Poet, filled with faith and hope in
the fortunes of mankind, rushed into noble verse. We
see how it told upon our poetry and told religiously, in
the finest expression of it, in the Prometheus Unbound of
Shelley: but the note here struck by Cowper in connection
with the idea of a universal mankind has never ceased to
echo in our poetry.

I turn, in conclusion, to that personal element in
Cowper's poetry, in which theology plays so sad a part.
But first let me say two things. In connection with
the poetry of Man as seen from the personal point
of view, no English Poet has ever excelled Cowper when
he writes of the daily human affections. In him, one
might almost say, began in English poetry that direct,
close, impassioned representation, in the least sensational manner, of such common relations as motherhood,
filial piety, friendship, married love, the relation of man
to animals—and in him they are made religious.
There is nothing more pathetic yet more simple in English poetry than the lines on his mother's picture, or the
sonnet and lines addressed to Mary Unwin. In the

lines on the picture and in the sonnet, the natural piety of the relations of a son to a mother, and of a friend to a friend, are bound up with religion ; and the infinite pitifulness of both are somewhat relieved by hope in God. In the later lines to Mrs. Unwin, when she was nearly as insane as he, there is no religion. It is " passionless despair, but the despair which loves to the last."

The second thing I remark leads me to the personal poetry of Cowper in its theological aspect. Much of it is a terrible record, stained with insanity, wretched with horror and despair. It has also, as we have seen, its gentler, sweeter, nobler aspect when he was happy with God ; but even here it is often morbid with overwrought feeling. But we must not think that this personal misery or the morbid element in his religion extended over his whole moral life, so as to make him or his poetry unmanly. He was partly saved from that by his humour—humour which is the guard of intellectual and moral sanity. But however saved, Cowper's treatment of all moral subjects is distinguished from his treatment of his personal religion by an essential manliness of tone. Nowhere in our poetry is there heard a finer scorn of vanity, ambition, meanness ; nowhere is truth more nobly exalted, or justice more sternly glorified. And his tenderness for the weak and poor and wronged is as sweet as his hatred of oppression is strong. We breathe throughout an invigorating air.

It is different when we return to his relation to God. That is almost darkness throughout. His Calvinism, which he seems to have had before meeting with Newton, combined with the tendency to madness in him, had produced a religious insanity, which, occurring at intervals through his life, finally fixed its talons on his heart and never let him go, even in the hour of death. He believed himself irrevocably doomed by God. We can trace the first hints of it in some of his earlier poems. At last an outward event hurried the evil to a head and he attempted suicide. During the madness which followed we have one poem written which is almost too terrible to read, lit with a lurid light and full of ghastly power.

> Hatred and vengeance,—my eternal portion
> Scarce can endure delay of execution,—
> Wait with impatient readiness to seize my
>   Soul in a moment.
> Damned below Judas; more abhorred than he was,
> Who for a few pence sold his holy Master !
> Twice-betrayed Jesus me, the last delinquent,
>   Deems the profanest.
> Man disavows, and Deity disowns me,
> Hell might afford my miseries a shelter ;
> Therefore, Hell keeps her ever-hungry mouths all
>   Bolted against me.
> Hard lot ! encompassed with a thousand dangers ;
> Weary, faint, trembling with a thousand terrors,
> I'm called, if vanquished ! to receive a sentence
>   Worse than Abiram's.
> Him the vindictive rod of angry Justice
> Sent quick and howling to the centre headlong;
> I, fed with judgment, in a fleshly tomb, am
>   Buried above ground.

Whether his madness would have passed away under the influence of a higher theology than that which Newton presented to him, it is fruitless to inquire. Again and again it settled down on his life in profound gloom; it always threatened him, and days when he

4

was happiest and best were often followed, even interspersed, by hours of misery. It is a dreadful thing to have the spirit mad and the intellect sound, and this was not rarely the case of Cowper. Some of his finest work was done when his soul trembled with the horror of coming hell, and it is possible here and there, in the midst of poems which breathe peace and simple gladness, to catch far off the note of that terror and pity which gives to the sequestered life of this lawyer's clerk the interest and power of Tragedy. No pity is more touching than that he bestows on suffering, none more childlike and pathetic than that which he lavishes upon himself. He speaks of his fate as if it belonged to another man, caressing, as the case is with many of the insane, his own misery with the gentlest words. I have quoted the passage before, but in a different connection :—

> I was a stricken deer that left the herd
> Long since ; with many an arrow deep infixed
> My panting side was charged, when I withdrew
> To seek a tranquil death in distant shades.
> There was I found by one who had Himself
> Been hurt by the archers. In His side He bore,
> And in His hands and feet the cruel scars.

What an infinite, long-continued self-compassion in the words! The note heard in them is low and sorrowful, and does not rise into passion; but the whole passage is exalted not into, but towards the region of great poetry, partly by its pictorial quality, but chiefly by the sudden yet natural introduction of Christ coming through the woods to heal him, and the association of his fate with that of the Saviour. In the " lines on receipt of my Mother's picture," where he uses one of his favourite sea similes, the same self-pity takes to itself the element of passion, but it does not touch its deepest depth, for a shadow of hope remains.

> But me scarce hoping to attain that rest,
> Always from port withheld, always distressed—
> Me howling blasts drive devious, tempest tost,
> Sails ripped, seams opening wide, and compass lost,
> And day by day some current's thwarting force
> Sets me more distant from a prosperous course.
> Yet oh ! the thought that thou art safe—and he !
> That thought is joy, arrive what may to me.

One sees that most of the intensity in that arises from the conviction that there is an irreversible fate against him. Continually, by hard striving, bringing himself near to port, continually driven away by a superior power; contending, weak as he was, with destiny till the last, yet knowing the contest to be in vain; he has unconsciously put himself into the position in which Greek Tragedy placed its heroes, but in the midst of an unheroic time and scenery, and with a heart not fitted to wage the battle of Œdipus; so that, though the mental position is tragic, the poetry wants the sublimity and the force of Tragedy. Still there is profound passion in it, working especially in the complete transference of himself into the soul of the tormented ship, and in the splendid use of the word " devious " in the third line. Unpretentious as the verses are, the stamp of passion is far deeper set upon them than in similar lines in Byron, where even his colossal power could not overcome the unreality of his self-pity.

But it is in the last poem which Cowper wrote, in the midst of the three last years of his madness and his life, that this self-compassion does reach the centre of intensity. In the "Castaway," a poem in its sphere of the very highest class, where simplicity of pitiful narration is set in melodious verse by an Art which had now become Nature—Cowper mingles up his fate with that of the drowned sailor of Anson's ship. He cannot help beginning in the first person; realizing the terrible night and the swift ruin as his own. He makes himself the sailor :—

> Obscurest night involved the sky,
>   The Atlantic billows roared,
> When such a destined wretch as I,
>   Washed headlong from on board,
> Of friends, of hope, of all bereft,
> His floating home for ever left.

He changes then to description in the third person, but we feel as we read of the long struggle of the swimmer, " supported by despair of life;" as he describes the pitiless blast which forbade his friends to rescue him, the useless succour of the cask and cord which served only to prolong his agony, the bitter thought that they were right to leave him—that we are looking into the heart of Cowper's life. With what exquisite simplicity of words, and yet with what a grasp of misery, is the next verse conceived—

> He long survives, who lives an hour
>   In Ocean, self-upheld;
> And so long he, with unspent power,
>   His destiny repelled ;
> And ever as the minutes flew
> Entreated help, or cried Adieu.

We are now relieved by a change from the doom of the sailor to the grief of Anson for his fate, and then, in a sudden rushing of misery, in which the impassioned imagination rises almost into a wild cry, and the verse in the last two lines becomes abrupt, and the voice choked, he again dashes himself into the fate of the sailor, and both perish in the seas:—

> No voice divine the storm allayed,
>   No light propitious shone,
> When, snatched from all effectual aid,
>   We perished, each alone ;
> But I beneath a rougher sea,
> And whelmed in deeper gulfs than he.

The poetic life of Cowper lies between this poem at the end, and those terrible Sapphics at the beginning. He entered it in despair, he left it in despair. For a time, during which he wrote most of the Olney Hymns, he enjoyed the sense of that " assurance " of salvation on which his friend Newton dwelt so much, and the humble ecstasy of some of the hymns is wonderfully touching. But the lines which have found a place in every hymn book—

> " God moves in a mysterious way,
>   His wonders to perform," etc.

mark the close of this period and prophesy the relapse which followed. When the attack was over, he never recovered his sense of acceptance with God. He even learned to acquiesce, at times, in God's condemnation of him to eternal misery. But the weight of this dreadful belief did not always oppress him. It came and went like dark clouds upon an April day of sunshine, and till the last three years, his life had many intervals of happiness. Many lovely landscapes lay between these three valleys of

the Shadow of Death, where he rested and was at peace;
sweet idleness and fruitful contemplation—tender friendships and simple pleasures—hours where charming humour
and simple pathos ran through one another, and inter-
changed their essence like the colours on a sun-set sea—
days of sweet fidelity to Nature in her quietest and most
restoring moods—times when the peace that passeth all
understanding made him as a child with God; but in the
end the darkness settled down, deep and impenetrable:
and the Poet, who of all English Artists, has written, to
my mind, the noblest hymns for depth of religious feeling
and for loveliness of quiet style; whose life was blameless
as the water-lilies which he loved, and the way of life of
which on silent streams he made his own; whose heart
breathed the sweetest air of natural piety, and yet could
sympathize with the supersensuous world in which
Guyon lived—died in ghastly hopelessness, refusing
comfort to the last.   On the physician asking how he
felt, he answered, "I feel unutterable despair."—
It is a strange commentary on the demand which the
school of his friend Newton make, that on the death-bed
there should be, or else one may scarcely dare to hope, a
triumphant confession of faith.

LECTURE IV.

COLERIDGE.

COLERIDGE has not written much poetry, but he has written a great deal of theology. We know him as a theologian and his views, and the difficulty, of course, in such a lecture as this, which keeps strictly to the theology in his poetry, is to prevent oneself from slipping into discussion of his philosophic prose, and to think and speak of him only as a poet. I shall try to get what I have to say about his poetic view of Nature, Man, and God, into one lecture.

First, he too, with the rest of the God-fearing English poets, saw in the proclamation of the revolutionary ideas the revelation of God; saw that the truth of universal brotherhood, and of the right of the meanest man to equal liberty, followed on and ought to be founded on the truth of God's universal Fatherhood. And when the first bright outburst of the Revolution took place, Coleridge was the poet who sang it with the stormiest glee and passion; something of the " storm and stress" (*Sturm und Drang*) period in Germany marks his verses, a violence of words and ideas, as if the more noise the more expression. Such lines as these show what I mean,—

> Thus to sad sympathies I soothed my breast,
> Calm as the rainbow in the weeping West:
> When slumbering Freedom roused by high Disdain
> With giant fury burst her triple chain !
> Fierce on her front the blasting Dog-star glowed ;
> Her banners, like a midnight meteor, flowed ;
> Amid the yelling of the storm-rent skies
> She came, and scattered battles from her eyes!

They are poor, but still they have a certain strength which will mellow—it is a shout of triumph, it is not the sensational shriek which exhausts itself. And they had a real enthusiasm at their root, that enthusiasm which delights to challenge established beliefs, as when Coleridge claimed heaven as the right of Chatterton the suicide ; which is full of wild projects, as when with Southey and some others he planned their communistic expedition, and society on the banks of the Susquehanna, where he hoped to realize his new dreams of human peace and equality,—

> O'er the ocean swell
> Sublime of Hope I seek the cottage dell,
> Where Virtue calm with careless step may stray ;
> And dancing to the moonlight roundelay,
> The wizard Passions weave a holy spell.
> O, Chatterton that thou wert yet alive
> Sure thou would'st spread the canvas to the gale
> And love with us the tinkling team to drive,
> O'er peaceful Freedom's undivided dale.

And it was an enthusiasm which, taking fire from the fire of the world, made him think, in the hope and joy which filled his heart, that all things were possible to faith so strong, and aspiration so intense ; but which failed in expressing itself, at least at first, with any of the poetic force that is the child of temperance.

Later on, in 1796, when the early excitement had lessened, and he had had time to learn his art, Coleridge
put into two Odes his past and present feelings about the
Revolution. They form the transition between his first
wild hopes and his later conservative despair.

The " Ode to the Departing Year " is the first of these,
and it has its historical interest as well as its theological.
It begins with the statement of his belief in God who
regulates into one vast harmony all the events of time,
however calamitous some of them may seem. It calls
on God by the voice of the "Spirit of the Earth" to
avenge the wrongs of the poor and the slave, to speak in
thunder to England who has been the oppressor, and who
now seeks to league herself against liberty. And its revolutionary character is strongly marked in this, that it
dissolves the tie of patriotism, in behalf of the interests
of mankind. It makes the nations rise to curse England,
abandoned of heaven, standing aloof at cowardly distance
from the interests of mankind.

Nor is the same character less forcibly seen in the
" Ode to France," where he looks back in 1797 on what
he had felt some years before.

> When France in wrath her giant limbs upreared,
>   And with that oath, which smote air, earth, and sea,
>   Stamped her strong foot and said she would be free,
> Bear witness for me, how I hoped and feared!
>   With what a joy my lofty gratulation
> Unawed I sang, amid a slavish band:
>   And when to whelm the disenchanted nation,
> Like fiends embattled by a wizard's wand,
>   The monarchs marched in evil day,
>   And Britain joined the dire array;

> Though dear her shores and circling ocean,
>   Though many friendships, many youthful loves
> Had swoll'n the patriot emotion,
>   And flung a magic light o'er all her hills and groves;
> Yet still my voice unaltered sang defeat
>   To all that braved the tyrant-quelling lance,
> And shame too long delayed and vain retreat !
>   For ne'er, O Liberty ! with partial aim
>   I dimmed thy light or damped thy holy flame;
> But blessed the pæans of delivered France,
>   And hung my head and wept at Britain's name.

Like Wordsworth, he divided himself, for the sake of
Man, from an attack on liberty, even when made by his
own country, for it was an attack on God; and unpartaking
of the evil thing, bewailed the vileness of his nation ; nor
did he remain in solitude, pampering his heart with feelings about human wrongs and liberty too delicate for use,
but, made active by his fervour, went among men, doing
what practical work he could.   Nor, at first, did the blas-
phemy, and Terror, and blood of the Revolution in Paris
daunt his hopes any more than they did Wordsworth's.
These evils, he thought, could not be helped ; they were
the necessary storms that precede the fulfilment of a vast
change for the better in human things, and behind them,
though they hid its light, the sun was rising.   And soon,
when France had quelled domestic treason, and the
Terror ceased, and her armies went forth, "insupportably
advancing" to overthrow the enemies of freedom, his
heart recovered, his hopes seemed fulfilled.

> And soon, I said, shall Wisdom teach her love
> In the low huts of them that toil and groan !
> And conquering by her happiness alone,
> Shall France compel the nations to be free,
> Till love and joy look round, and call the earth their own.

It was not, then, the horrors of the Revolution that shook his faith in it. But it was this—it was the attack of France, the champion of freedom, upon the freest spot in Europe, upon the " stormy wilds " of Switzerland and on her bloodless liberty. It was when she "mixed with kings in the low lust of sway," and insulted

> the shrine of liberty with spoils
> From freemen torn,

that Coleridge fell back in hopelessness of the world, in hatred of the Revolution, upon the sense of liberty in his own heart, and taking refuge in the solitudes of nature, declared, with a certain impatient petulance, that he could only truly feel the spirit of Freedom when he sent his being out of himself through earth and sea and air, and possessed

> All things with intensest love.

And the reaction was deepened when England herself was threatened with invasion, and when France that threatened her was no longer the apostle of liberty but the apostle of despotism. It seemed a duty then to lay aside wild hopes of universal love of Man, and to fall back on the old idea of patriotism; and doing so, the last large idea of the Revolution passed away from men like Coleridge.

They might have been able to be true to their first love, even when England was menaced, if France had been without Napoleon. But the Empire was more than human nature could bear. The hope had been so high, and the disappointment so deep, that it produced anger towards the ideas that had given birth to the hope, and men felt towards them as one does to a treacherous friend whose love

has promised much and ended in deceit. Mingled with
this was anger at the attack on England, a natural
feeling, and now justified as against a tyrant who, under
the name of liberty, was enslaving Europe; and both
these, combined with a backward look to the horrors of
the Terror for which there seemed now no excuse,
forced these men back at last, step by step, into a blank
conservatism for which they have been bitterly blamed
as traitors to the cause of liberty. But they had
something to say for themselves. After all, they said,
England has been bad and is bad enough. But she
is better than this; in her we find the bulwark of
freedom, the true defence against the despot. We
will, then, support her institutions through thick and
thin, give up hysterical efforts after liberty and put
them down. We have dreamt a dream; but we have
awaked and will keep ourselves awake by keeping things
as they are. And now, we turn and look at our own dear
land, and all our patriotism returns; of all our fears and
abuse of her we are ashamed. With her and round her
altars and homes we are content to live and die.

" O, native Britain," cries Coleridge,

> O, my mother Isle,
> How should'st thou prove aught else but dear and holy
> To me, who, from thy lakes and mountain hills,
> Thy clouds, thy quiet dales, thy rocks and seas,
> Have drunk in all my intellectual life,
> All sweet sensations, all ennobling thoughts,
> All adoration of the God in Nature,
> All lovely and all honourable things,
> Whatever makes this mortal spirit feel
> The joy and greatness of its future being?
> There lives nor form nor feeling in my soul
> Unborrowed from my country.

This, taken with the rest, is the poetical cry of an approaching conservatism, but of one which in men who had once held a higher view than that of mere patriotism, who had loved Man more than England, was likely as they grew older to sink into a blind opposition to all change, a blind hatred of all new ideas as dangerous. Neither in Wordsworth nor Coleridge did it quite become that. Coleridge was saved by his philosophy, Wordsworth by his poetry, and both by their Christianity, but still in both the change was great and sad. Yet we should be merciful when we speak of it. We should remember the bitterness of the disappointment, the heart-crushing sorrow that went with it, and not join in the outcry of Shelley and others, who, born later, had never been raised so high in hope and never experienced so fatal a reaction.

It was a rapid change, however, in the case of Coleridge, much more rapid than Wordsworth's. For Coleridge had been less firm, less quiet, less resolute, less clear-sighted, less temperate than Wordsworth. His hopes and their expression were like those of a wild boy; and their strength was the strength of violence. And when the shock came, he chilled quicklier, his force was quicklier drained. For Coleridge wanted will, and with will, perseverance and continuance. Nothing gave his will force but high-pitched enthusiasm, and with its death within him, with the perishing of his youthful dream, the enduring energy of life visited him no more. And this is specially true of him as Poet. Almost all his best poetic work is coincident with the Revolution; afterwards everything is incomplete. The weakness of will was doubled by disease and trebled by opium, and his

poetic life, even his philosophic work, was splendid
failure. That which, in self-reproachful pity, he says
of one of his unfinished poems was true of his whole life,
and it has its deep pathos, "To-morrow I will sing the
rest of this song, but the to-morrow has yet to come."
Slowly, surely, premature age crept upon him, the light
faded, and the only fine thing of his manhood's time is
the Ode to Dejection, one verse of which too well represents the ruin of his life.

> There was a time when, though my path was rough,
>   This joy within me dallied with distress,
> And all misfortunes were but as the stuff
>   Whence Fancy made me dreams of happiness :
> For Hope grew round me, like the twining vine,
> And fruits, and foliage, not mine own, seemed mine.
> But now afflictions bow me down to earth :
> Nor care I that they rob me of my mirth.
>   But, oh ! each visitation.
> Suspends what Nature gave me at my birth,
>   My shaping spirit of Imagination.
> For not to think of what I needs must feel,
>   But to be still and patient all I can ;
> And haply by abstruse research to steal
>   From my own nature all the natural man—
>   This was my sole resource, my only plan :
> Till that which suits a part infects the whole,
> And now is almost grown the habit of my soul.

And the only beautiful thing of his later years is the
deep regret which is sung in " Youth and Age."

Still more pitiful is the poem addressed to Wordsworth
on reading the Prelude. He reads this " orphic song,"
chanted to its own passionate music, and he is moved to
the depth of his heart ; his youthful passion comes again :
but he has no strength, he falls back, bleeding and worn ;
and his misery is deepened when he contrasts his now

broken work with the finished flower of Wordsworth's mind.

> Ah ! as I listened with a heart forlorn,
> The pulses of my being beat anew :
> And even as life returns upon the drowned,
> Life's joy rekindling roused a throng of pains—
> Keen pangs of Love, awakening as a babe
> Turbulent, with an outcry in the heart ;
> And fears self-willed, that shunned the eye of hope;
> And hope that scarce would know itself from fear ;
> Sense of past youth, and manhood come in vain,
> And genius given, and knowledge won in vain ;
> And all which I had culled in woodwalks wild,
> And all which patient toil had reared, and all,
> Commune with thee had opened out—but flowers
> Strewed on my corse, and borne upon my bier,
> In the same coffin, for the selfsame grave !

No dirge can be sadder than these lines ; they are the cry of one who once had a mighty idea, and who, in the shock of its overthrow, was struck with paralysis. He sees that Wordsworth after the same shock remained calm and sure, and saw beyond the lost idea a nobler vision that his very loss had led him to ; but it was not for him— nothing remained for him but prayer. The poetry-creating thought of an universal mankind, and of God as its king and guide, the theological idea of the poetry of Man had died in him ; and with its death his true life as poet ceased. It is a woeful thing to have known a high conception and to fall short of it. It is still more woeful when we have linked it to God and love it, for with its loss our idea of God is lowered from that it might have been. There is no lesson so solemn in the whole range of modern poetry as that given by Coleridge's poetry—genius without will—religion without strength—hope without perseverance—art without the power of finish. What he did well was unique, but it was very little; and the volume we have from him influences us with all the sadness that a garden does in which two or three beautiful flowers rise and flower perfectly, but in which the rest are choked with weeds or run to seed. And to those who can compare the things of Art with the things of the soul and heart, the analogy has its own profound moral lesson.

And now, I turn to him as the Poet of Nature. What was his poetic conception of the relation of Nature to God and Man? His theology in Nature went through two phases. The first in his wild young period, is very fantastic. There were multitudes of spirits, he conceived, belonging to the service of God; some contemplating spirits who gazed for ever on the fount of Deity; some in whose hands lay the guidance and the fate of nations, but others who were the forming spirits of creation, by whose operation all nature grew, and made itself, and died, and was born again.

> Ye of plastic power, that interfused
> Roll through the grosser and material mass
> In organising surge—Holies of God!

He conceives, that is, that the one all-conscious Spirit has within Himself and sends forth from Himself infinite myriads of self-conscious minds; some to weave the fates of Man and live in Man, others to live in and inform all the organic and inorganic forms of Nature. All these God informs

> With absolute ubiquity of thought
> (His one eternal self-affirming act).

So that the whole universe—through God's thought being always affirmed in all these spirits who make all things live—is always in God at every moment, and consists by Him. Nature, therefore, in all its myriad forms is ever alive in God; and each form, nevertheless, having a distinct spirit connected with it, seems to have its own peculiar life, and a self-centred end. Some, he says, speaking of these monads,

> Some nurse the infant diamond in the mine,
> Some roll the genial juices through the oak,
> Some drive the mutinous clouds to clash in air.

The theory has some relation to Shelley's, only that Shelley makes Nature self-existent, Coleridge an effluence from God.

" Glory to Thee," he cries,

> Father of Earth and Heaven,
> All-conscious Presence of the Universe,
> Nature's vast ever-acting energy,
> In Will, in Deed, impulse of All in All.

This is Coleridge's first idea.

He changes afterwards to the idea that it is the Thought of God in us which makes Nature to us. The existence of the outward world is only phenomenal, not actual. We have given us the forms of things in thought; and thinking these—we see, hear, and feel them, and build up the world of Nature from ourselves. Thus that which we call Nature only lives in us, it is we who make it; it can only be called alive because we are alive, and when we receive from it impressions, we receive, not something distinct from us, but our own thoughts. So that when we think and feel—Nature is.

In a remarkable poem, " The Æolian Harp," we have
the first touch of this theory. The music of the wind-
lute makes him think, as the wind touches it, of the
whole of Nature breaking into harmony under the
Thought of Man.

> O, the one life within us and abroad,
> Which meets all motion, and becomes its soul,
> A light in sound, a sound-like power in light,
> Rhythm in all thought, and joyance everywhere.

And carried further, he states the same idea more distinctly—

> And what if all of animated nature
> Be but organic harps diversely framed,
> That tremble into thought, as o'er them sweeps,
> Plastic and vast, one intellectual breeze,
> At once the Soul of each, and God of All.

In the last two lines the idea is made distinctly
theological. We, each in our thinking, make the outward world for ourselves ; but our thinking in this sphere
is in its source, the one Thought of God in which, infinitely varied through a myriad secondary forms of thought,
the universe consists.

In this poem the thought is philosophically stated ;
afterwards, in a poem of human feeling, the Ode to
Dejection, the same theory is stated from the side of
melancholy sentiment. They are lines which everyone
has read :

> O Lady ! we receive but what we give,
> And in our life alone does Nature live :

Ours is her wedding garment, ours her shroud !
And would we aught behold, of higher worth,
Than that inanimate cold world allowed
To the poor, loveless, ever-anxious crowd—
   Ah ! from the soul itself must issue forth,
   A light, a glory, a fair luminous cloud
     Enveloping the earth—
And from the soul itself there must be sent
A sweet and potent voice, of its own birth,
Of all sweet sounds the life and element !

There may be matter, that is, but matter only lives
when we think it and feel it. But our thinking and feeling of it are God's thinking and feeling of it through us.
When we think then those thoughts of God that projected
from us make the universe, we are thinking so much
of God. Whosoever then thinks of the universe thinks of
it as divine life : whosoever knows this as the truth,
rejoices in it, and from him goes forth over the whole
appearance which the world takes to him, "a light, a
glory, a fair luminous cloud," that makes glorious all
things,—a sweet and potent voice, the echo of God in
his own soul that turns the universe into music. Hence,
when we have given life to Nature from ourselves—its
"life the eddying of our living soul"—and our life is
itself one that feels its source in God, and has conscious
communion with Him—then there is nothing in Nature
which to our thoughts is not God's life, which to our
senses does not seem to speak or sing of Him. And
we, finding Him everywhere, transfer our own feeling of
thanksgiving and delight in His beauty and power to the
world itself, and say, with the Psalmist, "that the
Heavens declare His glory and the firmament sheweth
His handiwork," that all things praise and bless Him.

And Coleridge has written one noble psalm of Nature in his Hymn at sunrise in the Valley of Chamouni, in which ice plains, and meadow streams, and pine groves, and flowers and snow " utter forth God and fill the hills with praise;" in which, with an image almost too daring, he pictures the great mountain rising and ever rising, like a cloud of incense from the earth, and telling to all the stars and to the rising sun that

> Earth, with her thousand voices, praises God.

Secondly. The question arises, How, if Nature live only in our life, can she be said to have any influence over us ? and yet it is plain that she does affect us. Coleridge, as a Poet, replies in this way. The worldly man, who has lost his true self in devotion to the transient and the visible, does not of course recognise that Nature is the God within him speaking. It seems to him to be wholly different from himself or anything in himself. But being conceived of as different, he flies to it when wearied of self-seeking and of the busy human heart whose passions and follies have exhausted him; and he hears in it a voice strange to him, but beautiful, but which ought not be so strange. For it is in truth the voice of God in his own soul that he hears; it is, in truth, his diviner self he hears, only he does not know that. But when heard, it recalls him to himself; it puts him in mind of higher things, and without his will he worships. At first it only seems to him that there is a spirit of unconscious life in trees and wild flowers, in which life he longs to share :

> To be something that he knows not of,
> In winds or waters or among the rocks,—

for in such sharing he will lose something of the impor-
tunate, craving, lower self in another life than his own.
But as this longing passes into a real communion with
Nature, and he forgets his lower being, new hopes, new
pleasures come upon him, thoughts sublime, dreams in
which the soul forsakes itself, tearful raptures, boyish
mirth,

> Silent adorations making
> A blessed shadow of this earth;

and at last—though at first, as I said, he knows not
what it is that has lifted him above himself—a light
breaks upon him, he recognizes that it is God within
him who has spoken through Nature's images of
beauty or peace or sublimity; that the real lesson he
has received did not come to him from a dead Nature,
but from his own awakening soul, using the apparent
world as the means of teaching him that which his true
self is.* And when he has once learnt that lesson, then
—this is the peculiarity of his relation towards apparent

---

* As illustrating all that is said here, I quote a passage from one of
the few poems that rise above third-rate importance. It is from " Frost
at Midnight : "

> For I was reared
> In the great city, pent mid cloisters dim,
> And saw nought lovely but the sky and stars.
> But thou, my babe, shalt wander like a breeze
> By lakes and sandy shores; beneath the crags
> Of ancient mountains, and beneath the clouds,
> Which image in their bulk both lakes and shores
> And mountain crags : So shalt thou see and hear
> The lovely shapes and sounds intelligible
> Of that eternal language, which thy God
> Utters, who from eternity doth teach
> Himself in all, and all things in himself.

Nature—ever afterwards the impressions made on his senses by any beautiful object or landscape, do not remain as sense-impressions. The image of the thing begins to be supplanted by the thoughts it awakens, and of which it is in reality the appearance ; and ever growing less and less real, as it is replaced by the growing thoughts, becomes at last a vision in the mind, into which the whole soul for the time dilates, and in which, if the soul be religious, it is swept upwards towards God, in whom thought and image had their source. For example, he is thinking of Mont Blanc, and says

> O dread and silent Mount ! I gazed upon thee,
> Till thou, still present to my bodily sense,
> Didst vanish from my thought : entranced in prayer
> I worshipped the Invisible alone.
> Yet, like some sweet beguiling melody,
> So sweet, we know not we are listening to it,
> Thou, the meanwhile, wast blending with my thought,
> Yea, with my life and life's own secret joy :
> Till the dilating soul, enrapt, transfused
> Into the mighty vision passing—there
> As in her natural form, swelled vast to Heaven.

Or at other times, when the image seen is more homely, instead of a lofty mountain, a pastoral valley, or a pleasant glade where the thoughts and associations stirred are human; the visible image is gradually replaced by thoughts of real human love and joy and sorrow, by the vision of friendships gone and living, by hopes for man, by faith in his lofty destiny, by love of the whole race.

In both cases, we lose the sensuous impressions through the thoughts they awaken, and these thoughts are them-

selves the causes of the sensuous impressions, though that
is at first unknown to us.

Our best enjoyment of Nature, then, (if we take both
these cases as those which include the greater number of
smaller impressions and thoughts within them) is bound
up with two things, with the ineffable invisible life of
God, and with the image of a perfect human society. So
that we shall, first, gazing round

> On the wide landscape, gaze till all doth seem
> Less gross than bodily ; and of such hues
> As veil the Almighty Spirit, when yet he makes
> Spirits perceive His presence.

So that, secondly, life with Nature will seem like conversation with noble men and women, and we receive from
her human impulse and blessing, tenderer and kinder
feelings,

> A livelier impulse and a dance of thought,

" grateful," as Coleridge says :

> That by Nature's quietness,
> And solitary musings, all my heart
> Is softened, and made worthy to indulge
> Love, and the thoughts that yearn for human kind.

But the whole of this view which makes Nature the reflex
of Man, has two special evils. Its first evil is that
it fixes the mind when among natural beauty, on self, till
even in its highest expression, when it tells of joy and
life—the Poet closes by saying, that all the rapture we
have in Nature is but this:

> We in ourselves rejoice.

Nothing can be further than that from Wordsworth's
healthier view, which is the direct opposite.

Its second evil is, that always troubled with self-thought in the midst of Nature, philosophizing about himself and her, moving off to visit other things than her, the Poet can never see Nature exactly as she is, and consequently never describes accurately or vividly or closely. Wordsworth, on the contrary, gave himself up to what Nature was saying to him, and rarely thought of what he had to say about himself in connection with her till he had received all the impressions she chose to give him. He could look at a tree, a cloud, a flower, and see each as they were, unmixt with human feeling. Therefore we have from him close, direct description.

There are few passages in Coleridge of direct description; one, however, of special excellence, shows how he could have described if he could have got rid of the worry of self-thought, if he could have said, " I receive from Nature what I do not give ; she has her own life, and that is *not* mine ! " It is this description of the wayside spring that reads as if the mantle of Wordsworth had fallen on him as he wrote it :

> This sycamore, oft musical with bees,—
> Such tents the Patriarchs loved ! O long unharmed
> May all its aged boughs o'ercanopy
> The small round basin, which this jutting stone
> Keeps pure from fallen leaves. Long may the Spring
> Quietly, as a sleeping infant's breath,
> Send up cold waters to the traveller
> With soft and even pulse ! Nor ever cease
> Yon tiny cone of sand its soundless dance,
> Which at the bottom, like a Fairy's page
> As merry, and no taller, dances still
> Nor wrinkles the smooth surface of the fount.

Now and then even he seems to feel that the true poetic

position towards Nature was that which Wordsworth took up—that of one spirit, looking at and listening to another different from himself—and he expresses this in a few lines in his poem of "The Nightingale," when he speaks of the Poet, who echoing the thought of the sorrow-stricken man, calls the nightingale a melancholy bird. He is one

Who hath been building up the rhyme
When he had better far have stretched his limbs
Beside a brook in mossy forest dell ;
By sun or moonlight to the influxes
Of shapes and sounds and shifting elements
Surrendering his whole spirit, of his song
And of his fame forgetful! so his fame
Should share in Nature's immortality,
A venerable thing ; and so his song
Should make all Nature lovelier, and itself
Be loved like Nature.

It is curious that the poem in which Coleridge is truest to Nature is the "Ancient Mariner," written directly under Wordsworth's influence. It too shows us how much might have been done had he worked on a right path, had he not been led away, by a philosophy which mingled up Man and Nature, not to look at Nature but at himself. Let me recall to you, in conclusion, the natural description of that poem, and mark how it is at once accurate, imaginative, and of wide range.

Its range extends from the quiet scenery of a country wood to the fierce scenery of the tropics, and to that of the polar zone. Few poems embrace so much, and the work is all of the best class. There are just incidentally touched, but touched with perfect pictorial skill and truth, at least

5

a dozen aspects of the sea : the ship scudding before the
stormy wind towards the south, with sloping masts and
dipping prow; the iceberg-covered sea; the great snow
fog over the sea, dark by day, glimmering white by
night in the moonshine; the belt of calms with its dreadful rolling swell, and water "that like a witch's oils,
burnt green, and blue, and white;" the sea in the tor-
nado; the gentle weather of the temperate seas and the
quiet English harbour. Looking at the shortness of the
poem the range is very great; while its accuracy of description,—not the dull accuracy of mere portraiture, but
poetical accuracy, the thing itself described but lit up with
a glory of feeling or of association with other things—is
very remarkable.

I read this description of the ship in moonlight at sea,
in a tropic calm. The beauty of the illustration of the frost
is equalled by its truth, the motion of the moon is
almost heard in the verse, and yet the whole is a finished
picture:

> The moving moon went up the sky,
> And no where did abide :
> Softly she was going up,
> And a star or two beside—
> Her beams bemocked the sultry main,
> Like April hoar-frost spread;
> But where the ship's huge shadow lay,
> The charmèd water burnt alway
> A still and awful red.

But Coleridge is uncontent to leave the description of the
sky without throwing round it the light of the higher
imagination, and it is characteristic of the quaint phantasy
which belonged to his nature that he puts the thoughts
which lift the whole scene into the realm of the imagi-

nation into the prose gloss at the side — and it is perhaps the loveliest little thought in all his writings :

" In his loneliness and fixedness he yearneth toward the journeying " moon, and the stars that still sojourn yet still move onward ; and " everywhere the blue sky belongs to them, and is their appointed rest, " and their native country and their own natural homes, which they " enter unannounced, as lords that are certainly expected, and yet there " is a silent joy at their arrival."

Nor in contrast with this tropic scene and the fierce character of its landscape is the quiet harbour in the temperate zone less truly felt or less clearly expressed. Though some of the lines are weak, the whole impression is vivid :

> The harbour-bay was clear as glass
> So smoothly it was strewn !
> And on the bay the moonlight lay
> And the shadow of the moon.
> The rock shone bright, the kirk no less
> That stands above the rock :
> The moonlight steeped in silentness
> The steady weather-cock.

Then there are two other descriptions, one of the ship in a swift tropical squall in which the smallest details are true to fact, the other of the ship sailing quietly, which I throw together :

> And the coming wind did roar more loud,
>   And the sails did sigh like sedge,
> And the rain poured down from one black cloud,
>   The moon was at its edge.
> The thick black cloud was cleft, and still
>   The moon was at its side,
> Like waters shot from some high crag
> The lightning fell with never a jag,
>   A river steep and wide.

And the other:

> It ceased ; yet still the sails made on
> A pleasant noise till noon,
> A noise like of a hidden brook
> In the leafy month of June,
> That to the sleeping woods all night
> Singeth a quiet tune.

In both these descriptions, one of the terror, the other of
the softness of Nature, a certain charm, of the source of
which we are not at once conscious, is given by the introduction into the lonely sea of images borrowed from the
land, but which exactly fit the sounds to be described at
sea ; such as the noise of the brook and the sighing of
the sedge.   We are brought into closer sympathy with the
mariner by this subtle suggestion of his longing for the
land and its peace.   And we ourselves enjoy the travel of
thought, swept to and fro without any shock—on account
of the fitness of illustration and thing—from sea to land,
from land to sea.

Much more might be said on this, but it tells its own
tale.   The Poem illustrates still further—and this gives
it its special interest to us—the personal, simple religion
of Coleridge.   We see in it how childlike the philosophic
man could be in his faith, how little was enough for him.
Its religion is all contained in the phrase—" He prayeth
well who loveth well   Both man and bird and beast."
On this the changes are rung throughout ; the motiveless
slaughter of the bird is a crime ; the other mariners who
justify the killing of the bird because of the good it seems
to bring them are even worse sinners than the ancient
mariner.   He did the ill deed on a hasty impulse ; they

deliberately agree to it for selfish reasons. They sin a
second time against love by throwing the whole guilt on
him, and again for selfish reasons. They are fatally
punished, he lives to feel and expiate his wrong. And
the turning point of his repentance is in the re-awakening
of love, and is clearly marked. Left all alone on the
sea, "he despiseth the creatures of the calm, and envieth
that so many should live and so many lie dead," and in
that temper of contempt and envy Coleridge suggests that
no prayer can live. But when seven days had passed, he
looked again on God's creatures of the great calm, and
seeing their beauty and their happiness, forgot his own
misery, and the curse, and himself in them, and blessed
and loved them ; and in that temper of spirit prayer
became possible :

> O happy living things ! no tongue
> Their beauty might declare :
> A spring of love gushed in my heart
> And I blessed them unaware.
> The self-same moment I could pray.

The main thought and its details have their own beauty,
and they illustrate the new love of animals in English
poetry, but there is an often-noticed absurdity which
injures the sense of art in the mass of machinery which
is used to impress so simple a thought. It is like making
use of a calculating machine to add two and two together.

I have closed this lecture with the Ancient Mariner,
for in some sort he resembles his creator. Like him,
Coleridge's soul had been

> Alone on a wide wide sea,
> So lone it was, that God himself
> Scarce seemed there to be.

Like him, though not as Poet, Coleridge might say now:

> I pass, like night, from land to land;
> I have strange power of speech;
> That moment that his face I see
> I know the man that must hear me,
> To him my tale I teach.

And like him, finally, the much adventuring man, the Poet who had adventured so far into wild seas of mental and religious thought, came home at last and found peace in simple faith in God, in childlike humility, in mercy and love of man, and in reverence for all things :

> O sweeter than the marriage feast
> 'Tis sweeter far to me
> To walk together to the kirk
> With a goodly company !
> To walk together to the kirk
> And all together pray,
> While each to his great Father bends,
> Old men and babes and loving friends,
> And youths and maidens gay.
> He prayeth best who loveth best
> All things both great and small,
> For the dear God who loveth us
> He made and loveth all.

It would be no unpleasant thought to compare that close with that of Tennyson's "Two Voices."

LECTURE V.

WORDSWORTH.

In speaking of the poetry of Nature, we have at length arrived at Wordsworth, and in coming to him, we come to the greatest of the English Poets of this century; greatest not only as a Poet, but as a philosopher. It is the mingling of profound thought, and of ordered thought, with poetic sensibility and power (the power always the master of the sensibility), which places him in this high position. He does possess a philosophy, and its range is wide as the universe. He sings of God, of Man, of Nature, and, as the result of these three, of Human Life, and they are all linked by thought, and through feeling, one to another; so that the result is a complete whole which one can study as if it were a world of its own. As such, the whole of his poetry is full, not of systematic theology, but of his own theology; and to bring this out, while at the same time analysing his work as a Poet, is the object of the lectures I shall deliver upon him. My first subject will be the mode in which he conceives God in His relation to Nature, and necessarily what he means by Nature; the next will be the relation which Nature bears to Man, and the work of God on Man through that relation. Afterwards I shall speak fully of Wordsworth's poetry of Man and its theology. It may seem too much to those who know Wordsworth but little, to devote so many lectures to him alone, but the only feeling that one who loves this Poet can have is, that too much time can scarcely be spent upon him; and that if only a few are induced not to glance over but to study his work, more good may be done than by a hundred sermons. For in truth his poetry is, as Coleridge said of the " Prelude,"

> an Orphic song indeed,
> A song divine of high and passionate thoughts
> To their own music chanted.

The term Nature, in Wordsworth's use of it, means, sometimes, the Nature of Man, those inherent and indestructible qualities which are common to the whole race, and which form together that which we call Human Nature. In the realm of the imagination Wordsworth frequently conceives of this Human Nature as one person, acting as if directly from himself; the male being of the universe to whom Nature, that is, the spirit who informs the outward world, is as the female being of the universe wedded in love and holy marriage.

But the term he more commonly uses when speaking of Human Nature is the *Mind of Man.* For all the practical purposes of my lectures I may take the meaning of the term Nature to be concerned in Wordsworth's Poetry with the world outside of us. In most of the previous poets as in ordinary talk, it means the outward universe with its motions and laws, all that we know and feel beyond ourselves, organic and inorganic; and in this sense Wordsworth sometimes uses it. But that would not define his use of the term accurately, for then Nature might be conceived of as dead, or as the image of our own thought. Wordsworth added Life to the outward world, and separated it from our thought.

I traced in a previous lecture the growth of the conception of Nature as alive, and said that this conception which had only been in germ in others, reached its full growth in Wordsworth's poetry. In what way? The outward universe lay before the Poet's eye and ear. He felt it speak to him, through his senses to his soul, and feeling this, he asked, What is it? Who is it that speaks? Is it only the matter of the universe, which by itself is dead? No, he answered; Matter is animated by a soul, and it is this soul which thrills to meet me. "An *active* principle" subsists

> In all things, in all natures, in the stars
> Of azure heaven, the unenduring clouds,
> In flower and tree, in every pebbly stone
> That paves the brooks; the stationary rocks,
> The moving waters and the invisible air,
> *   *   *   *
> from link to link
> It circulates, the soul of all the worlds.

Now that which acts, lives; and the universe lives as much by its soul as we do by ours.

To this active principle, Wordsworth gave personality; that which all shared in was in fact one. It was one life, one will, one character, one person. And this personality he called Nature.

To Wordsworth as he wrote, she took a living form, and became the life-giving spirit of the world. Day by day she built up the universe; it was she who, from her own vast life, gave to everything its special life, a separate soul to each :

> Yet whate'er enjoyments dwell,
> In the impenetrable cell
> Of the silent heart, which Nature
> Furnishes to every creature.

Each had from Nature not only its own distinct soul, and character, but also its own distinct work to do; the elements had their business, " the stars have tasks, the silent heavens their goings on."

And not only had each separate thing the gift of a soul from Nature, but whenever a place, such as a lonely dell among the hills, had a special beauty and character of its own, it was it by reason of a special soul within it, of a more manifold soul than that which dwelt in a single flower or stone.*

The thought was still further varied; and the larger divisions of the world of Nature, the whole of the sky, the whole of the earth and of the sea, were gifted with distinct and more complex being :

> The gentleness of Heaven is on the sea :
> Listen ! the mighty Being is awake
> And doth with his eternal motion make
> A sound like thunder everlastingly.

And further still, the moving powers of Nature, the wind, when it dances over wood and hill, tossing trees and grass, bearing on its bosom the seeds of earth, becomes the "over-soul" of the things it touches, adds to them a new pleasure and a new life, a life of reckless sport and jollity.

> * " A spirit and pulse of good,
> A life and soul to every mode of being
> Inseparably linked."

Describing the dandelion seed, or the thistle beard in
their game upon the lake, Wordsworth writes—

> Suddenly halting now, a lifeless stand !
> And starting off again with freak as sudden ;
> In all its sportive wanderings, all the while
> Making report of an invisible breeze,
> That was its wings, its chariot, and its horse,
> Its very playmate and its moving soul.

Nor is this all ; Nature has her own personal pleasures,
emotions, thoughts, plans such as we might have. She
chooses places, as we might do, for her special delight in
the universe which is her kingdom, quiet places such as
that " glade of water," and one green field hidden far
among the trees, of which the Poet says—

> The spot was made by Nature for herself,

giving vivid personality by this touch of selectiveness to
the being he has created. She exercises watchful care
over the life of all things ; she loves, with passion pure
and calm, all her children.

And her love passes from her own works to Man. She
pours herself into the Poets, whom she chooses for her
special friends, and through whom she speaks to Man ;
and Wordsworth felt that he was chosen by her from his
birth. Others there were whose souls, though unable to
express themselves, were yet a favoured haunt of hers.
Such was his brother, who had early gone to sea:

> Nature there
> Was with thee : she who loved us both, she still
> Was with thee ; and even so didst thou become
> A silent Poet ; from the solitude
> Of the vast sea didst bring a watchful heart
> Still couchant, an inevitable ear,
> And an eye practised like a blind man's touch.

There were others also, whom she chose not as persons to express her, but as children on whom she could lavish all her love without asking from them a return. And no lovelier poem exists than that in which Nature makes her whole world unite to educate and make beautiful one little maiden :

> Three years she grew in sun and shower ;
> Then Nature said—"A lovelier flower
> On earth was never sown :
> This Child I to myself will take,
> She shall be mine, and I will make
> A Lady of my own.
> Myself will to my darling be
> Both law and impulse : and with me
> The Girl, in rock and plain,
> In earth and heaven, in glade and bower,
> Shall feel an over-seeing power
> To kindle and restrain."

There is no need to quote the rest, it is well-known ; but nothing can be more living than the personality with which this poem invests Nature, nothing greater than the difference in feeling and thought between this conception and the mechanical Nature of Pope, or the dead universe of Cowper. We are in contact with a Person, not with a thought. But who is this person ? Is she only the creation of imagination, having no substantive reality beyond the mind of Wordsworth ? No, she is the poetic impersonation of an actual Being, the form which the Poet gives to the living Spirit of God in the outward world, in order that he may possess a metaphysical thought as a subject for his work as an artist. We know that this theological idea is at the basis of Wordsworth's representation of Nature from many passages. Here is one:

> Wisdom and spirit of the Universe :
> Thou Soul that art the Eternity of thought !
> And giv'st to forms and images a breath
> And everlasting motion; not in vain,
> By day or starlight, thus from my first dawn
> Of childhood didst thou intertwine for me
> The passions which build up our human soul.

This is God, living, moving, and rejoicing in all his works; not God in Man, but God in Nature, a wholly distinct manifestation of His life. Again, he speaks of

> The Being that is in the clouds and air,
> That is in the green leaves among the groves.

And to this Being he allots the care also of the creatures whom He loves. Moreover, His

> Dwelling is the light of setting suns,
> And the round ocean, and the living air,
> And the blue sky, and in the mind of man
> A motion and a spirit, that impels
> All thinking things, all objects of all thought,
> And rolls through all things.

It is more, you observe, than a mere influence; it is a conscious life which realizes itself as a personality, in realizing itself within the sum of things. In fact, this Being who is the life of the universe, is the all-moving Spirit of God, the soul which is the eternity of Thought in Nature.* It may be the fashion to call this pantheistic,

---

* A few lines in the "Prelude" express this clearly :
> Hitherto,
> In progress through this Verse, my mind hath looked
> Upon the speaking face of earth and heaven
> As her prime teacher, intercourse with man
> Established by the Sovereign Intellect,
> Who through that bodily image hath diffused,
> As might appear to the eye of fleeting time,
> A deathless spirit.   Bk. v.

but it is the true and necessary pantheism which affirms God in all, and all by Him, but which does not affirm that the All includes the whole of God. It is true a certain amount of what is called the personality of God seems to slip away from Wordsworth, when he speaks of God being in Nature; but we must separate, in speaking of his theology, his idea of God in relation to man which he conceived of as distinctly a personal relation, from his idea of God in relation to Nature which he could not conceive of as an absolutely personal relation. In the case of man, God entering into what we call personality is thought of as personal—in the case of Nature, God entering into that which is impersonal is thought of as impersonal; or rather we are forced by our ignorance to use terms which imply impersonality, such as a motion, a Presence, and others.

Nevertheless Wordsworth's feeling of personality—that is of distinct self-consciousness of Being in God, was so strong, that he uses also such terms as the " Being who is in the clouds and air," and he would probably have said that the personality of God in reference to Nature consisted in God's consciousness of Himself at every moment of time in every part, as well as in the whole of the universe.

But as this is a metaphysical and not a poetic thought, and as Wordsworth wanted a thought which he could use poetically,* he transferred this idea of God realising His personality in the whole of the universe, to an actual person whom he creates, to a Being whom he terms Nature.

---

* The closing lines of the sonnet written at sea off the Isle of Man show how keenly Wordsworth felt the necessity of conceiving of Nature and of all her forms as living, if any intense poetry of Nature was to be

And hence there grew up in his mind the thought of one personal spiritual life, which had infinitely subdivided itself through all the forms of the outward world, which could realize an undivided life at any moment, but which also lived a distinct life in every part. It became possible then for him to have communication with any one manifestation of that life, in a tree or a rock or a cloud; to separate in thought the characteristics of any one form of it from another—or omitting the consideration of the parts—to think of or communicate with the whole, to realize the one spiritual life that conditioned itself in all, as a Person with whom he could speak and from whom he could receive impulse or warning or affection.

And when this was done, when Nature seemed one Life, then the necessary spirituality of the thought made him lose consciousness of the material forms under which this life appeared; and that condition of mind arose in which Nature was unsubstantialized in thought. And we find Wordsworth in many passages representing this as his experience, nor is it at all an uncommon one. For there are times when the sense of this spiritual life in Nature becomes so dominant that the material world fades away, and we feel as if we ourselves were pure spirit,

written, and how, as a Poet of Nature, he resented the mechanical theory of the universe.

> O Fancy, what an age was *that* for song!
> That age when not by laws inanimate,
> As men believed, the waters were impelled,
> The air controlled, the stars their courses held;
> But element and orb on *acts* did wait,
> Of *Powers* endued with visible form, instinct
> With will, and to their work by passion linked.

and all the objects of sense were not real things we could touch, but unsubstantial appearances.   In certain physical states—when they are accompanied with that upper meditation, if I may so call it, in which one seems to float apart from the body—the outward world is not felt, but only the life which inspires it.   We are forced to go to a tree to touch it, in order to realise that it is tangible.   We receive, that is, images through the senses, and the senses give them to the imagination and the intellect to deal with. These powers turn the sensible images into ideas and emotions, and so vivid do these ideas and emotions become, that they push the sensible things which awaked them out of the field of our consciousness.   Through the sense we lose the sense, through the visible we enter the world of the invisible.   It is an experience many of us have gone through.   It comes chiefly when the incessant small noises of Nature make less attack upon the ear, when we are high up on a mountain side, or when we sit at night by the sea when the low mist seems to hush the water into silence, or when in deep noon one sound alone, like the wandering voice of the cuckoo, smites on the ear.   One knows how Wordsworth felt this last—how the invisible bird became to him only a voice, a mystery; till the whole world was taken out of the region of sense and made as visionary as this herald of the spring.

> O blessed bird ! the earth we pace
> Again appears to be
> An unsubstantial faery place :
> That is fit home for thee.

It is an experience which often came to this poet as boy and man.   It marked his youth, as he tells us in one of

his letters ; it marked his manhood, and then he knew
better what it meant : then he felt that when the earth
grew unsubstantial in this hour of ecstasy, it was to reveal
the spiritual substance which lay within it, the life of the
living God—the ineffable act and thought of God by
which the universe consisted. He speaks of times
when

> The gross and visible frame of things
> Relinquishes its hold upon the sense,
> Yea, almost on the mind itself, and seems
> All unsubstantialized.

And the living soul communes directly with the living
soul of Nature, ' spirit to spirit, ghost to ghost.'

What is it then, to which we speak, with whom we have
communion? Not with Nature the poetic creation of the
imagination, but with the spirit of the God who abides
as Life in all. Here are some lines from the " Excursion " which express it, which embody the grandeur of
Wordsworth's theology of Nature in words as grand as the
thought :

> Such was the Boy—but for the growing Youth
> What soul was his, when, from the naked top
> Of some bold headland, he beheld the sun
> Rise up, and bathe the world in light ! He looked—
> Ocean and earth, the solid frame of earth
> And ocean's liquid mass, in gladness lay
> Beneath him :—Far and wide the clouds were touched
> And in their silent faces could be read
> Unutterable love. Sound needed none,
> Nor any voice of joy ; his spirit drank
> The spectacle : sensation, soul, and form,
> All melted into him : they swallowed up
> His animal being ; in them did he live,
> And by them did he live ; they were his life.

> In such access of mind, in such high hour
> Of visitation from the living God,
> Thought was not ; in enjoyment it expired.
> No thanks he breathed, he proffered no request ;
> Rapt into still communion that transcends
> The imperfect offices of prayer and praise,
> His mind was a thanksgiving to the power
> That made him ; it was blessedness and love !

I have now to ask, what are the special characteristics of this life of Nature, and how are they connected with the thought of a divine life ?

The first characteristic of this life of Nature is, that it is a life of enjoyment.   No instance of Wordsworth's belief in this is finer than the first poem upon the naming of places.   I give it as one example, though the thought runs through the whole of Wordsworth :

> It was an April morning : fresh and clear
> The Rivulet, delighting in its strength,
> Ran with a young man's speed ; and yet the voice
> Of waters which the winter had supplied
> Was softened down into a vernal tone.
> The spirit of enjoyment and desire,
> And hopes and wishes, from all living things
> Went circling, like a multitude of sounds.
> The budding groves seemed eager to urge on
> The steps of June : as if their various hues
> Were only hindrances that stood between
> Them and their object : but, meanwhile, prevailed
> Such an entire contentment in the air
> That every naked ash, and tardy tree
> Yet leafless, showed as if the countenance
> With which it looked on this delightful day
> Were native to the summer.—Up the brook
> I roamed in the confusion of my heart,
> Alive to all things and forgetting all.
> At length I to a sudden turning came
> In this continuous glen, where down a rock
> The Stream, so ardent in its course before,

Sent forth such sallies of glad sound that all
Which I till then had heard appeared the voice
Of common pleasure : beast and bird, the lamb,
The shepherd's dog, the linnet and the thrush
Vied with this waterfall, and made a song
Which, while I listened, seemed like the wild growth
Or like some natural produce of the air,
That could not cease to be.

Naturally, the same idea of frank enjoyment of life is given to things which have organic life. The hare runs races in her mirth, the flowers enjoy the air they breathe. The waves dance beside the daffodils, but they

Outdid the sparkling waves in glee,
A Poet could not but be gay
In such a jocund company.

The bluecap in the appletree cannot contain himself for glee, nor the lambs, in spring. Thus, he says of the linnet :

Thou, ranging up and down the bowers,
Art sole in thy employment ;
A Life, a Presence like the Air,
Scattering thy gladness without care,
Too blest with any one to pair ;
Thyself thy own enjoyment.

And though, when autumn had come, these gave no sign of open joy, yet it did not follow that they had no enjoyment, for other pleasures might be

Sweeter e'en than gaiety.

And all this life was praise to God, natural, unconscious praise, praise because the givers could not help giving it ; their enjoyment their greatest praise, as ours should be ; full and deep as that with which each morning the lark sang its hymn to God.

Happy, happy Liver !
With a soul as strong as a mountain river,
Pouring out praise to the Almighty Giver.

That was the religious aspect of this delight in life. But it passed from the religious to the theological when this infinite pleasure of the whole of Nature was felt to be by Wordsworth, not only symbolic of, but actually, the joy of God in His own life. It was God who renewed each moment in the boundless delight of all things, his "ancient rapture" in the continuous act of creation; it was God Himself who rejoiced in the brook and the tree, in the daisy and the lark. It is a thought which should add a new element to our happiness. For in our worst sadness we ought not to be too morose to be glad of the pleasure of all things—in our worst grief the sense of God's enjoyment which we receive from the joy of Nature ought to come with healing to our hearts.

The second characteristic of the life of Nature is its quietude. She has joy, ecstasy in her life, but it is untroubled-ecstasy. We are "pressed by heavy laws," tormented by doubt, and rent by struggle against conditions which we will not obey at once. Nature's life is at peace, for her children never wage a foolish strife with her; nor does self enter their hearts to make them weary of life. Deep calm is at her heart, the mountains rest in their own peace, the stars shine quietly, the sun "sinks down in his tranquillity," the flowers keep a still silence, and though there are storms which drive the clouds in passionate course, and torrents which rend the earth, and strong forces which sweep to and fro the elements in bewildering and endless, motion, yet

in the higher region of thought in which these things are
seen in their relation to the great whole, there is

> Central peace subsisting at the heart
> Of endless agitation.

And this, too—this tranquil being in each thing which
sends "its own deep quiet to restore our hearts," this
central peace, was not self-born in Nature—it was in
Wordsworth's thought the ineffable calm of God's existence which spoke to us and redeemed us.

The third characteristic is ceaseless intercommunion,
and that was founded on the unutterable love which flowed
through all things, and with which each thing acted on
each other. The whole world was linked together. Every
part, every element, gave and received, honoured and did
service to each other. Each plant and hill, cloud and
stream, has its own life and character, and they delight
in social intercourse like friends who love each other—
there is no jar, no jealousy, no envy there—their best joy
is in being kind to one another.

This idea is the loveliest of all which Wordsworth
introduced into English poetry, and it flowed from his
conception of everything in Nature having its own peculiar life. I might give a hundred instances of it, for it
runs like a living stream through all the woodland of
his poetry. It is varied in many ways; the waves are
brothers which run after one another; he says of the great
eminence which of all his hills last parleyed with the
setting sun that the meteors made of it their favourite
haunt, as if even those wild bodies had their power of
choice to love one cliff especially; the lake rejoices to

receive into her bosom the scenery which surrounds her :

> Through all her depths St. Mary's lake
> Is visibly delighted,
> For not a feature of the hills
> Is in her mirror slighted.

And Windermere prepares herself, like a woman for one she loves, to receive the evening :

> The lake though bright is of a placid blue
> As if preparing for the peace of evening.

In spring time the whole world gives and receives joy; and earth and sky and man feel their communion each with each :

> There is a blessing in the air,
> Which seems a sense of joy to yield
> To the bare trees, and mountains bare,
> And grass in the green field.
>
> * * * *
>
> Love, now an universal birth,
> From heart to heart is stealing,
> From earth to man, from man to earth—
> It is the hour of feeling.

But the noblest passage out of many is in the " Excursion " where the Solitary speaks of the two great brother peaks which overpeered the glen. I read it : mark how the wind rejoices in them, and they give back its wild pleasure; how all the things which touch and haunt them get their reply ; how they are loved and love; how busy are the mute agents there ; how proud the stars to shine on them :

> " Those lusty twins," exclaimed our host, " if here
> It were your lot to dwell, would soon become
> Your prized companions.—Many are the notes

Which, in his tuneful course, the wind draws forth
From rocks, woods, caverns, heaths, and dashing shores ;
And well those lofty brethren bear their part
In the wild concert—chiefly when the storm
Rides high ; then all the upper air they fill
With roaring sound, that ceases not to flow,
Like smoke, along the level of the blast,
In mighty current ; theirs, too, is the song
Of stream and headlong flood that seldom fails ;
And, in the grim and breathless hour of noon,
Methinks that I have heard them echo back
The thunder's greeting.   Nor have Nature's laws
Left them ungifted with a power to yield
Music of finer tone ; a harmony
So do I call it, though it be the hand
Of silence, though there be no voice ;—the clouds,
The mist, the shadows, light of golden suns,
Motions of moonlight, all come thither—touch,
And have an answer—thither come, and shape
A language not unwelcome to sick hearts
And idle spirits :—there the sun himself,
At the calm close of summer's longest day,
Rests his substantial orb ;—between those heights
And on the top of either pinnacle,
More keenly than elsewhere in night's blue vault,
Sparkle the stars, as of their station proud.
Thoughts are not busier in the mind of man
Than the mute agents stirring there :—alone
Here do I sit and watch."

The deep underlying thought of all this belief in the love and intercommunion of all things—the thought which makes Nature, in this conception of her, divine—was that this endless interchange of life and joy was in reality, not the type of, but actually, the never-ceasing self-reciprocation of God. He divides Himself into a myriad forms, and lives in each distinctly, and makes His own ineffable society and enjoyment by living with Himself from form to form, by loving Himself, and by self-communion through infinitely varied activity and beauty and sacrifice, giving and receiving Himself for ever in the universe. And yet, though I say self in these sentences, it is because we must so express it, in order to get the idea. There is no Self in our sense of the word in God, none except the consciousness of perfect Being : and we can best express what that consciousness of Being is by saying that it is for ever the unspeakable delight of everlasting thought unremittingly passing into creative activity, in which that which we call self is so lost as never to be known.

This is the idea of Life in Nature, which Wordsworth has given to the world. It fills the heart of his readers; it makes of Nature a new thing to them; it makes the commonest walk in the woods a delight, a teaching, a society; it fills the world with life and energy and joy; it uplifts us sometimes when alone among the hills—when Nature is in one of her wild moods, and her life most intelligent and most eager, into a kindred ecstasy in which we long to be borne away with wind and cloud to join the mighty stream of rejoicing Life. So was it once at least with Wordsworth : and with this I close.

> " Oh ! what a joy it were, in vigorous health,
> To have a body (this our vital frame
> With shrinking sensibility endued,
> And all the nice regards of flesh and blood)
> And to the elements surrender it
> As if it were a spirit !—How divine,
> The liberty, for frail, for mortal man,
> To roam at large among unpeopled glens
> And mountainous retirements, only trod
> By devious footsteps ; regions consecrate
> To oldest time ! and, reckless of the storm
> That keeps the raven quiet in her nest,
> Be as a presence or a motion—one

Among the many there ; and while the mists
Flying, and rainy vapours, call out shapes
And phantoms from the crags and solid earth
As fast as a musician scatters sounds
Out of an instrument ; and while the streams
(As at a first creation and in haste
To exercise their untried faculties)
Descending from the region of the clouds,
And starting from the hollows of the earth
More multitudinous every moment, rend
Their way before them—what a joy to roam
An equal among mightiest energies ;
And haply sometimes with articulate voice,
Amid the deafening tumult, scarcely heard
By him that utters it, exclaim aloud,
" Rage on ye elements ! let moon and stars
Their aspects lend, and mingle in their turn
With this commotion (ruinous though it be)
From day to night, from night to day, prolonged ! "

LECTURE VI.

In my last lecture I spoke of the meaning Wordsworth had for the term "Nature," of his conception of Nature as having a life of her own and of the characteristics of that life, its endless joy, central peace, and how all its forms, each having their own life, were knit together by unselfish love. But these are terms which are true of humanity also; we can say that human nature is capable of joy and peace and love, and Wordsworth does say that we see in Nature similar passions to our own. But though he thought them similar, he did not think them identical; he drew a clear distinction between them, between the life in Nature and that in Man. On this distinction I must now enlarge, in order that I may come to that part of my subject which treats of the education that Nature gives to man; a thought that pervades the whole of Wordsworth's poetry.

There are poets who impute to Nature their own moods and feelings, as when Tennyson makes the larkspur listen for Maud's footstep, or when Coleridge, giving to natural things the power of man, makes the Wind an actor or a poet. This is what Ruskin calls the "pathetic fallacy;" and a few instances, such as the phrase "forlorn cascades,"

where the lonely water-fall seems to him abandoned by
the world because he feels himself forlorn, exist in Wordsworth; but he always means to distinguish clearly between
his own feelings and those which he believes belong to
things outside himself. The Me and the not-Me are not
the same. It is not the poet who makes Nature this or
that by giving himself to her; it is she who builds up
part of his being by communicating herself to him. It is
not that the sea is in this or that special mood, because
he is in it, or that the birds sing of certain things of
which he is thinking, but that the sea has its own moods,
and that the birds sing their own emotions:

> The birds around me hopped and played
> Their *thoughts I cannot measure :*

He does not define their thoughts: he is only certain
that they do think, and have pleasure and pain of their
own:

> But the least motion that they made
> It seemed a thrill of pleasure.

It is the same thing with flowers and rocks and clouds;
he could not express their kind of existence, but he was
certain of its being a feeling existence:

> And 'tis my faith that every flower
> Enjoys the air it breathes.

He is, of course, obliged to use the same terms as we
use about our thinking and feeling, when he speaks of
the life which natural things live, but he does not identify
their thoughts and feelings with ours. They are similar
to ours but they differ from ours, being conditioned by the
different material through which they work, in a much

greater degree, though in the same way as the thoughts and feelings of a man differ from those of a woman.

It is important in reading Wordsworth to understand this clearly—this separate life of Nature and Man, this distinctness which enables a dramatic action to take place between them. We have wholly got rid of the thought of Coleridge that Nature lives by the projection of our self upon it: we do not receive what we give, we give and receive back something wholly different. It is not the reflection of ourselves which we have from Nature, it is the friendship of another than ourselves.

It is this which makes Wordsworth's poetry so fresh, so healthy, and of such a morning quality. He forgets himself in the beauty, joy, and life of things; he will not spoil Nature by tracing in her any likeness to his own moods; he would not willingly have written that stanza in " In Memoriam," beginning with these lines :

> Calm is the morn without a sound,
> Calm as to suit a calmer grief:—

they would have contradicted his philosophy—nor traced in the gathering storm and looming cloud the "wild despair" of grief which filled Tennyson's heart for the loss of his friend. Nor would he, even by permitting human associations to cluster thickly in certain places, prevent these places from making their own natural impression upon him—a thing which Tennyson does frequently. The whole of the descriptions of Nature in " In Memoriam " are tinged with one or the other of these faults : skies, flowers, clouds, and trees, are full of the self of the poet, or of recollections of his friend ; and the result is that a partly morbid impression is left on the reader, even in the triumphant passages at the end—an impression of the tyranny of Human Nature over Nature, of ourselves as being the only thing in the universe—which is a depressing element in the poem. It is painful to be deprived by this imposition of Man on Nature of the only chance we have of getting rid of ourselves, or of feeling another life than human life. It is the first excellence of Wordsworth that though he does not pass by this " pathetic fallacy " altogether, he only treats it as a transient and unhealthy phase.

The Poem on the picture of Peele Castle in a storm has been so explained as to be an example of this pathetic fallacy, but Wordsworth is true in it to his philosophy.

He sees in it the Sea at peace, but he does not see it as the image of his own peace. It has its own quiet from its own nature, not from his. Being thus distinct, it sends its impression of calm to influence his heart. That being received, the powers of his mind take it up, and add their own work to it, " the consecration and the Poet's dream." From both these things—from the impression passively received, and the active energy of thought upon it—another thing arises, the poetic picture, the work of Art.

> Ah ! then, if mine had been the Painter's hand,
>   To express what then I saw ; and add the gleam,
> The light that never was, on sea or land,
>   The consecration, and the Poet's dream ;
>
> I would have planted thee, thou hoary Pile,
>   Amid a world how different from this !
> Beside a sea that could not cease to smile ;
>   On tranquil land, beneath a sky of bliss.

> Thou shouldst have seemed a treasure-house divine
>   Of peaceful years ; a chronicle of heaven;
> Of all the sunbeams that did ever shine
>   The very sweetest had to thee been given.
>
> A Picture had it been of lasting ease,
>   Elysian quiet, without toil or strife ;
> No motion but the moving tide, a breeze,
>   Or merely silent Nature's breathing life.
>
> Such, in the fond illusion of my heart,
>   Such Picture would I at that time have made
> And seen the soul of truth in every part,
>   A steadfast peace that might not be betrayed.

It is an illustration, in a small way, of what he means in the lines soon to be quoted, when he says that the individual mind and the external universe are fitted, in difference, to each other, and when wedded together accomplish a *creation*—something different from both—with blended might.

The latter part of the Poem is another side of the same thought, only the Art work which he wished to do for the calm, is done by Beaumont for the storm. He can no longer look on a calm sea and find the impression of calm. Something has happened which forbids it ; the sea has engulphed his brother. But he neither imposes the storm in his own heart on the calm, nor sees the sea in the storm as in sorrow for his loss. The sea has *its own* anger and fury. But Beaumont has seen it in storm, and receiving from it an impression of anger, has added to that impression, by imagination, correlative human emotion, and composed both into one creation by Art. And on this creation Wordsworth loves to look. It, the human work, the artistic result of the blended might of Nature and of the human mind, consoles him by its sympathy with his sorrow. The conclusion follows easily from this analysis.

Nothing can be more remote than all this from the faded sentiment which we found in Warton and the other poets of his class. To sit in the shade of yew trees, and feel a charm in their gloom reflecting our own—as was the case with the youth on whom Wordsworth wrote his " Lines near Esthwaite "—to trace in the barren landscape an emblem of our own unfruitful life, is the most sickly of all pleasures :

> The man whose eye
> Is ever on himself, doth look on one
> The least of Nature's works, one who might move
> The wise man to that scorn which wisdom holds
> Unlawful, ever.

And he went further still : not only were we bound to resist this tendency, but Nature herself had against it a sad resentment. Against it she continually fought, her one effort being to redeem us from this self-consideration, to lead us to lose our stormy passions in her quiet, our consuming sadness in her joy. An instance of this in his own experience occurs in the Ode on the intimations of Immortality. He begins by feeling that a glory has passed from the earth since he was young : grief falls on him, and in the shade of disenchantment the splendour leaves the grass, and the freshness the sunlight. But with the very utterance of the thought he springs away from this diseased condition. Nature speaking to him, he hears her voice ; and joy returns, not the joy of early life, but a stiller, more grave delight. " No more shall grief

of mine the season wrong," he cries ; it would indeed be
an evil day if he were sullen,

> While the earth is herself adorning
> This sweet May morning.

There shall be no severing of his love from fountains,
meadows, hills, and groves :

> Yet in my heart of hearts I feel your might ;
> I only have relinquished one delight
> To live beneath your more habitual sway ;
> I love the brooks which down their channels fret
> Even more than when I tripp'd lightly as they ;
> The innocent brightness of a new-born day
> Is lovely yet ;

The lines have their own special connection, but through
them also runs the thought of which we speak—of the
distinctness of the being of Nature from the being of
Human Nature, and of the work which Nature, as distinct, does on Man. His own mood of morbid melancholy which he tried to lay on Nature, she had refused to
receive ; she sent him back, on the contrary, her mood
of joy. When he had opened his heart to that influence,
though the melancholy did not wholly depart, it was freed
from weakness and selfishness. His heart was opened,
his sadness was filled with strength and the hope which
comes of delight in other things than our own emotions.

All this may not be theological, but it is distinctly
religious. It is the very element in which a high religion
becomes possible, a freedom from looking into self which
enables men to love and lose themselves in others ; to win
power by taking into themselves a thousand influences ;
to conquer life by the possession of that sound mind which,

in freedom from the prejudices to which self-consideration gives birth, can see things and opinions directly as
they are. Hence, and especially because of this, the
religion of Wordsworth is the noblest we possess in our
poetry, and the healthiest.

And, apart from personal religion, if we pass into
the realm of theology, we are rescued in Wordsworth's
poetry from the sight of our Self in Nature, and enabled to
see God in it. The man who finds in Nature only the
reflection of his own passions and thoughts can only find
God therein in His relation to himself, or his fellow-men.
He sees God only as human, and missing thus all the absolute side of the Deity, his idea of God is very imperfect.
But he who, escaping through passionate love of Nature
from self, looks straight into Nature and sees her as she
is, beholds God not only as personal, but as impersonal,
not only as the human God, but as far beyond humanity ;
and realizes that there is an infinite Sublimity, an eternal
Calm, a glory of Order, Beauty, and Variety, to which
he dare give no name nor allot a human personality, but
which he truly knows is active and loving, wise and of
unweariable power. And our modern theology bitterly
wants that conception. It would tend to free it from its
ceaseless and diseased insistance on humanity alone, and
let us loose a little from ourselves.

II. Having now spoken of Wordsworth's separation of
Man from Nature, and its moral result on his poetry, I
ask what philosophic conception he founded on it. I
shall try to approach it by an analogy. We get a hint
in the first chapter of Genesis that God conceived of
Man and Woman as originally one being, as Man—who

held in one person all the male and female qualities, and as such, was a perfect ideal of Human Nature ; that afterwards He divided this one Being into two persons, having similar passions, volitions, and appetites, but differently conditioned by sex ; that each of these was the complement of the other and fitted to unite with one another, in order that by the mutual play of the divers qualities of each on the other the education of both might take place ; and that when both, through this mutual action on each other, became at one, Human Nature would be again, as it was at first, complete.

The conception of Wordsworth with regard to Man and Nature is much the same. The spirit which lives in each differs as Man differs from Woman, not indeed in the same, but in a similar manner, but—they differ for the purpose of union, and there is between them a preordained fitness. Each educates the other, and in their final marriage is the consummation of the perfection of the human mind and Nature. Here are the lines in which Wordsworth sketches this conception. It lies at the root of his Philosophy :

> For the discerning intellect of Man,
> When wedded to this goodly universe
> In love and holy passion, shall find these—

that is, Beauty, Paradise, the Elysian Fields, all ideal dreams of men—

> A simple produce of the common day.
> —I, long before the blissful hour arrives,
> Would chant, in lonely peace, the spousal verse
> Of this great consummation—and by words
> Which speak of nothing more than what we are,
> Would I arouse the sensual from their sleep
> Of Death, and win the vacant and the vain

To noble raptures ; while my voice proclaims
How exquisitely the individual Mind
(And the progressive power, perhaps no less
Of the whole species) to the external World
Is fitted :—and how exquisitely, too—
Theme this but little heard of among men—
The external World is fitted to the Mind :
And the *creation* (by no lower name
Can it be called) which they with blended might
Accomplish :—This is our high argument. *

So the whole grand idea is that God has made these two —Man and Nature—for one another and to develop each other, and His mighty object is that we should realise in the marriage of the mind and the external world the pre-arranged harmony. It is a sketch which is filled up in various ways in the minor Poems. It forms the true burden of the "Excursion" and the "Prelude." To reveal, to explain this underlying unity, to urge us to realise it by revealing the beauty in Man and Nature, is in Wordsworth's thought, the special work of poetry. "Poetry is the image of Man and Nature," and the object of the Poet is to produce such pleasure in the individual man by his imaging of Nature and Man as to induce love of Nature and union with her. "He considers Man and the objects which surround him as acting and reacting upon each other, so as to produce an infinite complexity of pain and pleasure." "He considers Man and Nature as essentially adapted to each

* Preface to the "Excursion." See also the Preface to the "Lyrical Ballads," where he says that the Poet is one "pleased with his own passions and volitions, and who rejoices more than other men in the spirit of life that is in him ; delighting to contemplate similar"—observe, he says similar, not identical —"volitions and passions as manifested in the goings-on of the universe, and habitually impelled to create them where he does not find them."

other, and the mind of Man as naturally the mirror of the fairest and most interesting properties of Nature."*

And when we look into our intuitions and emotions, when we are with an open heart alone with Nature, we seem to know that this is a true philosophy. We ask if Nature, so distinct from us, has no longing to unite herself to us, to find the complement of her Being in ours; and we cannot but trace this desire in the animals which love us, in the pleasure all of them, when we are kind, take in our company. And what we trace in the animals we need not fear to apply further, at least in the sphere of poetic feeling. There is a way in which things seem to look at us, and beg for our affection and sympathy. The trees nod to us, and we to them, as Emerson said. In hours when we have most shaken off the coil of self and the troubles of the world, we are impressed with delight by the love which all things seem to bear to us. A real emotion, as deep, but more clear and pure than that awakened by human love, is kindled in us by the knowledge that the trees are whispering their affection in our ear, and the brook singing its song to us, and the flowers adorning themselves to please our eye. Nor is there an atom of selfishness in this. We are frankly delighted with it, and accept it with healthy joy. We rejoice as much in the pleasure which Nature feels in uniting herself to us as in the pleasure she gives us. And when we feel so, we are ourselves purer and kinder, and less envious than at other times. She loves us and desires the time when her "mar-

* Preface to the second edition of the Lyrical Ballads.

riage " with us shall be complete; and when we are most conscious of that and most give back the wish, then we know best what St. Paul meant when he said—" The earnest expectation of the creature waiteth for the manifestation of the sons of God."

And we, on our part, we also possess this desire of union. Most of us have felt it at times to be unutterable, so secret and deep is its passion ; and when—rarely indeed, for they are the most consecrated moments of life—we have realised the emotion of harmonious alliance with the world, I know not if any purely human joy can be so exquisite. When we cannot realise it, the way in which our whole nature chafes against the secrecy and reticence of Nature shows how much the feeling partakes of true passion, while the very existence of such a passion prophesies the time when the marriage of the soul to the soul of Nature shall be accomplished. Men have tried to explain this longing by saying that it is the human element which we have projected into Nature, or that it is our own thought there to which we desire to reunite ourselves. It may be, they say, that the trees and the stream are really we, and that we love ourselves in loving them ; and Philosophy claps her hands and says that she has settled the question for Poetry. But the contradiction of that is rapid and instinctive; in the realm of feeling it is impossible to believe it ; one cannot love oneself in that manner. Moreover, whenever we are in that humour, when we try to say that the life of waters, clouds, and leaves is but " the eddying of our living soul," it is curious with what a mocking spirit they look upon us : walk in the woods with only that idea, or by the sea, and every tree and wave will say to you—"*you* find my secret, little fellow!" *

But a single rush of love to the great spirit who lives there will make her open her arms and heart to you. Turn to the trees and waves, as to friends, in that sudden expansion which one feels at times to human friends and in which all barriers melt, and there will not be a blade of grass nor a drift of cloud which will not partake its life with you, teach you its lesson, interpose between your heart and yourself its kindness, whisper to you infinite secrets and fill you with joy and calm.

> How bountiful is Nature ; he shall find
> Who seeks not, and to him that hath not asked,
> Large measure shall be dealt.

This is the task of Nature, and she fulfils it at the command of God, or rather it is God himself who in all her life gives us this education and help; and teaches us of Himself through her.

In the "Excursion," book iv., Wordsworth traces this work of hers into distant times. Long, long ago it began : Man was not left to himself to corrupt in apathy ;

> to feel the weight
> Of his own reason, without sense or thought
> Of higher reason and a purer will,
> To benefit and bless, through mightier power.

The Persian, when he sacrificed " to moon and stars, and to the winds, and mother elements," felt through

---

* One remembers Emerson's phrase—" Nature will not have us fret " or fume.   She does not like our benevolence or learning much better " than she likes our frauds and wars.   When we come out of the " Caucus, or the bank, or the Abolition Convention, or the Trans-" cendental Club, into the fields and woods, she says to us, ' So hot, my " ' little sir.' "

them "a sensitive existence and a God." The Chaldæan shepherds entered the invisible world through the thoughts which the moving planets and the still star of the Pole awakened in their minds; the Greek idolatrously served a hundred gods :

> And yet—triumphant o'er this pompous show
> Of art, this palpable array of sense,
> On every side encountered ; in despite
> Of the gross fictions chanted in the streets
> By wandering Rhapsodists ; and in contempt
> Of doubt and bold denial hourly urged
> Amid the wrangling schools—a *spirit* hung,
> Beautiful region ! o'er thy towns and farms,
> Statues and temples, and memorial tombs :
> And emanations were perceived ;—

For Nature spoke through the things of sense and told of spirit; and when the votary, thankful for his son's return, shed his severed locks upon Cephisus' river, then

> Doubtless, sometimes, when the hair was shed
> Upon the flowing stream, a thought arose
> Of Life continuous, Being unimpaired ;
> That hath been, is, and where it was and is
> There shall endure.

This was the work of Nature teaching an indefinite religion, telling of God to men who knew Him not, speaking of the infinite world beyond, through the emotions which the finite roused.

And now, in our later times, such training has gone so far, that we would not give to the trees or brook a wild half-human soul, and make a Dryad or a Naiad take their place ; for that would be to lose the tree or the brook itself. We keep the natural object, but we know within it is the life of God. It tells us in its own way part of the

character of our Father.   It is one of the forms He takes
to us.   Listen to Wordsworth speaking of the brook that
the poet and the painter sought :

> If wish were mine some type of thee to view,
> Thee and not thee thyself, I would not do
> Like Grecian artists—
>   No Naiad shouldst thou be—
> It seems the Eternal Soul is clothed in thee
> With purer robes than those of flesh and blood,
> And hath bestowed on thee a safer good,
> Unwearied joy, and life without its cares.

Then transferring in another place the same thought from
one object to all objects, he sees in the whole universe the
revealer of God to Man—the great Evangelist to Man.
" I have seen "—the lines are well-known—

> A curious child, who dwelt upon a tract
> Of inland ground, applying to his ear
> The convolutions of a smooth-lipped shell.
> To which, in silence hushed, his very soul
> Listened intensely ; and his countenance soon
> Brightened with joy ; for from within were heard
> Murmurings, whereby the monitor expressed
> Mysterious union with its native sea.
> Even such a shell the universe itself
> Is to the ear of Faith ; and there are times,
> I doubt not, when to you it doth impart
> Authentic tidings of invisible things ;
> Of ebb and flow, and ever-during power ;
> And central peace, subsisting at the heart
> Of endless agitation.   Here you stand,
> Adore, and worship, when you know it not ;
> Pious beyond the intention of your thought ;
> Devout above the meaning of your will.

It is God then who unites Nature to us, and directs her
teaching ; it is His life acting on ours.

But in order to be able to receive her training there

must be certain qualities in us. What are these in Wordsworth's philosophy? They are the qualities of the child.
The first is the simple heart which loves and to which the
world is sweet, it knows not why. We then accord the
measure of our hearts to the music of His power who attunes
the world to love; and loving things we know them. But
our meddling intellect, working without love, misshapes
the beauty of the world. It can only divide and subdivide,
and isolate for discussion thing from thing, element from
element. It cannot see the living, thinking, feeling
whole:

> It substitutes an universe of death
> For that which moves with light and life informed,
> Actual, divine and true.

The world, which Science "examines, ponders, searches,
vexes, criticises," is not the real life of things; and
Nature refuses to speak to those who prize

> the transcendent universe
> No more than as a mirror that reflects
> To proud self-love her own intelligence.

But to those who enter her kingdom with that listening
love of a child which watches and receives, she gives her
teaching:

> One moment now may give us more
> Than years of toiling reason;
> Our minds shall drink at every pore
> The spirit of the season.

But Wordsworth never meant to depreciate the nobler
Science, but only that which, striving after no vast ideal
conception of the whole, pored alone over what it could
hold in its hands and fixed itself exclusively on phenomena. Wordsworth disliked, as much as Socrates

did, the people who would believe in nothing or consider nothing but that which lay before their eyes.   But
the larger science of to-day, such as Faraday practised,
which works through imagination as well as through
experiment and observation, he would not have disliked.
From geometric science, for example, he drew

> A pleasure quiet and profound, a sense
> Of permanent and universal sway,
> And permanent belief—there, recognised
> A type, for finite natures, of the one
> Supreme existence, the surpassing life
> Which—to the boundaries of space and time,
> Of melancholy space and doleful time,
> Superior and incapable of change,
> Not touched by welterings of passion—is
> And hath the name of God.

Another quality which fits us to receive the training of
Nature is reverence, the food and source of admiration.
The scornful spirit is the blind spirit and the un-
thoughtful one; and to its blindness Nature displays in
vain her beauty, and Man his wonderful life ; contempt
sees nothing, and seeing nothing has no materials for
thought.   He who feels it for any living thing—and when
Wordsworth says " living thing " he means things which
we call inanimate, as well as things animate—

> hath faculties
> Which he hath never used, and thought with him
> Is in its infancy.

But he who bends in loving reverence before the beauty
and majesty of the universe, receives its teaching at every
pore.

But of all qualities, the two most necessary were purity

of heart and unworldliness of character, and in Wordsworth's thought they mingled into one. There is one
well-known sonnet which enshrines this belief of his
in a statement of its opposite.

> The world is too much with us ; late and soon,
> Getting and spending, we lay waste our powers :
> Little we see in Nature that is ours ;
> We have given our hearts away, a sordid boon !
> The Sea that bares her bosom to the moon ;
> The winds that will be howling at all hours,
> And are upgathered now like sleeping flowers ;
> For this—for everything, we are out of tune ;
> It moves us not.

And in a letter he says the same thing—" It is an
awful truth, that there neither is, nor can be, any genuine
enjoyment of poetry among nineteen out of twenty of
those persons who live, or wish to live, in the broad
light of the world—among those who either are, or are
striving to make themselves, persons of consideration in
society. This is a truth, and an awful one, because to be
incapable of a feeling for poetry, in my sense of the
word, is to be without love of human nature and reverence for God."

Now as these qualities are found chiefly in their purity
in the child, it is then that the work of Nature, as
Education, begins. Of what that work is, and how it is
carried on, he has given two examples—one in the first
book of the " Excursion," another in tracing his own
growth under the influences of Nature in the "Prelude."
Of these two I will give an analysis.

He traces in the first the history of a Highland child,
early thrown into solitary life among the hills. As he

came home at evening and saw the hills grow larger in
the mist, and the stars steal out in the infinite expanse,
and felt the horror of the pine wood in his heart, he
received impressions of greatness and its power, indefinite, but full of force to awaken and develop feeling.
These feelings, in their turn, reacted on the forms of
Nature till the impressions they made became like real
existences in his soul. Image after image thus received
and made into living things, soon made him unconsciously mingle up the living image in his soul with
the natural image of which it was the counterpart;
till he slowly began to feel that every image became
living in him, not only because he gave it life, but also
because the object which produced it possessed a life of
its own which, coming to the life in him, stirred and
kindled it into creation.

> And 'mid the hollow depths of naked crags
> He sate—and e'en in their fixed lineaments—
> Or from the power of a peculiar eye,
> Or by creative feeling overborne,
> Or by predominance of thought oppressed,
> Even in their fixed and steady lineaments
> He traced an ebbing and a flowing mind,
> Expression ever varying.

This was the work of the awe which Nature produces
in the child—a sense of sublimity, and of life as the
source of that sublimity.

As he grew, the fear which somewhat spoiled the awe
died away; and when it perished and awe alone was left,
then the whole vast world Being, when, at the sunrise,
it appeared to him from the mountain top, drenched in
light as with joy, and all its glory seeming to him—trained

as he was to feel that Nature was alive—not glory only but love, awoke unspeakable love in him. His mind became one mighty sacrifice of gratitude and love to God. And this reacted on the religion he had learnt and added to it the element of feeling. He had received revealed Religion at his mother's knee, had given it his reverence, but it yet was cold to emotion. But it was different now; emotion had come to him from Nature, and his spirit was stirred to feel it towards the things of Faith.

> A Herdsman on the lonely mountain tops,
> Such intercourse was his, and in this sort
> Was his existence oftentimes *possessed.*
> O then how beautiful, how bright, appeared
> The written promise ! Early had he learned
> To reverence the volume that displays
> The mystery, the life which cannot die ;
> But in the mountains did he *feel* his faith.
> All things, responsive to the writing, there
> Breathed immortality, revolving life,
> And greatness still revolving ; infinite :
> There littleness was not ; the least of things
> Seemed infinite ; and there his spirit shaped
> Her prospects, nor did he believe,—he *saw.*

That is the sketch given of this early education by Nature in the "Excursion." It resembles in one or two points the more elaborate one given in the "Prelude," which I analyse now, and which is the history of Wordsworth himself. Even from his birth he holds that Nature was his friend. The "ceaseless music" of Derwent flowed through his infant dreams, and gave him an unconscious foretaste, a dim earnest of the calm

> That Nature breathes among the hills and groves.

Then, as he became a boy her real work began to tell.

As before, it began with vague impressions of fear. When at night upon the moors, so profound was the vast impression of peace, he felt his bustling presence almost a trouble in the calm of skies and earth. There, when conscience touched him (having robbed the prey of another's trap than his own), Nature herself was felt as the avenger. Low breathings came after him, and steps, " silent as the turf they trod," were heard among the solitary hills.

Did he, as cragsman, shoulder the naked crag and cling to the perilous ridge?—then, if his courage held, Nature was his companion ; if it gave way, she became his destroyer. Did he, half by stealth, row on the lake when evening fell?—then, the huge peak which suddenly rose upon his view seemed to be instinct with voluntary power, and stride after him with a purpose of its own; and for days afterwards his brain

> Worked with a dim and undetermined sense
> Of unknown modes of Being,—

half glimpses of the Dweller on the threshold.

These were the vague impressions, mostly of dim yet delightful Fear, which repeated in many forms and woven together, not confusedly but as notes which fell into harmony, began to build up his character. For such impressions stirred in him germs of feeling—the sense of moral wrong, the sense of indefinite sublimity, the sense of a vast and invisible *life* without himself. And these germs of emotion, becoming conscious of themselves, were sent back to Nature, and made the impressions which were afterwards received from her more vivid, more infinite, more overwhelming : and they in turn stirred deeper emotion in him, and the deeper emotion again found itself met by a mightier answer—till in the mutual play of action thus established, his character grew daily into form. His mind *began* to be married to the external world and the external world to it; the first steps of that union were made which, when fulfilled, should make up that "calm existence which was to be his when he was worthy of himself."

It was the living Soul of the universe which was doing this work; a personal Being, ever melting on the skirts of consciousness into the impersonal. The eternal Thought that watches over the Thought of men, watched over his development; and itself linked to the majestic forms and scenes of Nature, acted through them upon his soul, and wrought in him the passions that build up character, and the ideals that ennoble it.

> Wisdom and Spirit of the universe !
> Thou Soul that art the Eternity of thought,
> That giv'st to forms and images a breath
> And everlasting motion, not in vain
> By day or starlight thus, from my first dawn
> Of childhood, didst thou intertwine for me
> The passions that build up our human soul ;
> Not with the mean and vulgar works of man,
> But with high objects, with enduring things—
> With life and nature—purifying thus
> The elements of feeling and of thought,
> And sanctifying, by such discipline,
> Both pain and fear, until we recognise
> A grandeur in the beatings of the heart.

Nor did this mutual intercourse cease its movement for a moment. By day and night, summer and winter, the silent education went on till at last he felt the " Presence

of Nature in the sky and on the earth," and saw the
" Visions of the hills," and spoke with the " Souls of
lonely places," and, in dim perception—but without an
intellectual form being given to the feeling—felt that
the whole world was alive and speaking to him as his
companion, greater than himself, but yet at one with
him.   Each of these presences, visions, souls, ministered
to him, haunted him, partook of his danger and desire,
and had a distinct desire and danger of their own ; till, at
last, as examples multiplied of this intercommunion (and
what the forms of nature said were met at once by a
response in his own heart, that fitted the impressions
made), the whole earth became like a great Being and,

> With triumph and delight, with hope and fear,
> Worked like a sea.

The whole of this is an explanation given in after life of that
which he insensibly felt as a child.   There was no reasoning possible then.   It was a wild tempestuous time, full
of giddy bliss, and the physical joy of being : and the
images he received from nature partook of this wild and
even vulgar character, images undignified by any association, made quiet by no thoughtfulness.

But (and here is another element in the education
Nature gives the child) in the midst of this wild extravagance of boyish life with nature, there were moments of
quietness in which a calmer beauty, of which he was then
unconscious, entered into his soul and took up there its
dwelling.

Looking back on them, he sees them as a part of that
great work by which the universe and the mind of Man

are wedded together. They are the result of that pre-established harmony which God has set between His thought in us and His thought in Nature. He calls them, in lines as beautiful as they are profound,

> Those hallowed and pure motions of the sense
> Which seem, in their simplicity, to own
> An intellectual charm : that calm delight
> Which, if I err not, surely must belong
> To those first-born affinities that fit
> Our new existence to existing things ;
> And, in our dawn of being, constitute
> The bond of union between life and joy.

By both were sown the first seeds of a deep love of nature which now began to take the place of a dim dread of her. The quieter impressions remained as they were ; the common and vulgar joys through which the others were received slowly died out of the memory ; but the impressions remained and their beauty. His mind became filled with solemn and lovely images ; he linked those images to the places from which he had received them, and loved the places for their sake. In this way, year by year Nature grew more dear, and with his love to her his soul grew into completer being.

It was thus the Poet's education began. How it went on, I shall tell in my next lecture. But does it not do one good to read of it ? How pure and fresh it is ; how healthy and natural, how true to Nature and how near to God. For so ought always to begin, if possible, the building of the soul. Natural Religion should go before spiritual ; vague feelings of joy and calm in the presence of One whom we know not yet, but who knows us—in these best begins the religion which afterwards in the

7

sadness and trouble of life teaches us to know that Presence in Nature as the Father in our hearts; in these best arises that spiritual life which, at first content with nature-worship,—learns, when it has become sadly conscious of sin and sorrow, to love God as the Redeemer, and to trust Him as the Comforter.

LECTURE VII.

WORDSWORTH.

THE simple ways in which the childhood of Wordsworth walked, and how he was taught by the rivers, woods and hills, were spoken of in my last lecture. The education thus begun by Nature was carried on steadily, and I shall explain its further course to-day. It divides itself into two parts, the first period when the influences of Nature were unconsciously received ; the second, when the new element of the relation of his own soul to Nature slowly introduced itself. For, becoming conscious of his own being, he became also conscious of its distinctness from the external world, and of the power and life which he was able to project from it over Nature—conscious, that is, of that action and reaction between the mind and the world without, the possibility of which was contained in the prearranged harmony which God had established between them. This point I shall fully speak of, and also how far this consciousness of the soul of its relation to Nature modified the continuous education which Nature gave him.

And throughout, and after nearly every point, I shall mark how the various lessons he learnt influenced or were likely to influence the poetic character of Wordsworth, the

growth of his religious life, and those theological ideas
which he held with regard to the relation of God and Man
to the Natural world.

Wordsworth begins the second book of the "Prelude"
by a description of the tumultuous joy and eagerness of
boyhood in its sports among a rich and varied scenery.
Looking back in tranquil manhood to this unconscious
time, he half sighs to think that these things are no more.
It tames our "pride of intellect and self-esteem of
virtue," to think how little we can give

> to duty and to truth
> The eagerness of infantine desire.

So that an ideal of eagerness in pursuit of things, and a
respect for the enthusiasm which makes us unconscious of
self, are part of the indirect teaching which we receive
from Nature in boyhood. They were two lessons which
formed part of his poetic training, for a poet is one who
is bound to lose himself in Beauty and Truth, and to see
things more eagerly than other men. And they have
also their moral influence, for it inspirits a man who has
strength enough for self-restoration, to know in after-life,
in times of depression and pain, that he has once possessed
joy and force; for then he believes in their existence in his
nature, and works towards their recovery. And this is
one of the continually recurring moral ideas of Wordsworth. You will find it running through a hundred
poems.

But this kind of teaching that Nature now gave him
was not consciously received by the boy; nor was it direct,
but incidental. It could not be consciously sought for;

but it came suddenly, in flashes of impulse in the midst of holiday delights. On Windermere were lovely and lonely islands, and to these he and his companions rowed in rivalry. But when they landed and wandered among the lilies or beneath the oaks or by the ruined shrine, emulation, jealousy, and pride were insensibly tempered by the stillness of the place, so that they did not care, after a time, whether they had the crown of boyish fame or no.

It was such silent influences of Nature frequently repeated that instilled drop by drop into Wordsworth's being that "quiet independence of the heart," that sense of

> The self-sufficing power of solitude,

so remarkable in him afterwards as man and poet.

Again, in the midst of noisy sport, a single, sharp impression came, the voice of Nature, not in rebuke of their delight, but in her desire to make herself felt, which stilled them for a moment into thoughtfulness. Once in St. Mary's nave the sudden song of the wren singing to herself, invisible, made one of those hushed surprises which no one can ever forget. Sometimes, pausing for a moment when racing home, the sound of streams among rocks and the "still spirit shed from evening air" made their presence felt in his heart. Sometimes when the games were over, and the minstrel of their troop blew his flute alone on the island, and they lay resting and listening upon the lake, the whole scene entered into his soul:

> The calm
> And dead still water lay upon my mind
> Even with a weight of pleasure, and the sky,
> Never before so beautiful, sank down
> Into my heart, and held me like a dream.

He imputes the same experience to the boy, his play-mate who lived by Winander, and of whom he tells in a famous passage. After describing him as in wild mirth he stood by the shore of the lake and blew hootings to the owls that answered till all the hills re-echoed—he marks how, suddenly, in the midst came a lengthened pause of silence. Then it was that the invisible quiet Life in the world spoke to him.

> Then sometimes, in that silence while he hung
> Listening—a gentle shock of mild surprise
> Has carried far into his heart the voice
> Of mountain torrents : or the visible scene
> Would enter unawares into his mind,
> With all its solemn imagery, its rocks,
> Its woods, and that uncertain heaven, received
> Into the bosom of the steady lake.

Those are the lines of which Coleridge said,—" Had I met these lines running wild in the deserts of Arabia, I should instantly have screamed out—Wordsworth." But the deep meaning of them is, that there is in the material universe a spirit at work on us, to calm, to exalt, and to suggest to our boyhood thoughts which sleep within like seeds, till future events develop them.

And now, accumulating from every quarter, these acci-dental impressions enlarged his sympathies till every day some new scene in Nature becoming dear, the conception of Nature as an organic Being, having a life beyond his, and existing in a direct relation to him, began, not to be realized, but to quicken in his mind.

A change then took place. Nature had been secondary in his life ; his boyish sports were first, and she had intervened among them with these surprises. She was the seeker, he the sought. But now, he sought her directly for the pleasure she gave. She had conquered his unthinking pleasure in play and replaced it by the enthusiasm of herself. He did not know well why he sought her, but a trouble came into his mind, which drove him away from the sports of boyhood. They had been the props of the impressions he had received from Nature. But, behold, when the scaffolding was removed, there was the building, sustained by its own spirit, the building of the love of natural Beauty and Life, a house not made with hands. Hence, the trouble was the first trouble of a youth who was leaving boyhood and who had begun to realize consciously all he had learnt unconsciously. It was such a trouble as moved the waters of the Bethesda spring.

The sensibility of his soul to Nature now went directly and with known purpose to commune with her. It was like two lovers who had seen one another only at intervals meeting at last for daily communion. Every hour brought new happiness, because it brought new knowledge of the life of things. And the source of the knowledge was love, refined to intense watchfulness by desire. Formerly he had received large indefinite impressions, now he saw into the "transitory qualities" of things, such as, if I may explain the phrase by an illustration, the subtle changes in colour of the lime-tree leaves as summer draws on day by day from spring, or the difference of the sound of a brook in winter and summer, or the way in which a passing cloud will alter the whole sentiment of a landscape, or even closer still, the way in which a sudden stroke of life will enlighten a lonely place; as when, in one of his own inimitable touches, he says of a lonely mountain lake—

> There sometimes doth a leaping fish
> Send through the tarn a lonely cheer.

Running along with these numberless small impressions, and derived from them, were " gentle agitations of the mind" from observation of these manifold differences, so that whatever came from Nature was answered by a different but correspondent feeling, and that marriage of the soul and the world began to grow towards its fulfilment.

One might object that this minute habit of observance would take away from the Poet the power of receiving a grand impression of the whole. On the contrary, when the soul is freely receiving, and this sort of work is done by the feeling, and not by the understanding, it prepares the soul, by kindling and quickening emotion, for a sublime impression. Nay more, since it brings the knowledge of particulars, it educates us for the moment when the vast, single conception of the Whole dawns like a sun upon the mind.

But this has its stages of growth in single impressions, made by separate scenes of sublimity and calm, and Wordsworth dwells on both. I would walk alone, he says,

> Under the quiet stars, and at that time
> Have felt whate'er there is of power in sound
> To breathe an elevated mood, by form
> Or image unprofaned ; and I would stand,
> If the night blackened with a coming storm,
> Beneath some rock, listening to notes that are
> The ghostly language of the ancient earth, .
> Or make their dim abode in distant winds.
> Thence did I drink the visionary power :

These moments were the origin of an ideal of sublimity. In after life, we forget what we felt, but not *how* we felt at such times : remembrance of the way in which we have been impressed creates and supports the obscure sense of a sublimity possible to the soul, to which with growing faculties the soul aspires—

> feeling still
> That whatsoever point they gain, they yet
> Have something to pursue.

To have such an ideal is in itself a kind of religion. And Wordsworth, in the "Excursion," taking up the same point, shows how an ideal of sublimity, won in early life from Nature, will make a man impatient of any pettiness of temper or life, of any wanting in noble simplicity, of any want of directness, of any of those meannesses, which, though they seem only paltry, have their root in some foulness or other. Nor will he ever become basely content. He shall feel

> congenial stirrings late and long
> In spite of all the weakness that life brings—

however tranquil—

> Wake sometimes to a noble restlessness.

Correlative with sublimity is calm ; it is the other side of the shield. The power which, in Nature, moves the mind to delight, and which arises from her inner order, made her hours of calm produce calm in him. And a certain love of calm in himself strengthened the impression. When, in early morning walks, he saw beneath him the valley sleeping in the lonely dawn—"How shall I seek the origin," he breaks out:

> Where find
> Faith in the marvellous things which then I felt?
> Oft in these moments such a holy calm
> Would overspread my soul, that bodily eyes
> Were utterly forgotten, and what I saw
> Appeared like something in myself, a dream,
> A prospect in the mind.

This was also destined to grow into an ideal, and it was necessary for his poetic work. One must have the power of compelling rest in the soul in order to work nobly. Nor is that self-control which can use passion and not be used by it, less needful for the man than for the Poet. It is not the calm of indifference which we want in order to be great, but the calm which Will and temperance produce in a nature capable of storm. The perfect moral work of life is done by him who has passion, but who subdues it to the workable point of heat.

From the time, now, that he had sought Nature directly, he had gained two things; a multitude of minute impressions awakening a multitude of thoughts : a sense of sublimity and of calm, which the work of his own soul was to change into moral ideals of them. So far the preparation for the grasp of Nature as a great whole had gone.

But something more was needed, *the influence of his own soul on Nature;* and this now began to be felt. Looking back, as he writes, on that time, he knew that his soul had been insensibly at work on the impressions Nature had given it. This was true, he thought, even of his infancy. The infant is frail and helpless then, yet he is

> An inmate of this active universe :
> For feeling has to him imparted power
> That through the growing faculties of sense

> Doth like an agent of the one great Mind
> Create, creator and receiver both,
> Working but in alliance with the works
> Which it beholds.

The lines re-illustrate the philosophic view of the distinctiveness of Nature and man on which I have dwelt, and in this mutual reaction of the two, and in having it, consciously in manhood, unconsciously in childhood, is the poetic spirit:

> Such, verily, is the first
> Poetic spirit of our human life,
> By uniform control of after years,
> In most, abated or suppressed ; in some
> Through every change of growth and of decay,
> Pre-eminent till death.

In becoming conscious, then, of this interaction he first began to be a poet.

Therefore he now knew that, unsubdued by the torrent of natural glory and beauty poured into his heart, he retained a plastic power, to form and shape the images he received. Nay more, though his mind was still subservient to Nature, it gave back a glory of its own to Nature :

> An auxiliar light
> Came from my mind, which on the setting sun
> Bestowed new splendour.
> And the midnight storm
> Grew darker in the presence of my eye.

Added to this was the power of imagination, which brought into poetic relation remotely connected objects, and which transferred his own enjoyments and passions to inorganic natures. Yet when he says that he did that, he feels that he is partly untrue to his special view of the difference

between man and Nature; and he says that this transference of himself to Nature was perhaps due to an excess
in the great social principle of life which naturally coerced
all things into sympathy—or, on the other hand, that he
did not really impose himself on Nature, but conversed
with things as they really were, with the enjoyments and
passions, that is, of Nature herself.   But however that
might be, the end of all this was, that what he had unconsciously felt as a boy became at last a conscious possession ;
he realized that all Nature was one great organic Being,
with whom he could commune through the means of love,
who directly communed with him, and whose ceaseless
prayer and anthem was the adoration and love of God.

> Thus while the days flew by and years passed on,
> From Nature and her over-flowing soul,
> I had received so much that all my thoughts
> Were steeped in feeling.   I was only then
> Contented, when with bliss ineffable
> I felt the sentiment of Being spread
> O'er all that moves and all that seemeth still ;
> O'er all that, lost beyond the reach of thought
> And human knowledge, to the human eye
> Invisible, yet liveth to the heart.
>   Wonder not
> If high the transport, great the joy I felt,
> Communing in this sort through earth and heaven
> With every form of creature, as it looked
> Towards the Uncreated with a countenance
> Of adoration, with an eye of love.
> One song they sang, and it was audible,
> Most audible, then, when the fleshly ear,
> O'ercome by humblest prelude of that strain,
> Forgot her functions, and slept undisturbed.

It is a wonderful picture of a youthful life—this young
and solitary creature, living in communion only with the

Being of the World, in a world which only lived to him and to God who sees the heart.

He had now reached his seventeenth year, and the results of his experience were these—he was conscious of the direct influence of Nature on him; of his own mind and the power it had to speak with and to answer Nature; and of both Nature and Himself as living powers acting on each other. With these was united a vague sentiment of religion, which chiefly appeared in a simple, pure and manly morality of life. This, he held, was the direct result of the work of Nature upon his soul, and looking back on his life then and afterwards, and summing up the result, it is to this early association with the beautiful and sublime things of the outward world that he traces the whole quiet, and faithful, and temperate character of his life, and of his self-training as a Poet. The passage is long, but it is necessary to quote it, and it completes the history of his boyhood. It follows directly on the last quotation.

If this be error and another faith
Find easier access to the pious mind,
Yet were I grossly destitute of all
Those human sentiments that make this earth
So dear, if I should fail with grateful voice
To speak of you, ye mountains, and ye lakes
And sounding cataracts, ye mists and winds
That dwell among the hills where I was born.
If in my youth I have been pure in heart,
If, mingling with the world, I am content
With my own modest pleasures, and have lived
With God and Nature communing, removed
From little enmities and low desires,
The gift is yours; if in these times of fear,
This melancholy waste of hopes o'erthrown,
'mid indifference and apathy,

And wicked exultation when good men
On every side fall off, we know not how,
To selfishness, disguised in gentle names
Of peace and quiet and domestic love,
Yet mingled not unwillingly with sneers
On visionary minds; if, in this time
Of dereliction and dismay, I yet
Despair not of our nature, but retain
A more than Roman confidence, a faith
That fails not, in all sorrow my support,
The blessing of my life ; the gift is yours,
Ye winds and sounding cataracts ! 'tis yours,
Ye mountains ! thine, O Nature ! Thou hast fed
My lofty speculations ; and in thee,
For this uneasy heart of ours, I find
A never-failing principle of joy
And purest passion.

                                    Prelude, Bk. ii.

He now passed, thus educated by Nature, out of her special guidance, and went to Cambridge as a student. It was a strange change from the solitary glen.   He was excited, full of spirit and hope, and when he saw the turrets of the University rising in the distance, he felt his heart racing before him.   He puts with one of his characteristic touches his own feeling into the place itself :

As near and nearer to the spot we drew
It seemed to suck us in with an eddy's force.

He entered, and was at once full of the blithe delight of a young fellow, fresh from the hills, to whom everything was new. "I was the dreamer, they the dream "—His new dress—and he became a dandy—the society, the lecture-rooms, the motley spectacle, the sound of frequent bells at night, the antechapel of Trinity where the statue stood—

Of Newton, with his prism and silent face,
The marble index of a mind for ever
Voyaging through strange seas of Thought, alone—

all dazzled him at first, and he forgot his early aspirations. But he soon returned to his more natural self, and felt even the more for this short forgetfulness, how native were his poetic instincts. Prizes, examinations and their fame, for these things he had no care; and the little interests of the place were not great enough for one accustomed to the solemn and awful interests of Nature. He was not, he felt, for that hour nor for that place. And we must hold that he was right. Special gifts have special duties, and they override the duties incumbent on ordinary men. It might be the duty of this or that youth to read for a prize; it was Wordsworth's instinct, and the instinct may be called a duty, not to do so. It marks the strong and independent character of his mind that he felt so early in life, that the bent of his genius set him apart, and must be followed. The mountains had taught him wisdom, and he turned—even in the fen-country, and among men—to Nature again, and looked in her for universal things, and called on the earth and sky to "teach him what they might." And when they spoke, he turned into himself, and asked what their revelations were in him, till he felt, as he had felt in his native glen, that they were in truth "visitings of the Upholder of the tranquil soul." And receiving these, he recognized with joy a new power in his own soul, and sending it forth to work on Nature, found in her life enjoyments and passions similar but not identical with his own.

To every natural form, rock, fruit, or flower,
Even the loose stones that cover the high-way,
I gave a moral life: I saw them feel,
Or linked them to some feeling: the great mass
Lay bedded in a quickening soul, and all
That I beheld respired with inward meaning.
And that whate'er of Terror or of Love
Or Beauty Nature's daily face put on
From transitory passion, unto this
I was as sensitive as waters are
To the sky's influence in a kindred mood
Of passion; was obedient as a lute
That waits upon the touches of the wind.
Unknown, unthought of, yet I was most rich—
I had a world about me—'twas my own;
I made it, for it only lived to me,
And to the God who sees into the heart.

Prelude, Bk. iii.

Sometimes he betrayed his joy in all this by gestures, and those who saw him called it madness. And it was madness, he says—

If childlike fruitfulness in passing joy,
If steady moods of thoughtfulness matured
To inspiration, suit with such a name.

Nor could that be well called madness, in which there was so intense a development of what one might call the logic of the eye—

For the bodily eye
Amid my strongest workings evermore
Was searching out the lines of difference
As they lie hid in all external forms,
Near or remote, minute or vast; an eye
Which, from a tree, a stone, a withered leaf,
To the broad ocean and the azure heavens
Spangled with kindred multitudes of stars,
Could find no surface where its power might sleep;
Which spake perpetual logic to my soul,
And by an unrelenting agency
Did bind my feelings even as in a chain.

Is not that a splendid commentary upon the passionate minuteness of his natural description—" Could find no surface where its power might sleep ? "

It was thus that Nature continued to exercise her power over him, and moulded even his University life. He was kept, by the continuance of her influence, from overwork, and from that tendency of a college career to lessen originality. At the same time the lively society, the first clash of life with other men, lessened the somewhat overwhelming influence of Nature, and not only prepared him for his future interest in mankind, but stirred to life those germs of it which had been insensibly sown in the north. The idle life was also, I think, good for him; he wanted idleness and repose; there was no need for him to do anything but drift and have that " wise passiveness " which he afterwards recommends, but which he took then as unconsciously as a child. In these first months then, he read the face of Nature, he read Chaucer, Spencer, Milton, he amused himself and rested—and since he was Wordsworth, he could not have done better.

But the time spent at Cambridge was not without its special influence : a human element, as I said, crept into his life. When, then, after eight months' absence, he returned to his mountain home, he found that certain changes had been wrought in his relation to Nature. He had a human heartedness about the love he bore to objects lately the absolute wealth of his own private being. He had loved rocks and brooks and stars as one Angel might love another—now human feelings and changes were connected with them, and a pensive shade stole over Nature. It was no longer only sublimity or calm which he felt, but

something kinder, sweeter — an inner touch of love,
delight or hope. His human soul, awakened by life
among men, began to wed Humanity to Nature, and
out of that came the first emotional feeling of a personal
religion. It was on a day when the hour of evening was
" sober, the air untuned." It influenced him like the
face of a friend in trouble, thrilling him through and
through with love and pain. And in the air of this
emotion, strength and comfort, which " he only knew he
needed when they came," entered his heart, and with
them came " inward hopes, and swellings of the spirit,"

> glimmering views
> How life pervades the undecaying mind—
> How the immortal soul with godlike power
> Informs, creates, and thaws the deepest sleep
> That time can lay upon her ;
>
> Prelude, Bk. iv.

—the sense of the majestic strength of man if he will but
live in the " light of high endeavour," and the glory of
the close that endurance wins.

The second religious impression was a deeper and more
important one. It made a crisis in his life, and it is
worth remarking that it came not as the first in the
sombreness of evening, but in the freshness of dawn.

When he returned from Cambridge, he had felt not
only more human, but also an inner falling off; less fiery
aspiration in his soul, some taint of the world, some
touch of vanity and its corruption. He could not, as
before, forget himself in Nature. But he was wrong in
this regret. It was a backward motion, but had it not
been, love of Nature could never have passed into love

of Man. We must often reach the higher by going back a little, and Wordsworth's " boundless chase of trivial pleasure " was a necessary parenthesis in his education. Through it the image of mankind had room to creep into his heart, and in reaction from it he drew nearer to God. It was in the very midst of this light and thoughtless gaiety, returning from a rustic ball—just as impressions of calm and beauty came on his boyhood in the midst of careless sport—that his highest early revelation broke upon him. For often in these opposing currents of the life of man,—and Wordsworth's life was now a parti-coloured show of grave and gay—at a moment when the force of the currents being equal, calm ensues, we are surprised by the voice of God in the hush of exhausted excitement. It is then that Solitude and Nature do their work, and we never can forget the surprise. I quote the lines in which he describes this baptismal hour when he was consecrated to his lofty work. He is going home after a night of merriment :

> Magnificent
> The morning rose, in memorable pomp.
> Glorious as e'er I had beheld—in front
> The sea lay laughing at a distance ; near
> The solid mountains shone, bright as the clouds,
> Grain-tinctured, drenched in empyrean light ;
> And in the meadows and the lower grounds
> Was all the sweetness of a common dawn—
> Dews, vapours, and the melody of birds,
> And labourers going forth to till the fields.
> Ah ! need I say, dear Friend ! that to the brim
> My heart was full ; I made no vows, but vows
> Were then made for me ; bond unknown to me
> Was given, that I should be, else sinning greatly,
> A dedicated Spirit. On I walked
> In thankful blessedness, which yet survives.

This was the God of Nature speaking in solitude. But solitude is still more solitary, says Wordsworth, where it has a human centre, and he finishes his account of his vacation time by narrating a dull story of his meeting an old soldier in a lonely road, and how far more deeply the loneliness sank into his soul, and with benign power separated him from worldliness, when this appropriate human centre impressed it on his mind. That would not have been the case some years before. I note it now to show how his mind was veering towards interest in Man as well as in Nature.

The next great religious impressions received through Nature were made on him during his journey on the continent, and were more distinctly connected with Man; one was sublime when he crossed the Alps, the other beautiful as he wandered through the Italian lakes. They were prefaced by a certain growth in his own soul; gladness and tenderness alike had made the air of thought more fine and pure. And further, the capacities of his own soul had now been so stirred that it began to assert itself as creator : the expressing power had begun to dawn.

It was then, that inspired with desire to see the larger forms of Nature, he went abroad. There his interest in Man was still further aroused, for he landed at Calais and went through France when the land was thrilling with the first youthful passion of the Revolution. He joined with the frank pleasure of youth in all the delight of the land, he felt the excitement of the ideas of the time even in the midst of the dark solitudes of the Chartreuse, he looked with the pleasure of a natural

Republican on the quiet valleys of Switzerland where men were free. But these things were but incidents in the devotion he gave to Nature and in the interest with which he watched his own soul working upon her. First, in lighter scenery, it was only that fantastic pensiveness which we all have felt that came upon him. There were hours of delightful dejection, like flowers " gathered from formal gardens of the Lady Sorrow." But these in turn were mixed with others in which a different impression came, not of the fancy, but wholly of the imagination. He crossed the Alps, and swept downwards towards Italy through the gorge of Gondo. There the stupendous powers of the world of the higher mountains, spoke one language to him :

> The immeasurable height
> Of woods decaying, never to be decayed,
> The stationary blasts of waterfalls,
> And in the narrow rent at every turn
> Winds thwarting winds, bewildered and forlorn,
> The torrents shooting from the clear blue sky,
> The rocks that muttered close upon our ears,
> Black drizzling crags that spake by the way-side
> As if a voice were in them, the sick sight
> And giddy prospect of the raving stream,
> The unfettered clouds and region of the Heavens,
> Tumult and peace, the darkness and the light—
> Were all like workings of one mind, the features
> Of the same face, blossoms upon one tree :
> Characters of the great Apocalypse,
> The types and symbols of eternity :
> Of first and last and 'midst and without end.
>
> Prelude, Bk. **vi.**

The majesty and awfulness of the place seized on him and ravished him beyond himself—he was lost in the revelation. The same note is struck in the last verse of

the hymn of the spirits to Asia, in the Prometheus of
Shelley :

> Lamp of Earth, where'er thou movest,
> Its dim shapes are clad with brightness,
> And the souls of those thou lovest
> Walk upon the winds with lightness,
> 'Till they fail as I am failing,
> Dizzy, lost, yet unbewailing.

That was something of Wordsworth's feeling. Nature
came upon him, imagination rushed into union with
Nature, and in the fierce ardour of their creative embrace
within him he lost all consciousness of self. Shelley could
have stayed there, did stay there ; the passionate pleasure
of being lost in the Spirit of Nature through love of it,
would have been enough for him. He would have kept
all his life the memory of that hour of rapture, and felt it
over and over again without ever subjecting it to thought.
It was different with Wordsworth ; having felt this wonderful emotion, and wholly lost himself in it at the time,
he returned to it afterwards that he might discover its
meaning. It is perhaps less poetical, it is certainly less
characteristic of the pure artist to do this ; but it is just
as well that all poets are not like Shelley, and instead of
contrasting the two methods to the disadvantage of either
we may be thankful to have the delight of both.

Afterwards, then, Wordsworth looked back on this
experience, and saw in it the glory of the soul in union
with God. It can usurp sense, and joining itself as
brother to the invisible and spiritual world, enter into that
infinitude of God of which Nature is the voice and symbol.
This is its greatness, this power bespeaks that its true

home is in the Eternal, that its rightful world is the world
of aspiration, desire, undying hope,

> And something evermore about to be.

And in this the soul is blest in thoughts,

> That are their own perfection and reward,
> Strong in herself and in beatitude
> That hides her.

It was here, then, that through a sublime impression of
Nature, the knowledge of the super-eminent power of the
human soul which had been growing up in his mind, was
fixed and recognized.

Descending into serener beauty, a tenderer revelation
came on him from a tenderer Nature. He felt the loveliness and calm of the world as similar to moral loveliness and calm. The things he saw were gracious as virtue
and goodness, sweet as love or the memory of a generous
deed, or those visitations of pure thought,

> When God, the Giver of all joy, is thanked
> Religiously in silent blessedness.

Nor were such scenes only analogous to moral qualities;
he seems,—and it is a thought which, though fantastic,
has its ground in his theory,—to imagine that characteristic types of landscape had the power of suggesting each
their correspondent virtue to the mind, and of giving to the
heart the sensation, as it were, of that virtue.

So far Nature acted directly upon him, but in all these
new scenes, as in the previous case, it was not without his own action on her work.   He asserts his right as

poet and man to offer no slavish worship in this temple. He was not prostrate, overborne as Shelley was, by the splendour of Nature; he never let loose the right of his own mind to co-operate with her. He began to feel that she was the complement of his soul, as natural religion is the complement of spiritual. He drew on still further to the full conception of that marriage of the mind of Man to the external world which he afterwards fulfilled. Whatsoever he saw or heard or felt was but "a stream which flowed into a stream kindred" to it in his own mind:

> A gale,
> Confederate with the current of the soul,
> To speed my voyage; every sound or sight,
> In its degree of power, administered
> To grandeur or to tenderness—to the one
> Directly, but to tender thoughts by means
> Less often instantaneous in effect;

And the action of all, in Wordsworth's deep religion, was to lead him, at last, to reach the point marked out for him by God.

One might say that having now become so conscious of the power of his own soul, he would naturally begin to have interest in Man more than in Nature. Everything that was then happening—the expectancy of the whole world, the sudden waking of the nations, the wonderful emotion of mankind—was, one would think, calculated to place Man first. But Wordsworth grew slowly; he reached that point afterwards, but not now. Nature was still predominant in his life. "Among the more awful scenes of the Alps," he says, in one of his letters, "I had not a thought of Man, my whole soul was turned to Him who produced the terrible majesty before me." It was the same in the peaceful beauty of the lakes. The happy, glorious time, and the universal cry for liberty that strengthened his interest in Man, were but an additional gleam of sunshine which enhanced his sense of the Beauty of the world. He was touched, "but with no intimate concern." He did not seem to need any human joy, for

> the ever-living Universe,
> Turn where I might, was opening out its glories,
> And the independent spirit of pure youth
> Called forth, at every season, new delights
> Spread round my steps like sunshine o'er green fields.

This is the close of the early education given him by Nature. What had it done for him? It had made him conscious of the might and dignity of his soul. It had shaped the views and aspirations of his soul to majesty. It had made him realize a Soul of beauty and enduring life without himself, and he knew, from the power by which it moved him, that that Soul was God. It had awakened in him ideals of sublimity in which self was lost, of calm and " ennobling Harmony" in which moral strength was gained, of tenderness in which joy and hope were born; and the sublimity and calm and tenderness were God. It had so spoken to him that he had separated himself for his work, and felt that he was a dedicated Spirit, and the Power that had done this through Nature was God. He had secured in this way a noble natural religion.

But Nature had not only educated his soul, it had also done service to his intellect. In scanning the laws and

8

watching the forms of Nature, by seeing things at first hand, he had gained a standard for measuring the value of things and thoughts; and he could now tell, as if by intuition—what in books " carried meaning to the natural heart "—

> What is passion, what is truth,
> What reason, what simplicity and sense.

Again, her order, which made itself felt within him, taught him to reverence the abstract truths of Science and filled them with the spirit of imagination. As he worked at geometric Science, he was able to clothe the nakedness of its austere truths with the hues and forms and with the spirit of the forms of Nature. The same calm which was impressed on him by Nature, in which he felt the ineffable oneness of its life—a thought created by the calm of Nature, and yet its source—he found again in the permanent and universal sway of law, that type of the supreme existence of God in whom all discords, untouched by passion, were harmonized and mingled.

The laws themselves were also made more interesting by being taken into the world of imagination. It did no harm to his work in the sphere of Science, that when away from it he clothed its laws with life, and asked, as he wandered and wondered among the hills, how did it happen that these great genii came to serve Man?

Again, as the solemn and simple aspects of Nature gave grandeur to Man's mind, and wrought to kindle and exalt the soul,—so the changes of Nature, rapid and forceful, which told of life, were powerful to stir and train the intellect:

Like virtue have the forms
Perennial of the ancient hills ; nor less
The changeful language of their countenances
Quickens the slumbering mind, and aids the thoughts,
However multitudinous, to move
With order and relation.

Prelude, Bk. vii.

And now that imagination and intellect were awakened, they could not rest content with Nature only, or their own work ; they turned to seek their food in books. And in this sphere also Nature intervened. He thanks God that he was allowed to run wild, and saved by Nature from a forced and artificial education; that he was handed over to the natural training of wild Nature and took up things as the external world woke interest in them. He lit by chance on books, and faëry tale and legend seemed more in harmony with Nature than manuals of science. She taught him not to lose her in over education, so that at least in his case old Grandame Earth had not to grieve that the

Playthings which her love designed for him

were unthought of, that the flowers and the river-sides were neglected. The pupil of Nature, his was a larger, grander teaching than that which merely trains the understanding. Books were good, he thought, yet how much less good than that invisible lesson which comes to us through the visible universe, even to the wild and careless child. But who gives that lesson, whose is the voice that works so silently ? In Wordsworth's deep religion it is God :

A gracious spirit o'er this earth presides,
And o'er the heart of man—invisibly
It comes—to works of unreproved delight,
And tendency benign, directing those
Who care not, know not, think not what they do.
                                        Prelude, Bk. **v.**

And surely he is right.   When we cram our children to
the throat with mere instruction, or make them move
over roads of learning like machines, we are really
shutting out from them God and God's teaching; we
are forgetting the wisdom that is gained by freedom ;
we are killing originality and the poetic spirit.   True
force and grandeur of character have their roots in early
freedom to drink in other lessons than those that in-
structors give, and come in the child and man, as they
come in the forest tree :

Not by casting in a formal mould
But by its own divine vitality.

We have no need to trouble ourselves to give so much to
our children, nor would we do so if we believed, as we
ought, that God is educating them Himself, that,

In the unreasoning progress of the world
A wiser spirit is at work for us,
A better eye than theirs, most prodigal
Of blessings, and most studious of our good
Even in what seem our most unfruitful hours.
                                        Prelude, Bk. **v.**

And lastly, as Wordsworth passed from childhood into
youth, the books that most attracted him were naturally
the Poets; and Nature stepped in here also and gave him
a deeper insight into them.   It is a splendid thought of his
when he describes how he, who had been intimate with

Nature in his youth, sees something more in the work of the great Masters of Song than mere glittering verse: he sees in them great Nature herself. Their words are viewless winds which visionary power attends; darkness and all the host of shadowy things make their abode in their poetry. In it, things, as in Nature, weave and unweave, change in shadow and sunshine of thought. That is one of the finest thoughts of Wordsworth, and the finest thing ever said of poetry. But it was Nature who taught him to feel and say it. It completes the history of this early education of Nature, and I quote it in conclusion:

> Here must we pause: this only let me add,
> From heart experience, and in humblest sense
> Of modesty, that he, who in his youth
> A daily wanderer among woods and fields,
> With living Nature hath been intimate,
> Not only in that raw unpractised time
> Is stirred to ecstacy, as others are,
> By glittering verse; but further, doth receive,
> In measure only dealt out to himself,
> Knowledge and increase of enduring joy
> From the great Nature that exists in works
> Of mighty Poets. Visionary power
> Attends the motions of the viewless winds,
> Embodied in the mystery of words:
> There, darkness makes abode, and all the host
> Of shadowy things work endless changes,—there,
> As in a mansion like their proper home,
> Even forms and substances are circumfused
> By that transparent veil with light divine,
> And, through the turnings intricate of verse,
> Present themselves as objects recognised,
> In flashes, and with glory not their own.
>
> Prelude, Bk. v.

LECTURE VIII.

I FINISHED in my last lecture our discussion of the early education which Nature had given Wordsworth, and traced its influence on his poetry of Nature. But Wordsworth was as much, if not more, the poet of Man as of Nature, and the poetry of Man took in his hands as great a development as the poetry of Nature. My task to-day will be to show,—always taking the "Prelude" as our guide,—how the love of Man grew up in his soul.

I begin by a quotation from an Essay of Wordsworth's, in "The Friend," which resumes a great part of that which we have been saying in the two last lectures with regard to the teaching of Nature.

"We have been discoursing of infancy, childhood, boyhood, and youth, of pleasures lying in the unfolding intellect plenteously as morning dewdrops, of knowledge inhaled insensibly like a fragrance, of dispositions stealing into the spirit like music from unknown quarters, of images uncalled for arising up like exhalations, of hopes plucked like beautiful wild flowers from the ruined tombs that border the highways of antiquity, to make a garland for a living forehead; in a word, we have been treating

of Nature as a teacher of truth, through joy and throu
gladness, and as a creatress of the faculties by a p
of smoothness and delight. We have made no mention of
fear, shame, sorrow, nor of ungovernable and vexing
thoughts; because, although these have been, and have
done mighty service, they are overlooked in that stage of
life when youth is passing into manhood, overlooked or
forgotten. We now apply for succour which we need, to
a faculty which works after a different course; that faculty
is Reason; she gives much spontaneously, but she seeks
for more; she works by thought, through feeling; yet in
thoughts she begins and ends."

The way in which Nature works, then, is this: She
makes an impression on the poet's mind, an impression
of calm, for example. That after a time insensibly touches
his sympathies, and the thought of his father's serene old
age or his child's peaceful sleep is awakened in his heart;
and led on in this process of soothing thought now
quickened by human tenderness, he thinks of other things
that belong to the sphere of calm—of the quiet balance
of the powers of his own being, of the mighty rest of
God; and these in turn create the resolve to attain
calm of heart, to reach, through endeavour and watchfulness, the peace which passeth all understanding.
"This is Nature," as Wordsworth says, for I have used a
different illustration from that he uses, " teaching seriously
and sweetly through the affections, melting the heart, and
through that instinct of tenderness, developing the
understanding."

"Let, then, the youth go back, as occasion will permit, to
Nature and solitude, thus admonished by reason, and

relying on this newly acquired support. A world of past sensations will gradually open on him as his mind puts off its infirmities : and he makes it his prime business to understand himself. In such disposition let him return to the visible universe and to conversation with ancient books—and let him feed upon that beauty which unfolds itself, not to his eye as he sees carelessly the things which cannot possibly go unseen,—but to the thinking mind ; which searches, discovers, and treasures up, infusing by meditation into the objects with which it converses an intellectual life, whereby they remain planted in the memory, now, and for ever."

This was the point which Wordsworth had reached when we left him. He had realized, through the affections which Nature had awakened, his own Reason in its relation to God and Nature, and he had felt the immense delight of redoubling the charm and sublimity of Nature by throwing upon it the force of his own mind. By this work the interest of more than half of his life was concentrated round the growth of his own being, and he studied himself with eagerness. But he did this in connection with the influences of Nature upon him, not in connection with the influences of Man. From these he was, at this time, nearly altogether free, or at least, not consciously influenced by them. Nature and God were first, Man second.

But the transition from the contemplation of his own being as a man to the contemplation of mankind itself was an easy one, and it now began to be made. His residence in London, in the midst of this great hive of workers, laid upon his soul the weight of humanity ; the residence in France which followed finished the work. Man became the first, and Nature the second.

This was the great change, and he was bound to explain it. It seemed sudden. Was it really so? And he looked back on his life in order to answer the question. To say that it was sudden would have contradicted his philosophy. For no one has seen more clearly than Wordsworth that the operations of the soul are gradual, that ideas do not spring to life at once, but grow, so that when they are recognised as conscious possessions, we find that they have been already for years developing themselves. We recognise them when they flower, we are not conscious of them in shoot, and stem, and leaves. But when they have flowered, we can go back and trace their origin and their growth. And Wordsworth now made it his business to ask how this idea of Man as the centre of the universe grew up in his mind; and to describe the religious aspect it finally took.

Looking back, he sees that it began in his childhood, and that just as interest in his own being was stirred in him by the love of Nature, so in this case also, it was the love of Nature which from the earliest times led him onwards to the love of Man. His childhood was passed among magnificent natural scenery, not so enchanting as the Eastern Paradises which he describes, but in this far lovelier that, unlike their gorgeous landscapes, its sun and sky and seasons found Man a worthy fellow-labourer among them; free, working for himself, led by all that surrounded him to individual and social ends of his own frank choosing, and educated through the simple gracious life of home. The men and mountains were at one in noble character. For the beauty of a country is elevated by the freedom of its inhabitants. No one can walk through Switzerland without feeling that the long, almost unbroken liberty of soul which marked her people, that the grave republicanism which marks them now, add a new element of greatness to her scenery. It is something to stand in the churchyard of Altdorf, as I stood two years ago, and look up the lake glittering blue in the morning light, and say to oneself, " this land has never been otherwise than free." It made wretched to many the loveliness of Italy, and Arnold records the feeling in his letters, to think that man was daily degraded there by a vile oppression ; it adds a new brightness now to her appealing Beauty to think that she is mistress of herself. So to Wordsworth the meadows beneath Helvellyn were lovelier far than the Paradise of Gehol, because, in one, the freedom of Nature's heart was in harmony with human freedom, in the other, her freedom was ceaselessly jarred by human slavery.

. It was in this free pastoral life that the roots of Wordsworth's love for Man struck deep. Shepherds were the men who pleased him first, not the Arcadian shepherd, nor such as Spenser fabled, but men " intent on little but substantial needs," whose life was yet full of beauty that the men had hearts to feel. In such a rude life imagination had much food from things connected with Man, for there was continually presented to the child (however unconscious of what he felt), the awful problem of the seeming helpless subjection of mankind to the wild powers of Nature. There was not a rock or stream or deep valley in the hills which was not vocal, in the traditions of the neighbourhood, with some tale of human suffering or human daring. Wherever the boy roamed, Man and his battle with Nature spoke to him. For here, where he lived, it was no "smooth life" the shepherd led, no piping by rivulets among sunny meadows, but a toilsome struggle for existence among hills where the snow buried sheep and shepherd, and where the winds howled around the companionless man who daily waited on the storms. Wordsworth saw him frequently when

> the lingering dews of morn
> Smoke round him, as from hill to hill he hies,
> His staff protending like a hunter's spear :

And followed him in thought throughout the day, till he felt
> his presence in his own domain
> As of a lord and master, or a power,
> Or genius, under Nature, under God,
> Presiding : and severest solitude
> Had more commanding looks when he was there.

In certain aspects he became to the imagination like an elemental genius, seen through the thick mist a giant form stalking on the hill ; or as he stepped from the shadow of the rock, glorified "by the deep radiance of the setting sun ; " or descried in distant sky,

> A solitary object and sublime,
> Above all height ! like an aerial cross
> Stationed alone upon a spiry rock
> Of the Chartreuse, for worship.*

---

* It is interesting to find the origin of this passage in the "Prelude" in Miss Wordsworth's diary. She and her brother are walking to Tarbert in mist and rain, and hear suddenly a loud hooting in the fields. "It came from a little boy whom we could see on the hill between us and the lake, wrapped up in grey plaid. He was probably calling home the cattle

In this way, man became ennobled outwardly before his sight, his heart was introduced

> To an unconscious love and reverence
> Of Human Nature.

" The sanctity of Nature was given to Man : " and yet this creature so glorified by the imagination was a man with the most common, a husband, father, one who worked, rejoiced and suffered ; and there was as much poetry in him, and his simple human relations, as there was in his relations to the imaginative world of Nature. It is one of Wordsworth's poetic customs to see things in the ideal and the real, and to make each make the other poetical.   He places the lark in a " privacy of glorious light," but he brings him home at last to his " nest upon the dewy ground."   It is the very thing that he always does for Man.

This was the first step whereby love of Nature led to love of Man.   To some it may seem far-fetched, but Wordsworth blessed God that in his childhood he started with faith in the nobleness of Man, that he began with an ideal of human Nature.   Were it otherwise, he says :

> And we found evil fast as we find good
> In our first years, or think that it is found,
> How could the innocent heart bear up and live !

---

for the night.   His appearance was in the highest degree moving to the imagination : mists were on the hill sides ; darkness shutting in upon the huge avenue of mountains ; torrents roaring ; no home in sight to which the child might belong ; his dress, cry, and appearance, all different from anything we had been accustomed to : it was a text, as William has since observed to me, containing in itself the whole history of the highlander's life ; his melancholy, his simplicity, his poverty, his superstition, and, above all, that visionariness which results from a communion with the unworldlinesss of nature."

It was well for him that he first saw his race through beautiful and noble objects, that he read the first pages of the book of man through Nature. For he had thus a safeguard against too rapid a disillusion of the sanctities of faith in human Nature ; he could resist

> The weight of meanness, selfish cares,
> Coarse manners, vulgar passions, that beat in
> On all sides from the ordinary world.

His face was turned towards the truth that though Man is base and sinful, yet that he is greater than his baseness and his sin ; that though at times we may despise him as the slave of his meaner self, yet that we must reverence him as destined to triumph over it, and claim his inheritance of Heaven. For true knowledge of human nature is the product, first, of a lofty but undefined ideal of Man ; secondly, of that ideal disappointed ; and thirdly, of that disappointment corrected by the calm judgment of a life which has never let love go, nor faith in a God who is the Father and the Saviour of men.

This was the root of Wordsworth's love of Man. But as we have seen, Nature was at first pre-eminent. Man was only an " occasional delight, an accidental grace " among the passion and the rapture in which Wordsworth moved, inspired by the beauty of the world. As he passed on from childhood and left its sports behind, and began to directly commune with natural objects, another step in this love of Man was made. When an inner impulse first urged him to embody in words his feelings, Fancy awoke and linked to Nature and her scenes human sentiment and human pictures. He could not see a grave without placing a widow there to weep ; nor the fox-glove dismantled of its bells without thinking of a vagrant mother whose children, careless of her sorrow, played around her; nor a rock, water-wet with springs and sparkling in the sunshine without fancying it the silver shield of a knight hung over his tomb, or an entrance into some fairy palace.   Thus " wilful and busy Fancy "

> Engrafted far-fetched hopes on feelings bred
> By pure imagination——turned
> Instinctively to human passions.

And though Wordsworth did not understand the cause of this, nor see that he was being slowly led towards that which he calls the point

> Of sound humanity to which our Tale
> Leads, though by sinuous ways—

he had now arrived through these earlier and later impressions at a vague ideal of Man, in which he unconsciously reverenced and loved him as sublime or good, and threw around his vague ideal the brilliant or pensive drapery of Romance.   It was at this stage in his progress that he went to Cambridge, and found in the university life a point of transition between his early remoteness from social life, and the great human disturbance into which he was soon to plunge.   It was, as he calls it, something that resembled "an approach to human business, a privileged world within a world, a midway residence with all its intervenient imagery, that suited far better his visionary mind than to be thrust out at once into the conflicts of substantial life."   He saw in it an image of the great world, and it touched him into that distant interest in humanity of which I have already spoken. But it was not at Cambridge, but afterwards, on his return to the mountains that the interest took a conscious form. The power and the life which lay in Man, as the crown of Nature, broke upon him at the very moment when he became through Nature a dedicated spirit. You will remember the passage already quoted, in which he describes the deep religious impression made on him by an early morning, his first clear realization of his mission in life. In an after passage in the " Prelude " he refers to the intense emotion of that hour. We then find that he not only realized himself, but also—in the excitement of the hour, being uplifted by the strength of the emotions that had wrought in him—rose into that conception of Man, as an ideal Whole, which a boy often conceives from history and poetry. Recall, he cries,

> My song ! those high emotions which thy voice
> Has heretofore made known ; that bursting forth
> Of sympathy, inspiring and inspired,
> When everywhere a vital pulse was felt,
> And all the several frames of things, like stars
> Through every magnitude distinguishable,
> Shone mutually indebted, or half lost
> Each in the other's blaze, a galaxy
> Of life and glory. In the midst stood Man,
> Outwardly, inwardly contemplated,
> As, of all visible natures, crown, though born
> Of dust, and kindred to the worm ; a Being
> Both in perception and discernment, first
> In every capability of rapture,
> Through the divine effect of power and love ;
> As, more than anything we know, instinct
> With Godhead, and, by reason and by will,
> Acknowledging dependency sublime.

With the dream of this conception in his mind he went

for the second time to Cambridge, and there a more practical contact with Man dispelled his ideal. Vice and folly were thrust upon his view, and he lost much of his early faith in human goodness : small characters, and the little bustling passions and the isolated aims of university life broke up the large impersonated idea of Mankind. Yet the Ideal was not quite lost, for first, Antiquity threw its solemn shadow over the present college life, and filled it with the shapes of the great men of the past, by whose life human nature was dignified; and secondly, the very vice and folly he beheld showed how lofty must be the nature which could fall so low. Nor was it possible for him to think of human life in its career to sorrow and guilt without a deeper and similar sense of that old indefinite terror and dismay, which once the storms and angry elements had wrought within him. He began to see mankind as he had seen Nature. Though then, the old imaginative ideal of simplicity and joy in human life had passed away, yet, through this new awfulness, another and a vaster thought of Man began to grow, which took to itself from the terror in it a touch of sublimity.

The journey to the continent, through France and Italy trembling with the first revolutionary excitement, added something to his interest in Man, and balanced, by the passing joy which he felt in that glorious time, the unhappy impression he had received at Cambridge. But Nature was still " sovereign in his mind " when he arrived in London. There his ideal was further shattered. The exposure of innocent life to shame, the degradation of womanhood, the tragic sufferings of men, the vast follies, the triviality mixed with horror, the vulgar thought, the mean interests, the sight of men unfaithful to their work—these broke down the unsubstantial palace of his ideal. But even as it was broken down, another building began to be raised. At his very first entrance a truer, loftier thought of Man arose—a tremendous sense of power as belonging to mankind—

> A weight of ages did at once descend
> Upon my heart—no thought embodied, no
> Distinct remembrances, but weight and power—
> Power growing under weight.

The "endless stream of men and moving things," the everyday appearance of the mighty city, and its wonder and awe, the "quick dance of colours, lights and forms," all the multitude of hurrying men, with every character of form and face, so that he could say, the face of every one

> That passes by me is a mystery;

the sight of the great men who moved Mankind; the orator, Burke, as he thundered against abstract rights; the peace of the London night, when all was still, and the business of the coming day was yet unborn; these were the things which, in this "theatre and burial-place of passions," moved him to the heart with that passion of the poet which answers the appeal of mankind for his interest and his love.

Daily and hourly, knowledge of man poured in upon him from a multitude of scenes, and he found (to his delight in the strength and glory of his youth) that he had power to grasp the whole. It was less knowledge of particular phases of human nature, than the impression of a vast spirit of humanity diffused through time and space, which he gained. It was the sense of all that had been done and suffered, was doing and suffering now in the great City and in the world, which brooded over him like a vast shadow and filled his soul with thought. A solemn, awful ideal of the majesty and power of humanity now began to replace the vague ideal of his boyhood, the shattered ideal of his youth. To him London now was thronged ; and the comparison is one of those sublime flights of imagination of which Wordsworth alone among modern poets has been capable :

> With impregnations like the Wilds
> In which my early feelings had been nursed—
> Bare hills and valleys, full of caverns, rocks,
> And audible seclusions, dashing lakes,
> Echoes and waterfalls, and pointed crags
> That into music touch the passing wind.

And the analogy which he felt is not obscure, for Nature, like mankind, bears the traces of a suffering past. Every rock-strewn valley tells of centuries of endurance and agony from storm and frost and lightning, in the rent channels of its streams and in the shivered peaks above it. And if in the past Nature has suffered, there is no moment of the present which does not tell of its intense activity ; we cannot linger by the sea or in the woods, without an impression, almost irritating, of unmitigated work and waste and reproduction. The same feelings as these were Wordsworth's in the city, when he passed through the forest, and wandered by the ocean, of humanity.

And as he had received higher ideas of God in spite of Nature, " red in tooth and claw," and seen love underneath its awful forces and the apparent ruin that they worked ; so in the city, owing to this early training, he was able, in spite of misery and guilt, to grasp the higher view of mankind, and to love mankind. He dwelt upon the real, but it led him to a new ideal. He saw what Man was, went down into the depths of his vice and guilt, and yet his trust in that which mankind might become was not overthrown. And when he turned from the darker to the lighter side, he saw that the Divine in Man was still Divine, nay, more beautiful even from the gloom through which it flashed to speak of Heaven in the hearts of men.

One more sublime idea came upon him and exalted the thought of Man. It was the idea of his unity. There was one Brotherhood held in one Father,—

> One Spirit, over ignorance and vice
> Predominant, in good and evil hearts :

one conscience shared by all alike, " as one eye for the sun's light." In this idea, among all the confusion of men, and whirl of good and ill, Wordsworth found rest, and in the rest and the blessedness of it, he found God, and saw Him as the Master of mankind. He had reached the third stage in our thought of Man of which I spoke, when the disappointment we suffer from the overthrow of our youthful ideal of Man is accepted and corrected.

Thus from his boyhood, his thoughts,—

> by slow gradations had been drawn
> To human-kind and to the good and ill
> Of human life——.

Nature had led him on ; through her he had found the

love of his race.   But still, though the love of Man was
growing day by day, it had not as yet reached that point
at which it became predominant.   He still was able to
fly from humanity to her, to find refuge in her mighty
calm from the guilt and anarchy of men.

> The world of human-kind outweighed not hers
> In my habitual thoughts ; the scale of love
> Though filling daily, still was light, compared
> With that in which *her* mighty objects lay.

And for a short period in this year, 1791, he went to
Wales and revived and sanctified his soul by communion
with the hills.   But the enthusiasm of Humanity, once
awakened, is not a passion that goes to sleep again, and
now the songs of liberty and the glory of the efforts
France was making rang with a more alluring murmur
in his ear.   He was irresistibly drawn to the theatre of
the Revolution, where the great questions which most
deeply move the race and all their passions, were play-
ing the first act in that mighty drama in whose
development we are now involved.   To this, and the
questions it involves, I shall devote my next lecture.

LECTURE IX.

At the beginning of these Lectures, we traced that which is called the Poetry of Man from Pope to the close of the life of Cowper. We found in his poetry a number of new ideas on the subject of mankind, the main characteristic of which was, that they all rested on the thought of an universal mankind, which in itself supposed the equality of all men in certain realms of thought and act. The ideas were new and revolutionary, but in Cowper they took no clear form. They floated in solution, they were not crystallized; they were the product of insensible not recognised influences of the time; mere green shoots of things which were to become mighty trees; the substance in faith of things hoped for, the evidence of things not seen; sparks of a kindling fire scattered only here and there, but full of a life whose first property was the will and the power to devour things too old and too corrupt to live. No one suspected then that they would burst into flame with such accumulating rapidity; but a few years only had passed by when they rose into a conflagration which, in the French Revolution, ran over the European world. In England the fire did not fall upon the State, but its inspiration, and the passionate emotion which

attended it, fell upon the poets; and out of the hearts of
Coleridge and Wordsworth the poetry of universal Man,
of freedom, of equal rights, of infinite promise, of the
overthrow of tyranny, leaped full-grown into a manhood
which has never endured decay. It is the history of its
influence on Wordsworth's mind which we have now to
trace and to explain.

We have seen that this development of the poetry of
Man in Wordsworth was preceded by that of the poetry of
Nature. I have worked out that in the previous lectures,
and an astonishing growth it is—so astonishing in comparison with the work on the same subject done by Cowper,
Crabbe, and Burns, that it seems, at first sight, inex-
plicable. But the first explanation of its rapidity is
one already alluded to in the history of the growth of the
poetry of natural description. It was in reality no
swift creation, but the flowering of a plant that had
already clothed itself with leaves and had nothing more
to do but flower. It is true that the whole plant was
covered almost in an instant with a mass of flowers,
and their extraordinary richness of flowerage needs a
further explanation. It is supplied when we realize
that the long European movement which so suddenly
took form in the French Revolution had reached in
Wordsworth's early life that point of expansion which
only needs a touch to cause the outburst. For at such a
time there is that profound but latent excitement in
which the minds of the Poets, who are the first to feel
excitements, become swiftly creative on all subjects within
their range; when the work of a century is often done in
a year. Supply a new and quickening element to the soil

of the Poet's thought, let the air which it breathes become nipping and eager, and things which have only been in leaf within him, will cover their every spray with flowers.

One more explanation of this apparent rapidity is that the revolutionary movement contained within it a particular excitement on the subject of Nature. It took form in France in Rousseau's love of wild nature, in his thought that Nature was wiser, simpler, and greater than Man; but in him it was mixed with the ugliest imposition of his own diseased feelings on Nature. It took form in Germany in the songs of the young Poets who stormed and raged in verse till Goethe, who had himself in his youthful time out-thundered the others, raised his tranquillizing head above the waves. It had been growing into form for the last hundred years in England; and we find that, partly influenced by Rousseau, it preferred, shortly before Cowper, the wild and lonely landscape in which men could feel sentimental; next, it preferred the wilder and lonelier scenes for their own sake, and having felt them profoundly, it then became connected with the poetry of Man. The Poets transferred their love of this wild nature to the men who lived in it, and looked on them as certain to be nobler and more independent than they could be in cities and the artificial world. It was there we ought to seek for the primæval and pure feelings of men; and Wordsworth, in the love which he bore to the shepherds, and the honour he paid to his own dalesmen, was following up to its legitimate conclusion that excitement on the subject of wild nature which was now one of the elements of the European disturbance.

We have thus been led, in thinking of the revolutionary

movement as it bore on the idea of Nature, to the very
point at which we left Wordsworth in the last lecture,
when he had been led by the love of Nature to the love
of Man. He had arrived, in solitude, and following his
natural individuality, at the same point to which the
world was being led by its new impulse, but the impulse
had of course its insensible influence upon him. He
was now fitted to become a part of it, and to consciously join in it. He had been led by the love of Nature
to the love of the simple men among whom he lived.
Passing into the world and mingling with men, he carried
with him the teaching of Nature, and applied it to his
conception of mankind. The self-investigation that
Nature had forced upon him; the sense of the pre-
eminent dignity of the human soul that he had learnt
from her; and the previous conception he had formed of
Nature as One, led him to investigate human nature,
to recognize then its pre-eminent dignity, and finally to
see mankind as One Being whose life and rights and
powers and place in the world, whose origin and whose
destiny he was above all bound to study. The revolutionary idea of one universal humanity began to germinate in his mind. A multitude of vague, formless thoughts
on this subject were floating in the air. He breathed
them, but as yet neither he nor anyone had been able to
realize them, for they were not made clear by being arranged
under a few leading thoughts.

It was this which the French Revolution did for him
and for the world. It gave sudden, clear, and terrible
form to the long-prepared ideas of Europe; it placed the
movement in which all had been sharing on lines on

which it could run along to a known end. It did the
work of the Prophet for the world; it gave voice to the
voiceless passion of a million hearts. It said, Man is
one and indivisible, and it attempted to carry out that
idea and all its resulting thoughts in politics and society.
How far it had anything to do with Christianity, and how
it influenced Wordsworth, is the subject of my lecture.

It did not, as I have hinted, come on Wordsworth unpre-
pared. He was himself a natural republican. He had been
born in a poor district, in a primitive homely corner of
English ground, and he had rarely seen, during his school-
day time the "face of one vested with respect through
claims of wealth or blood;" and when he passed to the
University it was, he says, one of its benefits, that it
held up to his view something of a Republic. All stood
there on equal ground, men were brothers there in honour;
distinction lay open to all alike, and wealth and title were
less than industry and genius. Moreover, he had learnt
obedience to the presence of God's power in the sovereignty
of nature; and again, fellowship with venerable books had
sanctioned—

> the proud workings of the soul
> And mountain liberty.

It could not be, he says,—

> But that one tutored thus should look with awe
> Upon the faculties of man, receive
> Gladly the highest promises, and hail
> As best, the government of equal rights
> And individual worth.

And to this natural republicanism he traces his first
indifference on the outbreak of the Revolution. It did

9

not seem so wonderful to him as the rest; for he had breathed unconsciously its air from the beginning.   He was scarcely dipped at first, he says, into the turmoil, and the result was that he then possessed a sounder judgment than those who lived in the full rush of the excitement. Even afterwards when, having fully shared in the excitement, his mind subsided, he recovered quickly the cooler judgment he had possessed; and for a long time, when other men in England despaired, retained his faith in freedom in spite of the Terror.   He had never been swept upwards on the shore so violently as others; he never was swept back so far as others in the reflux of the wave.

At the same time, and this is important for the comprehension of Wordsworth, there was a distant conservatism in his nature, that which belongs to the Artist and Poet who love the past for its romance, or for the nobleness it once possessed.   In the very midst of earnest dialogues with Beaupuis in the forests of the Loire, his imagination carried him away from the turbulent present; and he saw the woods full of the forms of old Romance, that Romance the Revolution was destroying.   Nor could he be unmoved when things, which had sacred or chivalrous associations growing round them like ivy round a ruin, were desecrated by the destroying element in the Revolution. Hence arose a conflict in his mind between delight in new-born freedom and its overthrow of corrupt states, and his sorrow for the many things which, once the origin of high emotions, went down in the same shipwreck.   But the conflict itself was productive of that mental and imaginative excitement in which fine poetic work is done; and the slight tinge of conservatism acted as a kind of

sobering restraint on the imagination, so that his sanity
as a Poet of Man was preserved in a time of furious
excitement. And again, the imaginative work his poetic
temper wrought around the old things of the past—a con-
vent, a *château*, a hermitage—served also to balance the
revolutionary passion.

> Imagination, potent to inflame
> At times with virtuous wrath and noble scorn,
> Did also often mitigate the force
> Of civic prejudice, the bigotry,
> So call it, of a youthful patriot's mind ;
> And on these spots with many gleams I looked
> Of chivalrous delight.

But these feelings were only slight weights in the opposite scale. His hatred of absolute rule, and of the barren
pride and oppression of the *noblesse*, and his longing for
the redemption of the people at almost any cost, grew till
they outweighed everything else, and in the first half of
his artist-life his republican ideas were always predominant. Living in these ideas, and in the excitement of that
contest in his own mind which I have pointed out, his
work was marked by a wonderful freshness and life. In
the second half, the contest ceased—he was shocked
back into conservatism ; the little germ of it in him
grew into an overshadowing tree under whose shade ideas
died. Maxims and formulas replaced them, and, being
essentially unpoetical, they all but killed his poetic
nature. With the passing away of his revolutionary
ideas, passed away the divine spirit of song, the strength
of his thought, the majesty of his style, the emotion
which thrilled through his verse and gave the kindling
impulse to his style. He became pedestrian and con-

templative, and we can no longer say of him, that he spoke "non verba, sed tonitrua."

Nor is it difficult to account for this. The Poet who is now to say great things of Nature or of Man, who is to be more than the mere describer of Nature, or the mere analyzer of human nature, produces nothing worthy, if he be not at heart influenced by the larger republican ideas.

To one holding no longer the great ideas, and feeling no longer the passions embodied in the words, Liberty, Equality, Fraternity, Nature could not speak as she did of old. For she is, to her core, republican. It is by the consent of all, and by its full value being given to the work of each, that her great community exists and moves and grows. Each thing, bird, and brook, and tree, sings and flows and clothes itself with its own beauty, by its own divine vitality, and at its own sweet will; all have equal rights in sun and earth, in rain and dew; all choose freely the dwelling-place most fitted for their self-development, and no one says them nay; and the seeming violations of this are nothing as against the rule, and indeed belong to the rule. All are brothers one of another and live and die for one another, and those things which have the mastery, like the sun, have it because they give away their life to others. They rule because they are the best givers.

And she deals with us with the same republicanism. We turn from the oppression of the world, from the selfishness of caste, and the exclusiveness of wealth to the blessed equalities of Nature; and find comfort in the knowledge that sunlight and rain fall as richly on the poor as on the wealthy, that her beauty is poured out on all, that she does not reserve the glory of the sunrise for the cultivated classes, nor the freshness of the dew for the nobility. It was this spirit of freedom, of the brotherhood of universal love, of unlimited life and beauty bestowed on all, contradicting by silent and hourly act the theories of the Tory, which strove in vain in later years to recover its early power over Wordsworth. He could not receive its teaching, and his poetry of Nature decayed as his life decayed.

As to the poetry of Man, it suffered still more. For in what high vein can he write, in whom the spirit of prophecy is replaced by the spirit of mere teaching, infinite hope for Man by melancholy moaning over his fate, belief in the future by belief in the past. These are not the things which kindle the life of Song, but depress it; they throw no consecrating light, but gloom, upon the landscape of Man; the sorrow born of them does not humanize the soul, but shuts it up within itself—and Wordsworth's verse suffered from their presence in his mind. He ceased to give voice to the deepest longings and hopes of men who cared for Man; and the Poet loses the very breath and impulse of song when men, listening to his words, no longer send back to him a wave of sympathy and joy.

It is most pitiful when the Poet, whose highest business is to hope and prophesy for Man, gives himself up to the melancholy pipe, and hymns only his own sorrow and the sorrow of the race by the riverside of time, as some of our modern poets do. There is no enduring life in such poetry, and so far as Wordsworth fell into despair of the Present and regret of the Past, his poetry lost its power and its life. He was saved from the worst form of this evil by that calmer judgment of which I spoke, which enabled him to resist the full force of the shock he received; but he was chiefly saved by his Christianity, for in the belief in a redeeming God and in a divine future he could still abide in hope, and live in faith of a diviner freedom, for the race. But he was only partly saved, for in rejecting the primary thoughts of the Revolution he rejected half the ideas of Christianity. If Christianity has any politics, they are democratic. It is very well to say that it has been the servant of tyrants over the body and the soul, because it has been made such by priests and kings. But the reason is not far to seek. They saw that it was the most dangerous element in the world for them and their power, and their one effort has been to prove that it was upon their side. But they could not do this without denying or travestying its primal ideas, and this they set themselves to do. They took out of it its universality, its love, its socialism; its proclamation of spiritual equality and of equal rights and duties before God; its contempt for wealth, its hatred of oppressors; its love for the poor, the ignorant, and the low-born. And they made an aristocratic, exclusive, oppressing phantom of it, and said to the world, believe in this, or you are lost for ever. And men not only believed in it, but believed that it was Christianity. It followed that when the thoughts of the Revolution swept away the political and ecclesiastical Christianity, men cried out that Christianity itself was dead and buried for ever. But it was not so. It rose again into a new life; it found its true home among the new ideas; it showed, as it grew, that it was not that thing which men had long believed it to be; but the supporter of freedom, of equality, of brotherhood, the most real force in this world against tyranny and superstition, the asserter, nay, the creator of the idea of an universal humanity, and of all the thoughts which are the children of that idea and of that of an universal Father. It is one of the most distinctive marks of Christianity that it has never failed to commend itself—not as a dogmatic system, but as a spirit which influences by great thoughts and stirs deep emotions—to free states. It is equally characteristic of it when it has been degraded by despots into a political engine, and treated by the people as such, to rise out of its degradation and overcome the popular hatred, and re-assert itself, undecayed, and with fresh hopes in its eyes, as the religion of Democracy. Even in France this was the case; in proportion as the political work of the Revolution grew firm, its irreligious work decayed. The Christian Church found its life renewed in republicanism; and if France is now un-Christian, that is not due to republicanism, but to the ceaseless despotism which, prevailing under various forms to the present hour in France, has again undone the religious work of the Revolution, and again travestied Christianity, so that men must hate it as an enemy.

If there is one thing which above all we need now, it is that there should be some who should boldly say that a Christianity which denies the root thoughts of the Revolution is not Christianity at all, but an odious idol which takes its name. Only we must also say that Christianity is more than these thoughts; that it takes in, for example, not only the rights of men, but as Mazzini said, hitting fairly the great omission of the Revolution, the duties of men as the masters and the limits of their rights. With this addition—it being understood that I speak here of Christianity in its relation to the whole of mankind as a social Being, not in its relation to personal feelings and wants, which forms a separate study,—the leading ideas of Christianity are the same as the leading ideas of the Revolution, only in the one case they are applied in the religious, in the other in the political sphere: or, to express it otherwise, the revolutionary ideas are the Christian ideas applied to the relation of men to one another, and to the state.

But we must look further into this thought, for it enables us at once to show the theology that naturally belongs to Wordsworth's poetry of Man. " The Revolution," says De Tocqueville, "had no peculiar territory, it was not made for France alone, but for the world, and its result was in some sort to blot out of the map all the ancient frontiers. In spite of laws, traditions, character, and language, it brought men together on a common ground, changed enemies into compatriots, and formed above national peculiarities an intellectual country common to all, of which all men of all nations could become citizens." That is as true of Christianity as of the Revolution, if we change the word intellectual into spiritual; because both started from the one idea of a common humanity which made all men brothers, and therefore claimed for all men equal rights to freedom, to self-development, and to the enjoyment of the common gifts of the earth and sky. Both Christianity and the Revolution built their foundation on Human Nature itself.

" It brought together," De Tocqueville continues, " nations which scarcely knew one another, and united them by interests common to the race. It was disengaged from every special bond to a people or a form of government, or a society, or an epoch, or a race ; it had no particular national end, no special French aim : its end was the general rights and duties of all men in political and social matters." That also was as true of Christianity as of the Revolution, if we leave out political matters with which Christianity did not directly meddle ; and it is true of both, because they started alike from the one great thought, that there was only one nation, the nation of mankind, and that all its citizens were bound to sacrifice themselves for one another. In Christ, there is neither Jew nor Greek, German, French or Englishman, but the one universal humanity which is all, and in all, and in which all men are one, equal, free, and brothers.

The ideas are the same in both, and whether politically, socially, or spiritually applied, they are Christian ideas. The difference lies in this, that the ideas of the Revolution were applied only to Man as Man, the Christian ideas sought for a higher unity than the mere basis of a common humanity. They found it in the common Fatherhood of God and in the union of all men in the humanity of Christ ; and until the ideas of the Revolution, as they have sometimes done, complete themselves in those two higher thoughts, they will fail to do their work. They cannot conquer of themselves that selfishness in man which supports exclusiveness, ensures oppression, and hates the freedom which equalizes men. They cannot prevent revolution from ending in despotism.

Naturally, along with these great thoughts of an universal mankind, of natural equality, of the brotherhood of the race, were two other lines of thought—one which went forward with passion to overthrow all institutions which repressed the growth of Man or kept him in any slavery; another which went forward with equal passion to prophesy a glorious future for mankind—and in both these lines of thought, Christianity and the Revolution were at one. They were both the work of God in the hearts of men, and they both became leading poetical ideas in the new poetry of Man in England.

These were the principles of the Revolution, and the great religious English Poet took them up and supplemented them at once with their analogous Christian ideas. Wordsworth could not help it; he did it almost unconsciously. He found the doctrine of an universal Man and an universal brotherhood in the doctrine of an universal Father. He saw in God the source of the rights of men to equality and liberty. It was God who was the avenger of slavery, the vindicator of man against the evils of caste, of enforced ignorance, poverty, and despotism over the bodies or souls of men; and he looked forward through God, because He was eternal Justice and Love watching over Man, to a glorious time of universal joy and mutual love, when the race should be regenerated. It was he who made the poetry of Man in England not only revolutionary but theological.

It was thus the Revolution came on the hearts of young and imaginative and religious men in England. But we, who live upon the broad river of its thought, can scarcely realize what it was to men when first it broke, a living fount of streams, from its rock in the desert, to quench the thirst of those who longed, but knew not, till it came, for what they longed. We who live in times which, though not dull, are sad coloured, can scarcely imagine the glory of that awaking, the stream of new thoughts that transfigured life, the passionate emotion, the love and hatred, the horror and the rapture, the visionary glories, the unutterable hopes, the sense of deliverance, the new Heavens and the new Earth, brimful of promise, which dawned on men :

> Before them shone a glorious world
> Fresh as a banner bright, unfurled
> To music suddenly.

In that early morning of hope, the love of liberty seized on men with a power, almost a violence, which prophesied a reaction, and forced itself forth in the young in violent poetry. I have already spoken of the uncontrolled and tempestuous verse of Coleridge on this subject. In his view also it was God who had awakened liberty. Freedom in France

> From the Almighty's bosom leapt
> With whirlwind arm, fierce minister of love.

Southey, and Lloyd felt the same ; vague expectations, wild schemes, flitted through their minds ; they projected a socialist communion on the Susquehanna to which they gave the name of the Pantisocracy, where all things were to be in common, and the " cluster of families, bound together by congenial tastes and uniform forms rather than in self-depending and insulated households," were to solicit their food from daily toil, a thing which De Quincey says might have been fortunate for Coleridge. But none felt the enthusiasm of the time more intensely, nor expressed it more nobly than Wordsworth. He was the true human Poet of the time. He felt every pulse of the movement in his own heart, and responding to that he felt—

> From hour to hour the antiquated earth
> Beat like the heart of man.

He describes its effect in the Excursion on a sorrow-stricken, lonely man. He was roused from his grief by the crash of the Bastille, and from the wreck rose a golden palace, as it seemed, of equitable law and mild paternal sway.

>   The potent shock
> I felt : the transformation I perceived,
> As marvellously seized as in that moment
> When, from the blind mist issuing, I beheld
> Glory—beyond all glory ever seen,
> Confusion infinite of heaven and earth,
> Dazzling the soul. Meanwhile, prophetic harps
> In every grove were ringing, ' War shall cease ;
> Did ye not hear that conquest is abjured ?
> Bring garlands, bring forth choicest flowers, to deck
> The tree of Liberty.'—My heart rebounded ;
> My melancholy voice the chorus joined ;
> —' Be joyful all ye nations ; in all lands,
> Ye that are capable of joy be glad !
> Henceforth whate'er is wanting to yourselves
> In others ye shall promptly find—and all
> Enriched by mutual and reflected wealth
> Shall with one heart, honour their common kind.

He was reconverted to the world in the general joy. He haunted all assemblies where busy men, inspired with universal hope, met to unite nations. In the victory of mankind over wrong, he found his faith in God again. He returned to public worship, and felt a new meaning in the Hebrew Prophets when they thundered against oppression, when they foretold a reign of peace.

Nor when Wordsworth describes its effect upon himself is he less enthusiastic—

> O pleasant exercise of hope and joy !
> For mighty were the auxiliars that then stood
> Upon our side, we who were strong in love !
> Bliss was it in that dawn to be alive,
> But to be young was very heaven !—Oh ! times
> In which the meagre, stale, forbidding ways
> Of custom, law, and statute, took at once
> The attraction of a country in romance !
> When Reason seemed the most to assert her rights,
> When most intent on making of herself
> A prime Enchantress—to assist the work
> Which then was going forward in her name !
> Not favoured spots alone, but the whole earth,
> The beauty wore of promise, that which sets
> (As at some moment might not be unfelt
> Among the bowers of paradise itself)
> The budding rose above the rose full blown.
> What temper at the prospect did not wake
> To happiness unthought of ? The inert
> Were roused, and lively natures rapt away !
> They who had fed their childhood upon dreams,
> The playfellows of fancy, who had made
> All powers of swiftness, subtlety, and strength
> Their ministers,—who in lordly wise had stirred
> Among the grandest objects of the sense,
> And dealt with whatsoever they found there
> As if they had within some lurking right
> To wield it ;—they, too, who, of gentle mood
> Had watched all gentle motions, and to these
> Had fitted their own thoughts, schemers more mild,

And in the region of their peaceful selves ;—
Now was it that both found, the meek and lofty
Did both find, helpers to their heart's desire,
And stuff at hand, plastic as they could wish ;
Were called upon to exercise their skill,
Not in Utopia, subterranean fields,
Or some secreted island, Heaven knows where !
But in the very world which is the world
Of all of us,—the place where in the end
We find our happiness, or not at all !

That was written in 1805 as he looked back on all he
had felt, and the enthusiasm of the time is not dead in
its noble verse. It was a dream, but it is a dream which
hour by hour is fulfilling itself; and dream or not, it
did a mighty work on Wordsworth. It built him into a
man ; it added the enthusiasm of Man to the enthusiasm of Nature; it took him away from contemplation
of his own soul to live in the hopes, to proclaim the
faith, to seek the love of mankind ; it gave him the
impulse to write some work, which should give form to
the faith he now possessed in the glory of the future,
and in the majesty of the powers, of Man. It led him
all his life long—even when his Conservatism got the
upper hand,—to be the champion of liberty, the hater
of oppression in the present—however in his imaginative
Toryism he might glorify the past. It made him the
singer of simple life, of honest manners, of poverty and
its sorrows, of the honour of humanity in all ranks—it
taught him to see the face of God in every man.

It gave, De Quincey says, " to the whole system of
his own thoughts and feelings a firmer tone, and a sense
of the awful *realities* which surround the mind," of the
awful sorrows and guilt and the still more awful goodness

which belong to Man in times of profound emotion, and underlie his nature always. And in this new and lurid but absorbing light, the passion for Nature was quenched. It reawoke afterwards, and how, we shall hereafter see; but at present, the destiny of Man, his origin, his duties, his rights, his possibilities, the agony of his battle, and the God with him—these were all in all to Wordsworth. He saw through a glass darkly, he only knew in part, but he had put away childish things for ever. He had entered on the dignity and sincere thinking of matured manhood. He was now trained not only to be the revealer of Nature, but also the Poet of Man.

LECTURE X.

⸺◆⸺

THE Revolution with which Wordsworth came into contact in France, made a revolution in his mind. It carried him forward from a life with Nature to a life with Man. I discussed last Sunday some of the ideas that seized on him, and I traced their relation to theology, and their effect on Wordsworth. I propose to-day to continue the subject, and to connect what is to be said, partly with Wordsworth's life in France during 1791—92, and partly with his poetry.

We have seen that in 1789 the influence of Nature was predominant; but after his stay in London, where he was brought into closer contact with mankind in mass, the revolutionary movement sucked him into its whirlpool with amazing force, and shortly after Louis XVI. had taken the oath of fidelity to the new Constitution, he went to France to find the whole nation mad with joy. At first his ardour for freedom was more a sentiment than one of those profound convictions which create an enduring passion. In the guise of an enthusiast, he made a relic of a stone picked up where the Bastille had stood; but things of this kind seemed to touch him less than the sentimental paintings in the Louvre. He was not as yet conscious of the power which had begun to move within him. But, passing on to live in Orleans, the passion of the time soon developed it. On his arrival, he haunted society where politics were tabooed; but he was soon wearied, and withdrew to a noisier world.

At first he associated chiefly with the officers stationed in the city, who were bent on restoring the old régime, their only wish being to undo that which had been done. One among them, however, who became his special friend, was of a different type, and his case is important as illustrating how the awful temper of the time mastered men who would otherwise have been frivolous. He had been a noted gallant, but now—in the conflict which raged within him between old feelings, traditions of caste and honour, and the new ideas and the revelation of the wrongs of mankind—his person, spirit and character changed. He was like a man ravaged by inward pain. With every post from Paris,—

> the fever came,
> A punctual visitant, to shake this man,
> Disarmed his voice and fanned his yellow cheek
> Into a thousand colours; while he read,
> Or mused, his sword was haunted by his touch
> Continually, like an uneasy place
> In his own body.

Such agitation in others soon awoke the same in Wordsworth. Indeed none could long remain at peace, for

> The soil of common life was, at that time
> Too hot to tread upon .   .   .   .   .
> The land all swarmed with passion, like a plain
> Devoured by locusts.

Small men, unheard of now, became for the time powers;

the fire ran from Paris to the provincial towns, and from them to the remotest nook and village of the land; and Wordsworth, resisting the arguments of those who supported the past, threw himself into the arms of the republicans.

> Became a patriot, and my heart was all
> Given to the people, and my love was theirs.

He and his friend Beaupuis, who was rejected with hatred by his brother officers, lived almost together. Both were enthusiastic, both were full of hope, and the description which Wordsworth gives of him is in itself so beautiful, and illustrates so well the best type of the men of the earliest times of the revolution, that I cannot refrain from quoting it,—

> A meeker man
> Than this lived never, nor a more benign,
> Meek though enthusiastic. Injuries
> Made *him* more gracious, and his nature then
> Did breathe its sweetness out most sensibly,
> As aromatic flowers on Alpine turf,
> When foot hath crushed them. He through the events
> Of that great change wandered in perfect faith,
> As through a book, an old romance, or tale
> Of Faery, or some dream of actions wrought
> Behind the summer clouds. By birth he ranked
> With the most noble, but unto the poor
> Among mankind he was in service bound,
> As by some tie invisible, oaths professed
> To a religious order. Man he loved
> As man ; and, to the mean and the obscure,
> And all the homely in their homely works,
> Transferred a courtesy which had no air
> Of condescension ; but did rather seem
> A passion and a gallantry, like that
> Which he, a soldier, in his idler day
> Had paid to woman : somewhat vain he was,

> Or seemed so, yet it was not vanity,
> But fondness, and a kind of radiant joy
> Diffused around him, while he was intent
> On works of love or freedom, or revolved
> Complacently the progress of a cause
> Whereof he was a part : yet this was meek
> And placid, and took nothing from the man
> That was delightful.

They talked together, while France stood on the brink of its great trial, of Man and his noble nature, as it was in itself; of the abstract political theories founded on the conception of an universal mankind; and of the oppression and tyranny that had for centuries hindered Man's development. On these three lines of thought I shall build what I have to say in this lecture and the following one.

I. And first with regard to Man, Wordsworth approached, he tells us, the shield

> Of human nature from the golden side,

and would have fought even to the death to attest that it was gold. And charmed with the golden view, he was led to ponder, first on the individual man, on what was best in him—

> Wise in passion and sublime in power,
> Benevolent in small societies
> And great in large ones.

And he did this, stripping him of all adventitious ornaments, of rank and wealth, and traditional honours— looking at him as he was in himself, not as he was by that which he possessed. This habit which had grown upon him among the hills, but which he did not then consciously possess, became now the conscious habit of his life, and to express its results one of the principal objects of his poetry.

It was rooted in him by that which he saw at this time in France, when the whole nation sprang as it were into new being. He and Beaupuis rejoiced together, when after long conversations on " the honourable deeds and noble spirits of ancient story," on the rise of sects and nations, and the natural union of men under the influence of forming ideas—they turned to the movement going on around them, and beheld, responding to the aspirations of their own minds—

> A living confirmation of the whole
> Before us, in a people from the depth
> Of shameful imbecility uprisen,
> Fresh as the morning star. Elate we looked
> Upon their virtues ; saw, in rudest men,
> Self-sacrifice the firmest ; generous love,
> And continence of mind, and sense of right,
> Uppermost in the midst of fiercest strife.

It was this that he carried back to England with him and wrought into his poetry. He moved among men, he says, with genial feelings ; when erring, erring in the better part, and in the kinder spirit ; indulgent to their weakness, rejoicing in their goodness ; as much a child of Nature as before, only now giving to Man a stronger affection than he gave to Nature.

> Diffusing only those affections wider
> That from the cradle had grown up with me,
> And losing, in no other way than light
> Is lost in light, the weak in the more strong.

Trusting in the grandeur of the one human heart that he had learnt in France belonged to all, he made it his main subject, but he turned from it as seen in cities to its more natural aspects among the poor. He was the first in England—not excepting Crabbe, whose sternness, even whose cynicism of portraiture, leaves too little of that tenderness and pity, or of that reverence for the men which is necessary for poetic treatment of the poor—he was the first who threw around the lives of ordinary men the glory and sweetness of song. He was the first who poured around the dalesmen's cottages, and the wandering life of the pedler, and the unheard struggles of the country and the mountain folk, the consecration and the Poet's dream. He was the first who isolated life after life in tender and homely narrative, and made us feel that God was with simple men and women; that in their lives were profound lessons; that the same equal heart beat in the palace and the hamlet hidden in the hills; that all men were brothers in the charities which soothe and bless, in the moral duties which God demands, in the feelings which nature awakens in their hearts; that a spirit of independence and stern liberty is the birthright and the passion of the poorest shepherd, as well as of the patriots who fill the pages of history.

One of the best examples of this is the way in which he sympathised with the love of the *statesmen* for their land. In his "Repentance," a pastoral ballad, he describes the misery, the consuming dullness of the small farmer's life who has parted with his estate, and lost with it the tie that bound him to his ancestors. In "Michael," when misfortune comes on the shepherd, Wordsworth describes, and in lines that show how deep his sympathy was with the humble feeling, how strong it was—

> Isabel, said he,
> I have been toiling more than seventy years,
> And in the open sunshine of God's love
> Have we all lived ; yet if these fields of ours

> Should pass into a stranger's hands, I think
> That I could not lie quiet in my grave.
> > The land
> Shall not go from us, and it shall be free ;
> He shall possess it, free as is the wind
> That passes over it.

Nor did he in after-life lose this close sympathy with the independence of the individual. The last book of the " Excursion " is full of passages that maintain the rights of men to individual development, to freedom from the oppression of unremitting toil, to all the means of education that the State can give. The worst fate that could befall a poor as well as a rich man, was to be turned into a mere instrument,—

> > Our life is turned
> Out of her course, wherever man is made
> An offering, or a sacrifice, a tool
> Or implement, a passive thing employed
> As a brute mean, without acknowledgment
> Of common right or interest in the end ;
> Used or abused as selfishness may prompt.

Lines which might be taken as a motto by the Trades' Unions.

This was the practical way in which he carried out the revolutionary idea that each man was to have the freest room for self-development, to be considered separate from the rest, not lost in a class. And he embodied these views in his Poems. The first book of the " Excursion " will never let us forget the power, the simple dignity, the capacity for refined feeling which may be in the poorest whom we meet. Two neglected Poems, " The Brothers," and " Michael," are exquisite from the sense they leave in us of the human reality and passionate tenderness which are to be found in the humblest lives. It was indeed republican to gather round the sorrows of children and their innocent talk, round names like " Matthew" and " Lucy Fell " and the " Idiot Boy," the interests and the feelings of England. His very theory of Poetic diction—that it should be that which men commonly use when in rustic life they express themselves simply, and in accordance with which the Lyrical Ballads were written—was itself due to his republican opinions. Both the theory and the poems astonished men at first; but they made their way, till a truer sentiment of Equality and Fraternity knit together the rich and the poor. He felt, and truly felt, that his writings of this kind "would co-operate with the benign tendencies in human nature and society; that they delineated not merely such feelings as all men sympathize with, but revealed such feelings as men may sympathize with, and such as there is reason to believe they would be better and more moral beings if they did sympathize with;" he wrote with "a view to show that men who do not wear fine clothes may feel deeply; that the spirit of resolution and independence was rooted in many parts of the country, and that the State should endeavour to support and not eradicate it;" with the design to "recover for the poor the rights of the human family and the franchises of universal brotherhood, of which they had been robbed by the wealthy and the noble; to impress the world with a sense of their dignity in suffering, and the moral grandeur of their honest poverty."

Love had he found in huts where poor men lie.

Connected with the whole of this love for the lives of common men was his love for the lowlier flowers. We see the influence of this element of his republicanism in the thoughtful and tender poems that he wrote about the common people of the fields and hedgerows—the daisy, the celandine, the daffodils, the primrose, and the snowdrop. These also he exalted by the influence of his imagination as much as the poor who loved them, and it was his delight to make them and their ways the image of mankind.

Nor did he neglect the lower ranges of mankind. None was so low as to be scorned without a sin, none without offence to God cast out of view. The old beggars who wandered uselessly about Cumberland awoke his poetic pity. In describing one of them, Wordsworth saw in him a man who, though he perhaps did no good himself, was yet the cause of good in others, and to whom at least Nature was always kind.

> Then let him pass, a blessing on his head !
> And while in that vast solitude to which
> The tide of things has borne him, he appears
> To breathe and live but for himself alone,
> Unblamed, uninjured, let him bear about
> The good which the benignant law of Heaven
> Has hung around him : and, while life is his,
> Still let him prompt the unlettered villagers
> To tender offices and pensive thoughts.
> —Then let him pass, a blessing on his head !
> And, long as he can wander, let him breathe
> The freshness of the valleys ; let his blood
> Struggle with frosty air and winter snows ;
> And let the chartered wind that sweeps the heath
> Beat his grey locks against his withered face.
>
> *   *   *   *   *

> Be his the natural silence of old age !
> Let him be free of mountain solitudes ;
> And have around him, whether heard or not,
> The pleasant melody of woodland birds.

He saw in the idiots who roved about the villages those whose life was hidden in God. He had compassion on the immoral; the gipsies who idly went through the country were the children of free Nature : the farmer of Tilbury Vale who had run away from his debts was one in whose frank ease of heart, and in whose simple affection for Nature, good lay hidden. And with an exquisite touch of loving-kindness he brings around those whom society had cast aside the gentleness and love of Nature, till, learning from her, we feel pity and kindness for the outcast. Every one knows the " Reverie of Poor Susan," but the description of the old farmer in London and of the love of Nature for him, is not so well known, and is characteristic of Wordsworth's tenderness to the erring.

> In the throng of the town like a stranger is he,
> Like one whose own country's far over the sea ;
> And Nature, while through the great city he hies,
> Full ten times a day takes his heart by surprise.
>
> This gives him the fancy of one that is young,
> More of soul in his face than of words on his tongue
> Like a maiden of twenty he trembles and sighs,
> And tears of fifteen will come into his eyes.
>
> 'Mid coaches and chariots, a waggon of straw,
> Like a magnet, the heart of old Adam can draw ;
> With a thousand soft pictures his memory will teem,
> And his hearing is touched with the sounds of a dream.
>
> Now farewell, old Adam ! when low thou art laid,
> May one blade of grass spring up over thy head ;
> And I hope that thy grave, wheresoever it be,
> Will hear the wind sigh through the leaves of a tree.

Nor did this reverence for " the power he served, that

10

sacred power, the Spirit of Humanity;" nor his love of the
simple poor, and his sense that Nature loved them
though man might not, cease to abide with him as he
grew old. There is a sonnet, written in 1831, which
embodies this continuous interest. It ought to be read
along with another written nearly thirty years before on
the same kind of subject, not only for the interest of
comparing the same thought in different expressions, but
for the interest of comparing the change of style—the
earlier one being in his best manner.* Even later, in
1842, when he is mourning over the state of England,
he feels himself the apostle of humanity. He describes
his poems as coming from one whose voice

> —Devoted to the love whose seeds
> Are sown in every human breast, to beauty,
> Lodged within compass of the humblest sight,
> To cheerful intercourse with wood and field,
> And sympathy with man's substantial griefs—

he hopes will not be heard in vain.

* I place these Sonnets opposite one another :—

ADMONITION.	HIGHLAND HUT.
Well may'st thou halt—and gaze with brightening eye !	See what gay wild flowers deck this earth-built Cot,
The lovely Cottage in the guardian nook	Whose smoke, forth-issuing whence and how it may,
Hath stirred thee deeply : with its own dear brook,	Shines in the greeting of the sun's first ray
Its own small pasture, almost its own sky !	Like wreaths of vapour without stain or blot.
But covet not the Abode :—forbear to sigh,	The limpid mountain rill avoids it not ;
As many do, repining while they look ;	And why should'st thou ? — If rightly trained and bred,
Intruders—who would tear from Nature's book	Humanity is humble, finds no spot
This precious leaf with harsh impiety.	Which her Heaven-guided feet refuse to tread.

These were the results of the reverence for human nature which he had learnt from the Revolution, and to which he had added the strong religious element I have sufficiently indicated. I quote in conclusion of this first part of my subject, and as resuming and confirming much that has been said, a passage from the Preface to the Lyrical Ballads :—

" The principal object, then, proposed in these Poems was to choose incidents and situations from common life, and to relate or describe them, throughout, as far as was possible, in a selection of language really used by men, and, at the same time, to throw over them a certain colouring of imagination, whereby ordinary things should be presented to the mind in an unusual aspect ; and, further, and above all, to make these incidents and situations interesting by tracing in them, truly though not ostentatiously, the primary laws of our nature : chiefly, as far as regards the manner in which we associate ideas in a state of excitement. Humble and rustic life was generally chosen, because, in that condition, the essential passions of the heart find a better soil in

Think what the Home must be if it were thine,
Even thine, though few thy wants !
—Roof, window, door,
The very flowers are sacred to the Poor,
The roses to the porch which they entwine :
Yea, all, that now enchants thee, from the day
On which it should be touched, would melt away.

[1804 ?

The walls are cracked, sunk is the flowery roof,
Undressed the pathway leading to the door ;
But love, as Nature loves, the lonely Poor ;
Search, for their worth, some gentle heart wrong-proof,
Meek, patient, kind, and, were its trials fewer,
Belike less happy.—Stand no more aloof !

[1821.

which they can attain their maturity, are less under restraint, and speak a plainer and more emphatic language; because in that condition of life our elementary feelings co-exist in a state of greater simplicity, and consequently, may be more accurately contemplated, and more forcibly communicated; because the manners of rural life germinate from those elementary feelings, and, from the necessary character of rural occupations, are more easily comprehended, and are more durable; and, lastly, because in that condition the passions of men are incorporated with the beautiful and permanent forms of nature.   The language, too, of these men has been adopted (purified indeed from what appear to be its real defects, from all lasting and rational causes of dislike or disgust) because such men hourly communicate with the best objects from which the best part of language is originally derived; and because, from their rank in society and the sameness and narrow circle of their intercourse, being less under the influence of social vanity, they convey their feelings and notions in simple and unelaborated expressions.   Accordingly, such a language, arising out of repeated experience and regular feelings, is a more permanent, and a far more philosophical language than that which is frequently substituted for it by Poets, who think that they are conferring honour upon themselves and their art, in proportion as they separate themselves from the sympathies of men, and indulge in arbitrary and capricious habits of expression, in order to furnish food for fickle tastes, and fickle appetites, of their own creation."

II. With regard to the second point, Wordsworth found

France steeped in the abstract political theories which her literary men had poured out upon her for half a century. They were not politicians in the sense of mingling in political action, but they occupied themselves almost altogether in writing about government, the origin of society, the natural rights of man, the limits of authority, the true principles of laws, the relations of man to man.

Every man had a different theory, but one general idea lay beneath them all,—" the substitution of some simple and elementary rules of government in accordance with reason and the law of nature, for the complicated and worn-out traditions which directed their present Society." That was the political philosophy of the 18th century, as De Tocqueville reads it.

These writings spread everywhere. All France read and thought, and by-and-by there grew up in the imagination of the people an imaginary society, in which all laws were simple, conformed to reason and nature; in which all men were equal, were brothers, and were free. It was a dream that seized on the hearts and minds of all men. They lived in an ideal city, the palaces of which were built by theory; and when what they dreamt was realized, as they thought, in America, the Revolution took substance. And Wordsworth with his friend took up these theories, and discussed with the ardour of youth the government of nations, what it ought to be, and how far the weal or woe of a people depends " upon their laws and fashion of the State." In long talks with Beaupuis he argued—

> about the end
> Of civil government, and its wisest forms ;

> Of ancient loyalty, and chartered rights,
> Custom and habit, novelty and change ;
> Of self-respect, and virtue in the few
> For patrimonial honour set apart ;
> And ignorance in the labouring multitude.

The noble passage I read last Sunday, in which he describes the romantic ardour with which all men were rapt away into schemes that did not then seem Utopian for the regeneration of mankind, is a picture of his own impassioned hopes at a time when the " senselessness of joy was sublime." He looked forward and saw Liberty building her palace upon strong foundations, and sending from her council-chamber laws which should make

> Social life,
> Through knowledge spreading and imperishable,
> As just in regulation, and as pure
> As individual in the wise and good.

How far these political theories and hopes entered into and formed part of Wordsworth's mind is now our subject. They made him ever afterwards interested in men, not only as persons, but as citizens of a State. They made him take the greatest interest, far greater than any other English poet of the time, in all political and national movements in England and Europe. Living apart from the world, retired as a noontide grove in the solitudes of Grasmere, he yet threw himself, and that with the passion of a poet, into the fate of France, of Switzerland, of Spain, of St. Domingo, of the war on the Continent. He wrote a long pamphlet on the Convention of Cintra, and cast the main thoughts of the pamphlet into poetic form in his sonnets. The internal government of England

and the duties of the State to English citizens were continually before his mind. Every one remembers the dreary discussion in the "Excursion" upon Education; few have read his long essay on the Poor Law, in which he treats of the state of the paupers, of the workmen congregated in manufactories, of joint stock companies, of the relation of capital and labour, and of the Church and Dissent. They were strange subjects for a poet, and he threw many of them into poetical form; and at least they prove that the seed sown in his mind on the banks of the Loire when wandering with his friend Beaupuis had grown into a tree. But the whole of its growth was modified by Wordsworth's individuality. After a gloomy passage in his life, when disappointed in France, he gave himself wholly up for a time to mere social theories—an experience of his that I shall speak of in another lecture—the theoretical element was cast aside, and the practical English sense of the man brought his early dreams to the test of fact. Nothing can better illustrate the difference between the two nations than the experience of Wordsworth. For a short time he was wholly French, indulging in those theories which, applied without political knowledge, make violent revolutions; returning to this country he became, though still republican, practical. Wishing for the overthrow of the Monarchy and the aristocracy, believing that "hereditary distinctions and privileged orders of every species counteracted the progress of human improvement;" he yet spoke strongly against the hasty destruction of them, and "recoiled from the very idea of a revolution." In 1814 his theory of Equality, as we see from the last book of the "Excursion," was based, not on the vague phrase of the rights of Man, but on the facts that God has given the same gifts to all alike—love of natural beauty, reason, imagination, freedom in the will, conscience, death, immortality, the primal duties, the common charities of life. He who works from this ground will come to a very different conclusion from that which landed the French Revolution in a new and enthralling despotism. For it is the ground of common duties making common rights among men, and the common duties are founded on the common Fatherhood of God and the Brotherhood and Equality of men in Him. This is exactly the principle which, in my last lecture, I said needed to be added to those of the revolution to secure their permanence; and it is a theological idea which Wordsworth added to the poetry of Man.

As to the right to political liberty which was then contended for in France, and based on the theory of the rights of Man without any distinct reference to God, indeed, afterwards with a distinct repudiation of God; it was supported by Wordsworth, as we have seen, with all his heart, but it was supported as the will and work of God. In the "Descriptive Sketches," written in October as he was wandering on the banks of the Loire, all Nature is made more beautiful to him by his dreams of the advent of perfect liberty; a milder light fell from the skies, the river rolled with more majestic course, the foliage shone with richer gold. But as he wrote he heard the gathering of the enemies of freedom, he foresaw that the land would soon be wrapt in fire, and that all the promise in his heart could not be fulfilled. Yet,

undespondent, he appealed to God as the source and
protector of the work that France was doing against
the oppressing kings of Europe.

> Great God ! by whom the strifes of men are weighed
> In an impartial balance, give thine aid
> To the just cause ; and, oh ! do thou preside
> Over the mighty stream now spreading wide :
> So shall its waters, from the heavens supplied
> In copious showers, from earth by wholesome springs,
> Brood o'er the long-parched lands with Nile-like wings !
> And grant that every sceptred child of clay
> Who cries presumptuous, " Here the flood shall stay,"
> May in its progress see thy guiding hand,
> And cease the acknowledged purpose to withstand ;
> Or, swept in anger from the insulted shore,
> Sink with his servile bands, to rise no more !

As to the various theories of government of which
he heard, we do not find that they had much influence
on him. He did not care for indulging in Utopias
upon paper ; and the only place where we meet cut
and dry systems of government is when he began in
and after 1832, to put forward a kind of strong Conservative programme in opposition to Reform, in such
pieces as the " Evening Voluntaries," and the " Sonnets
dedicated to Order," and the " Warning to England."
In the early times, however, from 1801 to 1813, he put
forward no political theories at all, either of government
or of liberty. He turned from them to ask more practical
questions, as he thought; to discover by what inward
forces a nation was free, by what moral powers a state
grew into the best organization. The complete break-
down of theory in France when the whole nation without
a word gave itself into the power of one man, " of men

the meanest too," forced him into this inquiry; and no
wiser or nobler answer exists on the subjects than in
that magnificent series of sonnets dedicated to national
independence and liberty. They begin with 1802, when
he was again in France and found the nation bending
before Napoleon as First Consul. He looked on the
people and found them wanting in all that could establish
true political greatness or true liberty, and the lines
in which he characterizes France have only too much
meaning now. Speaking of A. Sidney, Marvel, Har-
rington, and Vane, as those " who knew how genuine
glory was put on," he adds—

> France, 'tis strange
> Hath brought forth no such souls as we had then.
> Perpetual emptiness ! unceasing change !
> No single volume paramount, no code,
> No master spirit, no determined road ;
> But equally a want of books and men.

Their master spirit was himself a slave (and nothing is
finer in Wordsworth than his consistent scorn of Napoleon), and the nation that obeyed him must be without
the true elements of political liberty. They could not
exist where power was worshipped as mere power. Unless
it was applied for ends useful and kindly to men, it was
not great, but an idol whose service debased and enslaved
a people. It was even worse when it was founded on
warlike glory or force.

> 'Tis not in battles that from youth we train
> The governors who must be wise and good,
> And temper with the sternness of the brain
> Thoughts motherly and meek as womanhood.

> Wisdom doth live with children round her knees :
> Books, leisure, perfect freedom, and the talk
> Man holds with week-day man in the hourly walk
> Of the mind's business ; these are the degrees
> By which true sway doth mount ; this is the stalk
> True Power doth grow on ; and her rights are these.

For under a Power founded on mere glory in war, a nation lost its own liberty and combined to take liberty from others. This was the sight he saw in France, and he turned within himself and to history to find the contrast. The liberty and greatness of a nation, he answered, were in its harmony with the laws of God, such moral laws as the Prophets of Israel laid down ; the ground of its existence and success was a moral ground, the test of its liberty was in the virtue and unselfishness of its citizens. By the soul only, by patience and temperance, by

> Honour that knows the path, and will not swerve ;
> Affections which, if put to proof, are kind,
> And piety towards God ;

by lives given to labour, prayer, to nature and to heaven, by virtuous homes, and political wisdom founded on moral law, are nations great and free. It was not riches, which were akin, " to fear to change to cowardice and sloth," for did not ennobling thoughts depart " when men changed swords for ledgers and the student's bower for gold ?"— but " plain living and high thinking " that were the vital power in a people against oppression. It was not in warlike force, but in the patience, temperance, hope and fortitude of men who loved liberty for the sake of men and not of themselves, that a people found power to win their freedom against oppression. Not from

> fleets and armies and external wealth,
> But from within proceeds a nation's strength—

Nor is it intellectual power, or scientific research which in evil days does most for the cause of Man—but simple moral force and the strength of natural human feeling towards things loved by all.

> A few strong instincts and a few plain rules,
> Among the herdsmen of the Alps, have wrought
> More for mankind, at this unhappy day
> Than all the pride of intellect and thought.

He sought.for these in England, and in 1802 he could not find them.   One knows the sonnet in which, deploring the evils of his country, he asserts the necessity of the opposite qualities for the greatness of a people.

WRITTEN IN LONDON, SEPTEMBER, 1802.

> O Friend ! I know not which way I must look
> For comfort, being, as I am, opprest,
> To think that now our life is only drest
> For show ; mean handy-work of craftsmen, cook,
> Or groom !—We must run glittering like a brook
> In the open sunshine, or we are unblest :
> The wealthiest man among us is the best :
> No grandeur now in nature or in book
> Delights us.   Rapine, avarice, expense,
> This is idolatry : and these we adore :
> Plain living and high thinking are no more :
> The homely beauty of the good old cause
> Is gone ; our peace, our fearful innocence,
> And pure religion breathing household laws.

Equally fine is the sonnet written in the same year to Milton, and those which follow calling on his countrymen to remember the great men of the past who taught us how rightfully a nation shone in splendour ; to be worthy to speak the tongue

> That Shakespeare spake, the faith and morals hold
> Which Milton held.

But the despairing view soon passed away, and when the country went to war with the despot, he became ashamed of his "unfilial fears" and found in her the "bulwark for the cause of men;" one, at least, who held that it was

> an accursèd thing to gaze
> On prosperous tyrants with a dazzled eye.

Shall the Godhead, he asks, who dwells in Nature and the affections and the soul of man, pour his bounty on city and on field, and yet have no thought of the awful contest for the liberties of man ; is it to be our doom, to have no hope, to have faith in no promise of God ?

> Nay, forbid it Heaven !
> We know the arduous strife, the eternal laws
> To which the triumph of all good is given,
> High sacrifice, and labour without pause,
> Even to the death—else wherefore should the eye
> Of man converse with immortality ?

He followed the whole continental struggle of the nations against Napoleon, step by step ; and as year by year the ambition of Napoleon declared itself as the will of France, as the nation which had preached liberty laid itself at the feet of one man, and went forth to enslave; as year by year the nation which had declared the equal rights of man, fought to take away those rights; as year by year, the nation which had said that there was but one nation, the nation of mankind, laboured to prove by violence that there was only one nation—the nation of France—that mankind was created for France and not France for mankind; as year by year every principle of the Revolution was reversed—Wordsworth felt more and more strongly the uselessness of mere political theories to give birth to permanent liberty, and he put them out of his mind.

But it was a somewhat perilous thing for a poet of Man to lose his interest in theories of Man. For it is on theory and the ideas it presupposes that the poet who would speak of mankind exists. They are his nectar and ambrosia, and when he can delight in them and assimilate them no longer, he sinks out of the ideal life and world, where art abides, into the common and the commonplace. But if he have once lived therein, he brings with him and retains for a time the celestial light, and he may manage, as Wordsworth did, to find poetry in life's familiar face for many years. Yet, as time goes on— never soaring into the impossible or towards it, never lost in an Idea—he wins no Promethean fire, breathes none of that diviner air which would enable him to glorify the common, to see the infinite hope in the mean reality. Then the light he has had lingers, but it slowly dies away, and the prose of life overcomes his human poetry in the end. It was very well for Wordsworth to give up theories about the future of man, but he did so too completely, and the end thereof was Prose.

LECTURE XI.

IN speaking last Sunday afternoon of the three great lines of thought on which Wordsworth's interest ran, when in France he was brought into contact with the Revolution, I omitted the last, for which there was no time. It was the moral aspect of the Revolution as the avenger of oppression, and the general hatred of the oppression of nations by tyrannous rule. It was a hatred which he learnt from what he saw in France, and it lasted almost his whole life, though it changed its form. And it was accompanied—though he had put aside theories of liberty and the rights of Man—by a steady ardour for liberty, which diminished but never altogether died. These are the points on which I shall enlarge in this lecture.

The Revolution which began in a dream of the Golden Age ended in the Reign of Terror. Arising as the saviour, it became the inveterate destroyer. And this was the reason of the change—that the theories which the literary class had conceived the ignorant and brutalized lower classes carried out, and the natural result was the fury and blood of the Terror. The lower classes were ignorant and slaves; at every point of daily life they were met by the greed of the nobles, and by the irresponsible action of the law; tax after tax wrung from them the fruits of all their labour; and the taxes, being exacted not so much by government as by the class of the *noblesse*, fixed their hatred on a class with whom they had now neither political nor social ties. The government itself educated them for the revolutionary work they did in the Reign of Terror. It seized on property at its own arbitrary will. All the land was by right the king's, and whenever the State wished to make a road, it drove it right through one small property after another, generally without paying a penny. Every poor proprietor, so damaged, learnt the doctrine that private property must give way, without any claim, to public interests. It was a root idea of the Revolution. Again, in the case of crimes against the State, there were exceptional tribunals; the villages were visited by night, men were carried off without a warrant and never seen again, their condemnation was done in half an hour under a mere form of trial. No man's liberty was safe from the caprice of those who had power or interest with those in power.

In this way, a taste for this sort of work was actually taught to the people—they were educated for the revolutionary tribunals. The forms of these things were given by the old *régime;* the Revolution added to them, says De Tocqueville, the atrocities of its genius.

With all this and its results Wordsworth was brought into contact. He touches on all the points I have mentioned in the "Prelude;" he and his friend discussed them with fiery indignation, till at last, "hatred of absolute rule where the will of one is the law of all," and where the nobles were on the side of absolute

dominion as against the people, seized on them,
mingled with pity and with love for the miserable multitude. They met a hunger-bitten girl, driving her heifer
through the lane in despairing solitude—"'Tis against
that that we are fighting," said Beaupuis in agitation;
they heard a dreadful and pathetic story of two lovers,
Vaudracour and Julia, where, by the monstrous law that
enabled a father's tyranny to imprison a son, the man was
driven to fatal crime, and both man and woman to hopeless misery. Seeing these things the two friends were
thrown into passionate opposition, and into as passionate
hopes that at least the time was come when—

> Captivity by mandate without law
> Should cease; and open accusation lead
> To sentence in the hearing of the world,
> And open punishment, if not the air
> Be free to breathe in, and the heart of man
> Dread nothing.

More even than this negative hope they dreamed—

> I with him believed
> That a benignant spirit was abroad
> Which might not be withstood, that poverty
> Abject as this would in a little time
> Be found no more, that we should see the earth
> Unthwarted in her wish to recompense
> The meek, the lowly, patient child of toil;
> All institutes for ever blotted out .
> That legalised exclusion, empty pomp
> Abolished, sensual state and cruel power,
> Whether by edict of the one or few;
> And finally, as sum and crown of all,
> Should see the people having a strong hand
> In framing their own laws; whence better days
> To all mankind.

When Beaupuis left him and afterwards " perished in

supreme command" in the war against La Vendée, Wordsworth went to Paris at the end of 1792. The September massacres were just over, the King in prison, and the quarrel between the Girondists and the Mountain in full swing. It was a time well calculated to excite to a higher level the mind of Wordsworth, and the passage in which he describes the intensity with which he felt the passion of the whole city is one of the finest in the "Prelude."

> But that night
> I felt most deeply in what world I was,
> What ground I trod on, and what air I breathed.
> High was my room and lonely, near the roof
> Of a large mansion or hotel, a lodge
> That would have pleased me in more quiet times ;
> Nor was it wholly without pleasure then.
> With unextinguished taper I kept watch,
> Reading at intervals ; the fear gone by
> Pressed on me almost like a fear to come.
> I thought of those September massacres,
> Divided from me by one little month,
> Saw them and touched : the rest was conjured up
> From tragic fictions or true history,
> Remembrances and dim admonishments.
> The horse is taught his manage, and no star
> Of wildest course but treads back his own steps ;
> For the spent hurricane the air provides
> As fierce a successor ; the tide retreats
> But to return out of its hiding-place
> In the great deep ; all things have second birth ;
> The earthquake is not satisfied at once ;
> And in this way 1 wrought upon myself,
> Until I seemed to hear a voice that cried,
> To the whole city, "Sleep no more." The trance
> Fled with the voice to which it had given birth ;
> But vainly comments of a calmer mind
> Promised soft peace and sweet forgetfulness.
> The place, all hushed and silent as it was,
> Appeared unfit for the repose of night,
> Defenceless as a wood where tigers roam.

His very inmost soul was agitated, but not for a moment against the principles of the Revolution. He took the side against Robespierre, but felt that Robespierre was the strongest; and a hundred hopes and desires went rushing through his mind, as he thought how the earlier form of the movement might be preserved. Would not all nations come and help France to carry out her first great resolutions? Will not some one man, trusting in ideas and strong in such trust, self-restrained, nobly trained for rule, arise and dominate the struggle, even though he met with death? Would not death be nothing to such a man, for he would gladly obey the Sovereign Law that calls for sacrifice? For one thing was only to be sought for—the overthrow of Tyrants. One thing was sure— for he had no doubt of the end—freedom must win the day as against oppression. He threw himself into the party of the Brissotins, and it was only " by the gracious providence of Heaven," or as it seemed then to him, " dragged by a chain of harsh necessity," that, compelled to leave France, he escaped the fate of his friends. From thence he watched the growth of the Reign of Terror in France, but though he hated its excesses, he was not shocked by it into any retreat from his opinions. He saw in it all, though he confessed its enormity, the neces- sary work of vengeance—the vengeance of God Himself upon the guilty. However done, these long cruelties had to be expiated, and the abuses which caused them crushed, and if there were men who still supported them, so much the worse for the men. They must die—who innocently or guiltily subserve oppression ; nor should war be avoided with those who from without hindered the march of freedom, even though his own country took part in such a war. Therefore it was that when he returned to England, and war, after the execution of the king in 1793, was declared by England against France, he received a blow which shocked his whole moral nature. Was it possible that his country was on the side of oppression against the destroyers of oppression; and so deep was the feeling, that he, than whom none was a truer patriot, but who yet was more a prophet of Humanity than a patriot, wished and prayed that the arms of England might fall lifeless in the battle, and her hosts be scattered by the young Republic? He exulted in the victories of the Republic, he followed them with as great delight, as was the sorrow with which he groaned over the insults heaped on liberty by the crew of Robespierre. But even the Reign of Terror at its worst did not make him lose hope; when the tyrant fell, he prophesied a new deliverance for France.

But when the career of Napoleon began, though his ardour for liberty did not alter, it changed its form. Oppressed France became the oppressor, and the work of Napoleon stirred into a warmer flame the hatred of oppression which the Révolution had awakened in Wordsworth. In wrath and pity he threw himself into the cause of distressed nationalities; he remembered the starving people—the cruelty which came of irresponsible will and greed, and he saw in Napoleon the concentration into one man of all the elements of the evil which had darkened the old *régime*. All men, all people who fought against him were on the side of God, even though they had been on the side of the devil for years before.

An indignant sonnet recorded his horror at the attack upon the Swiss, another mourned for the fate of Venice, once the eldest child of liberty; another poured its pity upon Toussaint, imprisoned by Napoleon, and in a noble outburst bid him live and take comfort, for the worlds of Nature and of Man fought upon his side.

> Thou hast left behind
> Powers that will work for thee: air, earth and skies,
> There's not a breathing of the common wind
> That will forget thee; thou hast great allies;
> Thy friends are exultations, agonies,
> And love, and man's unconquerable mind.

A whole series followed with eager hope and encouragement the struggle of Hofer and the Tyrolese; another series records his passionate interest in the efforts of Spain against the oppression of France. One of these I quote, partly because it was a favourite of Wordsworth's, but chiefly because it hits sharply the vile falsehood by which Napoleon most defamed the Revolution when he declared that he came as the Apostle of freedom to the nations over whom, the moment they were lured into his hands, he set up an exhausting tyranny. It is entitled "The Indignation of a High-minded Spaniard."

> 1810.

> We can endure that He should waste our lands,
> Despoil our temples, and by sword and flame
> Return us to the dust from which we came;
> Such food a Tyrant's appetite demands:
> And we can brook the thought that by his hands
> Spain may be overpowered, and he possess,
> For his delight, a solemn wilderness
> Where all the brave lie dead. But, when of bands

Which he will break for us he dares to speak,
Of benefits, and of a future day
When our enlightened minds shall bless his sway;
Then, the strained heart of fortitude proves weak;
Our groans, our blushes, our pale cheeks declare
That he has power to inflict what we lack strength to bear.

At last, the year after the "Excursion" was published, the long contest closed at Waterloo, and the Oppressor was overthrown. Two "Thanksgiving Odes" show how greatly he was moved, and both bear that deep religious stamp which marked his work; both prove how closely he knit together the fate of nations with the government of God; both are full of genuine enthusiasm for his country and of joy at her success, but it is an enthusiasm and a joy which are gathered together in humble gratitude to God, in faith that it is He who has done the work of liberty against tyranny by the hands of England.

Our greatest Poet since Milton was as religious as Milton, and in both I cannot but think the element of grandeur of style which belongs so pre-eminently to them flowed largely from the solemn simplicity and the strength which a dignified and unbigoted faith in great realities beyond this world gave to the order of their thoughts. Coleridge was flying from one speculation to another all his life. Scott had no vital joy in his belief, and it did not interpenetrate his poetry. Byron believed in Fate more than in God. Shelley floated in an ideal world, which had not the advantage of being generalized from any realities—and not one of them possesses, though Byron comes near it now and then, the grand style. Wordsworth alone, combining fine artistic power with profound religion, walks when he chooses, though he limps wretchedly at times, with nearly as stately a step as Milton. He had the two qualities which always go with the grand style in poetry—he lived intensely in the present, and he had the roots of his being fixed in a great centre of power—faith in the eternal righteousness and love of God.

And he had this, I believe, more than any other Poet of the time—more practically far than Shelley—because the cause of man was so dear to him, and because he saw that the cause of man was the cause of God. That truth, the profoundest truth of Christianity, he had grasped with his greatest strength. His poetic work did not enthral him—did not in itself alone possess its own desire; he bent it to larger ends than those of giving transient pleasure. He not only reflected faithfully the feelings of human nature, he went further. A great poet, he says, ought to do more than this; he ought "to rectify men's feelings, to give them new compositions of feeling, to render their feelings more sane, pure and permanent; in short, more consonant to Nature, that is, to eternal Nature and the great moving spirit of things." And he has proved by his work, that the great poet ought to do more than even this; he ought to expand men's sympathies over the great interests and movements of nations, to beautify the great truths on which the moral and political progress of nations rest, to add emotion to the ideas of liberty and brotherhood, to bid men look forward and labour for not only their own country's highest good, but for the restoration of all things, to keep the hope and faith of a millennium ever before our eyes, to be the Prophet of mankind.

And this was something of Wordsworth's work, only it was not done by vague prophecies like Shelley's; it was done by taking up the events of the day and applying to them principles which led him to give as much interest and emotion to the struggles of distressed Europe with an overwhelming Imperialism as he gave to the struggles of the dalesmen of Grasmere with the overmastering forces of Nature.

The pity of it is, that this power did not last till the very close. After Napoleon's overthrow he grew somewhat sick of the present, and for the first time turned to the past for his subjects. It was then that such poems as "Laodamia" and "Dion" were written. As time wore on, he became less widely human and more Wordsworthian: the intense one-sidedness with which he always treated his subjects grew more conscious of itself, and at last pleased with itself; the want of living in the world, among men and movements, the want of being himself moved by any great impulse such as had transported him in youth, fixed him down into illiberal opinions at last. He still maintained his hatred of oppression, his love of liberty, but in practice both the hatred and the love broke down. The moral, temperate element in him, the abhorrence of violence and disorder, the love of the old—which in the first part of his life had formed a useful check upon his revolutionary enthusiasm, so that he always kept his head, grew,—now that the Revolution and the Empire itself had horrified him — into devouring prominence, and he lost in his old age that balance of opinions which mark sanity of mind. It is not strange to find him opposing the bill for admit-

ting Nonconformists to the Universities without any
subscription or declaration of conformity to the Church,
but it is strange that he should think that this would
endanger the monarchy and social order. It is strange to
find him maintaining that civil disabilities ought to be
removed from every class, and yet that they ought not
to be removed from the Roman Catholics, because to
give liberty to them promoted the cause of spiritual
tyranny. It is curious liberality which in order to pro-
mote liberty violates liberty. It is stranger still, when
we look back to the enthusiast of the Revolution, to find
him saying in 1832 that the Constitution of England
would be destroyed by the Reform Bill, and writing
letters on the subject which are even duller than such
Poems as the " Warning," and the " Sonnets to Order,"
and that is saying a great deal. What a change from
the earlier dignity of his poetry, how curiously infe-
licitous the phrases, how meagre the style—a kind
of poor extemporary prayer in verse—are the following
lines :—

> O for a bridle bitted with remorse
> To stop your Leaders in their headlong course !
> Oh may the Almighty scatter with his grace
> These mists, and lead you to a safer place,
> By paths no human wisdom can foretrace—
> May He pour round you, from worlds far above
> Man's feverish passions, His pure light of love !

Nevertheless it is but right to say that Wordsworth's
dislike to the liberal movements in 1832 and afterwards,
was in his own mind, founded on love of constitutional
liberty. It is the statement of the Conservative, but still
it would be unfair to call him a bigoted Conservative.

11

He wished, for example, that representation could be thrown more fairly into the hands of the property of the country, and less into the hands of the great proprietors. It was a change from the time when he thought it degrading to human nature to set up property in preference to person as a title to legislative power, but it was not a bigoted change. He could speak plainly even in 1844 as to the duties of the great landowners and manufacturers to the poor. "One would wish," he writes, "to see the rich mingle with the poor as much as may be on a footing of fraternal equality. The old feudal dependencies and relations are almost gone from England, and nothing has yet come adequately to supply their place. Why should not great landowners look for a substitute for what is lost of feudal paternity in the higher principles of Christianised humanity and humble-minded brotherhood?" It was on these principles that the old man himself lived among the poor that surrounded him, when young and old met at Rydal to keep his birthday.

Nor was it change he disliked, but reckless sweeping change; and the changes wrought by the Reform Bill seemed such to him. We must remember that he was then sixty-two years old, and had lived too much apart from men. Much may be pardoned to old age that one does not pardon to youth, and Wordsworth himself says that he had lost "*courage* in the sense the word bears when applied by Chaucer to the animation of birds in spring time." He had seen a Revolution in a foreign country, and he had not courage now to face another in his own. He expected that something of the same violence which had made him recoil from France, would

prevail in England after the Reform Bill, and he advo-
cated, if change was necessary, a slower, wiser change.
The following sonnet, not so poor poetically as others of
the same period, is interesting as embodying his views
and referring to the French Revolution.

> Long-favoured England! be not thou misled
> By monstrous theories of alien growth,
> Lest alien frenzy seize thee, waxing wroth,
> Self-smitten till thy garments reek dyed red
> With thy own blood, which tears in torrents shed
> Fail to wash out, tears flowing ere thy troth
> Be plighted, not to ease but sullen sloth,
> Or wan despair—the ghost of false hope fled
> Into a shameful grave. Among thy youth,
> My Country! if such warning be held dear,
> Then shall a Veteran's heart be thrilled with joy,
> One who would gather from eternal truth,
> For time and season, rules that work to cheer—
> Not scourge, to save the People—not destroy.

When things, however, were not so close to him, when
he came into contact with the struggle of liberty in a
foreign country, his sympathy with the oppressed seems
to have been nearly as strong as ever. One would scarcely
conceive Wordsworth, when almost seventy, as a supporter of the Carbonari, but such was the case, and those
who love Italy and Wordsworth cannot but be pleased to
bring them together. In 1842 he mourned over the
decay of Italy, and saw in the Lago Morto its emblem.
" Be its depths quickened," he cries out with some return
of his ancient energy—

> What thou dost inherit
> Of the world's hopes, dare to fulfil : awake,
> Mother of Heroes, from thy death-like sleep !

And in another sonnet, the last part of which I quote,

he breaks into a prophecy which God has fulfilled in our
own time—

Fallen Power !

Thy fortunes, twice exalted, might provoke
Me to glad notes prophetic of the hour
When thou, uprisen, shalt break thy double yoke,
And enter, with prompt aid from the Most High,
On the third stage of thy great destiny.

But in the case of Italy also, taught, as he held, by the
fate of France, he was against all rash schemes and
popular passion. Writing about the insurrections in
Bologna in 1837, he declares that by no mere fit of
sudden passion is freedom won, and urges gradual progress, noiseless pains, and moderation. And the advice
he gives is noble enough and characteristic of him, nor is
it one which the Italians would despise. It was at the
root of all Mazzini's later teaching to his people. " O,
great Italian nation," Wordsworth writes,—

Let thy scope

Be one fixed mind for all : thy rights approve
To thy own conscience gradually renewed ;
Learn to make Time the father of wise Hope ;
Then trust thy cause to the arm of Fortitude,
The light of Knowledge, and the warmth of Love.

It has seemed to me worth while, though at some length,
to look into the question of Wordsworth's later Conservatism, and to show that he did not merit the violent
expressions used about his change. Apostate, renegade,
were terms equally unjust and unworthy to be applied to
one who had done so much for Man. Still he suffered
from the change. I have already said that with the decay
of his natural republicanism, and with the loss of the
ideas of republicanism as the leading thoughts of life,

decayed his poetical power when he spoke of man, even
to a certain degree when he spoke of Nature.   With
their overthrow decayed also that larger Christianity in
him, which is not personal, but human ; but at the same
time his personal Christianity grew deeper.   Nor must
we blame him much for this.   'Twould have been better
had he been as before, the Prophet of liberty and right,
the declarer that the cause of man is the cause of God ;
but it is but natural that, as age grows on, our thoughts
should centre more round the relation of God to our own
soul than our relation to the world of men, that the
"Evening Voluntaries" should succeed the "Sonnets
dedicated to Liberty and Independence."

LECTURE XII.

In my last lecture, I was carried far forward to the close of Wordsworth's life by my wish to bring under one theme his earlier and later feelings with regard to the Revolution. It is necessary now to return to his personal history, as it touches on the poetry of Man and of Nature. In doing so there will be some unavoidable repetition, but that which is repeated will be used in a different connection and for a different purpose. I have in this lecture to trace how the failure of his hopes for Man impaired his love of Nature and his love of Man; how they were restored, and, finally, how that marriage of his human mind and Nature, to which we have been looking forward for so long, was at last fulfilled.

I must, therefore, in order to arrive at the causes which impaired his love of Nature and Man, return to his personal history. We left him when he was driven by stress of circumstances from France to England in 1793. He had nearly been involved in the fate of his friends, the Brissotins, and he followed with intense eagerness the progress of affairs in France. He refused to seek the country, and remained in London. It is characteristic of him at this time, that he took but little interest in the movement for Negro Emancipation, for he felt that if France prospered, slavery must perish. The principles there fought for, if established, would strike at the root of all oppression, and with the destruction of the root, all the branches of the tree of human slavery would be destroyed, Negro slavery among the rest.

But as he watched in passionate desire, two things deprived his watch of all delight and threw him into almost despair. The first was the union of England with the confederate powers against France; the second was the Reign of Terror. He never heard the sunset cannon from the English fleet, as he watched it riding in the Solent, ere it went to war,

> Without a spirit overcast by dark
> Imaginations, sense of woes to come,
> Sorrow for humankind, and pain of heart.
>
> Prelude, Book x.

It was this first threw him out of his love of Man and soured his heart. It was misery to him to sit among the worshippers who gave praise for his country's victories, "like an uninvited guest whom no one owned, to sit silent, and to brood on the day of vengeance yet to come." It was still worse to be tossed between love of England, and delight that she was beaten by her enemies because she was false to liberty: a woeful time which those who afterwards attacked Wordsworth had never gone through.

Nor did he ever cast his eyes on France without misery: misery because God seemed to have forgotten Man, because liberty seemed to have forgotten herself and to wear the robes of tyranny, because the deeds then done would be brought in charge against her name. For years his dreams were haunted with the ghastly visions of that time ; he saw the dungeons, the executions, the unjust tribunals, and in sleep he seemed to plead in long orations before their judges,

> With a voice
> Labouring, a brain confounded, and a sense,
> Death-like, of treacherous desertion, felt
> In the last place of refuge—my own soul—

Moved in this way to the very centre of his being with the passion of humanity, troubled, even tortured with conflicting emotions, he compared this new love of Man with his early love of Nature, and both in their relation to God.

His love of Nature, whose veins were filled from the fountain of the grace of God,

> Was service paid to things which lie
> Guarded within the bosom of God's will.
> Therefore to serve was high beatitude ;
> Tumult was therefore gladness, and the fear
> Ennobling, venerable ; sleep secure,
> And waking thoughts more rich than happiest dreams.
> Prelude, book x.

But this new love of Man, how unspeakably unlike! With what a different ritual did one serve, through it, the Power Supreme who made man divine ! Faith and calmness seemed to leave his heart when he felt how full of doubt, dismay, and sleepless trouble, how sorrowful the tumult, how dreadful were the dreams, which belonged to this new service of mankind.

Yet, as he looked deeper—and that he could do this marks the temperate courage of Wordsworth as a thinker, and the mastery of his intellectual will over mere emotion, he saw no reason to despair of Man. As the Prophets, who in their highest inspiration worked with a human heart troubled for the woes of man, wanted not consolation in that they saw God in the punishment of evil, and the triumph of moral law; so Wordsworth saw beneath the misery of France, God in moral retribution, and God educating the nation. That was one theological aspect in which he viewed events.

He looked again, and saw another star of hope for Man in the self-sacrifice and virtues of those who suffered. He saw in a hundred instances that God had not forsaken human nature. Green spots appeared in the desert, bright islands of " fortitude, and energy, and love," of honour, faith, and sanctity,

> And human nature faithful to herself,

amid the dark and stormy seas of the time. For a time he was thus kept true to his belief of God in Man, in spite of repeated shocks : his worship and his love, though dark, were touched with breaks of sunlight.

Then came to support this hope the news that Robespierre was dead. He heard it as he crossed the estuary of the Leven, and hope revived within him, more than hope—enthusiasm.

> Great was my transport, deep my gratitude
> To everlasting Justice, by this fiat
> Made manifest. " Come now, ye golden times,"
> Said I, forthpouring on those open sands
> A hymn of triumph ; " as the morning comes
> From out the bosom of the night, come ye—
> Thus far our trust is verified."
>
> Prelude, book x.

The world would now, he thought, go forward to righteousness and peace and liberty.

But he was still doomed to disappointment. Preserving amid the weakness of the new government his trust in the people, he found it slowly ebb away; and when Frenchmen changed " the war of self-defence for one of conquest, and lost sight of all they struggled for;" when, finally, to close her gains, a Pope

> Was summoned in to crown an Emperor;

when he saw a people, that once looked to Heaven for manna,

> take a lesson from the dog
> Returning to his vomit,

then the crash was too great; he lost faith for a time in God, in moral right; the old miseries returned to add their weight to the new; the hopes that had risen again against the shocks he had received, died now finally; and he lost his true love of Nature, his true love of Man, or rather he lost the true foundations on which they were based. It will be my business to trace how these two affections were impaired, and how they were restored, and how, after passing through this trial, they mingled into one.

In the account given of this mental crisis in the " Prelude," in books xi., xii., and xiii., the two subjects of the Love of Man and Nature are mingled up together as poetic emotion led him to speak of each. For the purposes of the lecture we must isolate them from each other, but it must be always remembered that they went on together, *pari passu*, in his mind. With regard to the love of Nature, it lost its natural, intuitive quality; it became a business of the intellect as stimulated by sensible images, more than of the heart as impressed by the same. The first step towards this impairing of his love of Nature—and it shows how the two things were mingled up in his mind—was made when he lost hope for and love of Man in the present and began to look beyond it, in a merely critical spirit, for a coming race. He became absorbed in the picture of an ideal mankind in the future, wholly different, he hoped, from the wretched creature he knew in the present. He looked back also to the sages, patriots, and heroes of the past, and it seemed to him, so dark his mind, that their "best virtues were not free from taint." He went to the Poets to find purer creatures, but if "Reason be nobility in Man," can anything, he asked, be more ignoble than the creature they delight to picture,

> the miserable slave
> Of low ambition and distempered love.

This was the wretched carping condition into which he fell; he judged mankind by the intellect alone, and shut out the heart as co-assessor with the intellect. It was by the understanding alone that he tried to solve those mysteries of being that make of the human race one brotherhood, and in so doing he cut himself off from his poetic nature, and

> From all the sources of his former strength.

He even, by the exercise of his critical faculty on Man, lost the power of conceiving Man as a whole, for it is only in belief in things not subject to the critical faculty work-e, such things as the universal sense of right rong, of truth, of common and natural emotions, of rod, that we have any absolute grounds for holding the doctrine of an universal humanity.

The slave then of this critical faculty, he could not help applying it to Nature. Long ago he had believed in a soul in Nature, aud looked beneath her outward forms in order to feel this soul and its "impassioned life," with heart and intellect at one in the work, and the Soul of Nature answered to his love and told to him her secrets. * But now, he had abandoned the thought of a soul within the world, and love could no longer rule his life with her. He criticised its surface beauty like an art critic, "even in pleasure pleased unworthily." He liked here and disliked there as artistic rules led him, applying rules of art "to things above all art." He

---

* I place the passage here in order that it may be read in connexion with the lecture in which I have maintained that Wordsworth gave a Life to Nature different from ours.

> O Soul of Nature ! excellent and fair !
> That didst rejoice with me, with whom I, too,
> Rejoiced through early youth, before the winds
> And roaring waters, and in lights and shades
> That marched and countermarched about the hills
> In glorious apparition, Powers on whom
> I daily waited, now all eye and now
> All ear ; but never long without the heart
> Employed, and man's unfolding intellect :
> O Soul of Nature ! that, by laws divine
> Sustained and governed, still dost overflow
> With an impassioned life, what feeble ones
> Walk on this earth ! how feeble I have been
> When thou wert in thy strength.
>
> Prelude, book xii.

compared landscape with landscape, to the disadvantage
of one—

> Bent overmuch on superficial things,
> Pampering myself with meagre novelties
> Of colour and proportion—to the moods
> Of time and season, to the moral power,
> The affections, and the spirit of the place
> Insensible.

Prelude, book xii.

In this way that spiritual Imagination was impaired
which penetrates to the living heart of Nature, and feels
it beating against the human heart.

Another phase of the same thing also beset him. The
eye took despotism over the rest of his senses and powers,
and held his mind in slavery to its special pleasure. It
had vivid but not profound pleasure in roving from one
landscape to another, and in craving new combinations
of beauty. Still worse, it took pride in this power, and
began to think it nobler than the power of feeling, so
that, at last, it grew so important to him that it laid the
inner faculties asleep.

It is an experience which we see repeated at the present day, and its lesson should not be lost on us. A
more complex worldly life creates often, and is creating
now among us, a worldliness of the eye. It lusts after
mere outward beauty, harmonies of colour, picturesque-
ness, exquisiteness of form. And in its insatiable pursuit of these, which only touch the senses, the influence
of Nature on the heart is lost. It cannot rest quiet and
content with any beauty; nor assimilate the teaching
Nature gives to the heart and conscience: for it has
no true love of Nature, and without that it only looks

long enough to satisfy the eye. It is only love which enables us to dwell on a thing without weariness. And this delight in mere outside beauty soon finds satiety, and flies to something else, and, flying thus incessantly, it never remains long enough by anything to be able to comprehend it. For a time this was Wordsworth's failing, and the cause of it lay not only in that of which I have spoken, but also that the troubles of human life in which he was now involved overrode the silent influences of Nature, and made his life with Nature share in the excited life he was leading with Man. He contrasts this " thraldom of the sense "—this feverish worldliness of the eye—with the life which his sister lived with Nature. In her—

> The eye was not the mistress of the heart ;
> Far less did rules prescribed by passive taste,
> Or barren intermeddling subtleties,
> Perplex her mind : but wise as women are
> When genial circumstance hath favoured them,
> She welcomed what was given, and craved no more ;
> Whate'er the scene presented to her view
> That was the best, to that she was attuned
> By her benign simplicity of life,
> And through a perfect happiness of soul,
> Whose variegated feelings were in this
> Sisters, that they were each some new delight.
> Birds in the bower, and lambs in the green field
> Could they have known her, would have loved ; methought
> Her very presence such a sweetness breathed,
> That flowers, and trees, and even the silent hills,
> And everything she looked on, should have had
> An intimation how she bore herself
> Towards them and to all creatures.   God delights
> In such a being ; for, her common thoughts
> Are piety, her life is gratitude——.
>
> Prelude, book xii.

So it was with him of old, when he "worshipped among the depth of things," without criticising overmuch; but now it was different. Yet the evil did not last long; the Poet was too strong in him and Nature herself too close. She fought, he held, against the tyranny of any one sense over the others—

> Summons all the senses each
> To counteract the other, and themselves,
> And makes them all, and the objects with which all
> Are conversant, subservient in their turn
> To the great ends of Liberty and Power.
>
> Book xii.

There is an exact analogy to this in Christianity. It employs all the virtues, and by insisting on a harmony of them all in the character, endeavours to thwart the tyranny of any one virtue, which dwelt on exclusively passes into a vice. But the harmony of all, each doing its own work in mutual service, makes action free, and gives to the Will power towards righteousness.

But what redeemed him chiefly were the recollections of early impressions which he had received from certain scenes in Nature. He had known, in youth, too forcibly,

> Visitings of imaginative power,

for this evil habit to endure their remembrance. Youth and its powers return to the true heart, however troubled it has been; the memory of passionate feeling waked by the influences of grandeur or beauty in Nature, inspires such joy, that we cannot but return to win from her again the same passionate feeling as of old. For there are certain spots of time, and I analyse here a long passage, the recollection of which possesses a renovating virtue; there are passages of life which give,

> Profoundest knowledge to what point, and how,
> The mind is lord and master—outward sense
> The obedient servant of her will. Such moments
> Are scattered everywhere, taking their date
> From our first childhood.
>
> Prelude, book xii.

In these moments Nature impresses herself as a living Force of passion on the soul. The impressions are deepest when we are alone and Nature is dreary. For when we are alone the soul is most receptive, and when she is dreary there arises in us, aroused by her touch, a wild, involuntary, apparently causeless sorrow. It is, in Wordsworth's thought, the spirit mourning in itself for that imperial Palace whence it came, the recollection of a time of disembodied joy and purity, before it came to earth. These are the intimations of our Immortality in childhood. Nature, working on us from without, sends a kindling touch that awakens the slumbering powers of the soul. We are lifted beyond our life of thoughtlessness, and feel, half unconsciously, the greatness of the soul. To these hours we look back, and there is in them, all sorrowful and vague as they are, virtue to recall us— when they are refashioned by association and added to by experience—to higher thoughts, to nourish and repair imagination when it has been dulled by the wear and stress of life ; to lead us, through their memories, to find beauty again in the commonplace, the ideal in the dull reality of life, and the presence of the soul and the passion of the heart in communion with the life of Nature.

Such regenerating memories were Wordsworth's, and they wrought in him that " working of the spirit," those "inward agitations," which carry us beyond ourselves into that region of the spiritual which we always touch but so seldom enter, into that region of the heart which lies so close to us but which too often we despise for the region of the understanding.

Influenced by them, the Poet escaped at last from the critical, analysing spirit with which he had for a time confronted the soul of Nature. I shook the habit off, he says—

> Entirely and for ever, and again
> In Nature's presence stood, as now I stand
> A sensitive being, a *creative* soul—

with power as of old to receive sensitively all impressions from Nature, with power to create, by the working of imagination on the impressions, new images of thought. So was it with his love of Nature.

The trial through which his love of Man went ran on much the same lines. As in the love of Nature so in the love of Man, he slipt out of the region of intuition in which the Poet most keenly lives, into the region of speculative opinion. It is not difficult to understand how he got into that region; for it is characteristic of human nature in youth, when enthusiastic opinions which have been loved have received a shock from the contradiction of events, to fight against that contradiction, even though the heart is failing under the blow it has received. This was the case with Wordsworth. Events seemed to prove that the principles he would have laid down his life for were null and void, and a vague despair began to move in his heart. Along with this was combined the sneer of men who had hated the Revolution from the beginning. They turned on Wordsworth with ridicule and mocked his opinions. And he replied indignantly : he fought for his views, clung to them as a man clings to religious opinions of which he has an inner doubt, saying to himself, " If I am wrong, then all is lost." But having this inner doubt, his heart and conscience were forced to cease to take part in his battle against the world, and his intellect alone was engaged. And then, in the heat of contest, opinions became all he cared for, till round his mind

> They clung, as if *they* were its life, nay more
> The very being of the immortal soul.

He threw himself into speculative schemes of socialism, formed an ideal of Man, exalted his reason as the sole lord of his acts, and strove to conceive a community in which, like Robert Owen's, social liberty should be built on personal, laws should be wholly directed by circumstances, man live by his intellect alone, and, shaking off all degrading pursuits, be absolutely free,

> Lord of Himself in undisturbed delight.

But before realizing this scheme, it was necessary to make an accurate study of society, and he did this by the help of the understanding alone. He brought all systems, creeds, and laws before the bar of the reasoning faculty and asked them to prove their rightness. He demanded that the soul should give formal proof of its powers. How did it know that it could distinguish between right and wrong, how did it know it was immortal? Had morality or religion any ground in fact?

What was the result? It was, that looking into these things without love, and leaving out of the investigation the imagination and the spirit as means of judging, he saw not life but death in the world; he lost all certainty. As one piece of evidence was strong he believed in the greatness of the soul, as one piece was weak he disbelieved in it. He found himself endlessly perplexed with questions about impulses, and motives, whether what seemed wrong was not sometimes right, and what seemed right, wrong. He could not decide whether there was any eternal rule of Duty, whether it had any ground in the nature of things, whether what seemed its sanctions, were sanctions, or whence the sanctions came; till at last, he became a sceptic, and yielded up all moral questions in despair. Man was either—

> The dupe of folly or the slave of crime.
>
> Book xii.

This was the lowest depth he reached, and from this he was saved, first, by the common sense so characteristic of him among the Poets. It led him to employ his puzzled reason on some subject whose elements were not disturbed by human passion. He took to the study of abstract science, and in realizing its calm realities, his mind grew calm. He was saved, secondly, by the influence of human love, which restored to him that reverence for the heart which he had lost. It was through his sister's influence that this sacred work was also wrought. She who lived from the heart, moved ever by his side; she believed for him when he disbelieved; she saw that his scepticism

was more the flight of clouds across his mind, than any
vital change in his mind itself; she went with her own
eager sympathy through all his trouble,—

> Then it was—
> Thanks to the bounteous Giver of all good—
> That the beloved Sister in whose sight
> Those days were passed, now speaking in a voice
> Of sudden admonition—like a brook
> That did but *cross* a lonely road, and now
> Is seen, heard, felt, and caught at every turn,
> Companion never lost through many a league—
> Maintained for me a saving intercourse
> With my true self——
>
> Prelude, book xi.

she "whispered still that brightness would return," and
herself, loving Nature intensely, as her delightful Diary
proves, not only restored to him his ancient love of
Nature, but also opened to his heart again the fountains of human love and bade him drink them and
be whole; brought him back to his real work,—

> preserved him still
> A Poet, made him seek beneath that name,
> And that alone, his office upon earth.

It was thus he began to find his love of Man again.

But another power now joined in his sister's work. He
had refound, as we have seen, his love of Nature, and Nature
led him now again, as she had done of old, to the love of
Man. In his youth he had seen in her Beauty and
Sublimity; he now, influenced by his study of Science
on the one side, and by desire to be freed from confused
opinions on the other, saw in her not only Beauty and
Sublimity but divine and quiet Order. She seemed to him
the image of right reason, the witness to calm obedience

to eternal Law; she held before his eyes no disturbing
passion, but a " temperate show of objects which endure."
It was a view which sank deep into his troubled human
heart; he took it with him to the world of man, and it
taught him to seek in it, beneath the wild disturbance of
the surface sea of life,—

> Whate'er there is desirable and good
> Of kindred permanence, unchanged in form
> And function, or, through strict vicissitude
> Of Life and Death, revolving.
>
> > Prelude, book xiii.

And having found these things in human life, he turned
again to Nature, and in feeling his brotherhood with
Man, felt his brotherhood with her complete. Those
" watchful thoughts " were re-established, which had
early tutored him—

> To look with feelings of fraternal love
> Upon the unassuming things that hold
> A silent station in this beauteous world.

Both had been fully regained—the love of Man, the love
of Nature.

Freed thus from unregulated emotion, he sought with
quiet judgment to find the great truths which underlie
human life, and the permanent feelings of human nature,
and to rest on these amid the storm of passions and
opinions, for there, among much evil, was the abiding
good in Man, the dwelling-place of God.

> Thus moderated, thus composed, I found
> Once more in Man an object of delight,
> Of pure imagination and of love——

but it was now a wiser love; it had given up theories of

Man, it only sought now a humbler object—to find out what Man was when unspoilt, through the power of a sympathising human heart. And seeking thus, he recovered his clear belief in right, his clear sight of wrong, his faith in the eternity of pure feelings and the divine nature in the human. Sanguine schemes, ambitious projects for the regeneration of mankind, pleased him less; the wild dream of promise which had flown before him in the Revolution, "retired into its due proportion." "I sought," he says,—

> For present good in life's familiar face
> And built thereon my hopes of good to come.

Where now was he to seek this present good, where find the divine wealth of pure feeling and honest life of which he was now convinced? Where, he answered, but among the natural abodes of simple men, the men among whom my life was passed; thither I turn from national interests to individual, and perhaps in finding there personal lives true to duty, the heart, and conscience, I may best learn what makes the true worth and dignity of Man, and why this glorious creature should not be counted by thousands, not by one only in ten thousand. I will "inspect the basis of the social pile, and ask how much of mental power and genuine virtue they possess who live by bodily toil,"—

> therefore did I turn
> To you, ye pathways and ye lonely roads;
> Sought you enriched with everything I prized,
> With human kindnesses and simple joys.

There he learnt the wisdom of the Poet, the wisdom to feel deeply and to know things and men through love;

healing and repose came to his wounded heart as he
wandered over the moors, or sat on the cottage bench, or
by the well-spring, and talked with all he met. This was his
school, it was here he read the passions of mankind, and
the depths of the human heart, and heard—

> From mouths of men obscure and lowly, truths
> Replete with honour.

He sketches such a life in the character of the Pedler, in
the first book of the "Excursion," and he drew it from himself. It was the life he would have chosen, and no words
can describe better than the following—a few lines being
excepted—the character of Wordsworth at this time:—

> He wandered far ; much did he see of men,
> Their manners, their enjoyments, and pursuits,
> Their passions and their feelings ; chiefly those
> Essential and eternal in the heart,
> That, 'mid the simpler forms of rural life,
> Exist more simple in their elements,
> And speak a plainer language. In the woods,
> A lone Enthusiast, and among the fields,
> Itinerant in this labour, he had passed
> The better portion of his time ; and there
> Spontaneously had his affections thriven
> Amid the bounties of the year, the peace
> And liberty of nature ; there he kept
> In solitude and solitary thought
> His mind in a just equipoise of love.
> Serene it was, unclouded by the cares
> Of ordinary life ; unvexed, unwarped
> By partial bondage. In his steady course,
> No piteous revolutions had he felt,
> No wild varieties of joy and grief.
> Unoccupied by sorrow of its own,
> His heart lay open ; and, by nature tuned
> And constant disposition of his thoughts
> To sympathy with man, he was alive
> To all that was enjoyed where'er he went,

> And all that was endured ; for, in himself
> Happy, and quiet in his cheerfulness,
> He had no painful pressure from without
> That made him turn aside from wretchedness
> With coward fears.   He could *afford* to suffer
> With those whom he saw suffer.   Hence it came
> That in our best experience he was rich
> And in the wisdom of our daily life.

It was thus for a time he lived, till at last, inspired by such communion with "men as they are men within themselves," he resolved, seeing what holy worship was offered unto God in the wayside chapels of humble and loving hearts among poor and simple men, to make his song of these. This then was his work, this the aim he had at last found for his poetic life ; to—

> Deal boldly with substantial things; in truth
> And sanctity of passion, speak of these,
> That justice may be done, obeisance paid
> Where it is due : thus haply shall I teach,
> Inspire, through unadulterated ears
> Pour rapture, tenderness, and hope,—my theme
> No other than the very heart of man,
> As found among the best of those that live,
> Not unexalted by religious faith,
> Nor uninformed by books, good books, though few,
> In Nature's presence : thence may I select
> Sorrow, that is not sorrow, but delight ;
> And miserable love, that is not pain
> To hear of, for the glory that redounds
> Therefrom to humankind, and what we are.
>
> Prelude, book xiii.

It was a work to which men " accomplished for communion with the world, most active when they most are eloquent," but needing admiration to develop them, might not care to listen. But there were others who would ; men who uphold themselves, and by their own solitary might and joy create—others too and those chiefly found among the walks of homely life—

> men for contemplation framed
> Shy and unpractised in the strife of phrase ;

who cannot speak, nor tell their secret heart, but whose

> is the language of the heavens, the power,
> The thought, the image and the silent joy :
> Words are but under-agents in their souls ;
> When they are grasping with their greatest strength
> They do not breathe among them—this I speak
> In gratitude to God, who feeds our hearts
> For His own service ; knoweth us, loveth us,
> When we are unregarded by the world.
>
> Book xiii.

This was his work, to make unworldly men listen to the beating of the heart of natural humanity.

And now having taken the world of humanity into himself, the world of Nature, which he had received and loved before, united itself to the world of humanity within him, and the marriage of the Mind to the Universe of which we spoke so much was complete in Wordsworth. He saw how Nature consecrated and made grand the human life which was lived among her beauty and sublimity. He felt also that the visible world and all its forms gave teaching and pleasure to the mind in proportion as human passion worked upon them, and that, in turn, the forms

> Of Nature have a passion in themselves,
> That intermingles with those works of man
> To which she summons him ; although the works
> Be mean, have nothing lofty of their own ;
> And that the Genius of the Poet hence

12

> May boldly take his way among mankind
> Wherever Nature leads ; that he hath stood
> By Nature's side among the men of old,
> And so shall stand for ever.

And he dares to hope—

> That unto him hath also been vouchsafed
> An insight that in some sort he possesses,
> A privilege whereby a work of his,
> Proceeding from a source of untaught things,
> Creative and enduring, may become
> A power like one of Nature's.

Book xiii.

Feeling, hoping thus, he looked into the world of Nature, and felt within it a living spirit, moving unseen, but making all its life.   He looked again, and below the surface of the world of Man he gained sight of a new and living world also, a world ruled by those fixed laws

> Whence spiritual dignity originates,
> Which do both give it being and maintain
> A balance, an ennobling interchange
> Of action from without and from within ;
> The excellence, pure function and best power
> Both of the object seen and eye that sees.

Hence when these two spiritual worlds were bound together in holy wedlock in the Poet's heart, he could speak from both of them alike, and reveal the mutual action on each other of Nature and the human mind, and his work, issuing from such origins, not only be a creation of the human mind, but also a Power like one of Nature's, speak to men, as the winds and ocean speak ; move them as the beauty of the evening moves them; and make them thrill, as does the thunder in the tempest, with a sense of grandeur ; soften, soothe, and bless, as the quiet of the stars or the ripple of the water. For the Poet is the living voice of Nature as he is the expressing voice of Man.

Profoundly, then, impressed with Man, he did not desert his first love, Nature. He threw on her the light and emotion he had won from knowledge of the sorrows, passions, battles and destiny of Man, till she trembled not only with her own emotion but with his. He saw in her— thus infinitely sympathetic to those who loved her, and brought the power of humanity to her—the teacher, the guide, and yet the servant of Man. And in this light, the intercourse he had with her was not as in boyhood a wild passion, nor a solitary one—it had now a softer, gentler, more enduring feeling, as if felt to a lover or a friend. She was no longer apart from Man, but thrilled through all her veins with sympathy for Man in good: no longer apart from God, but a life whose life was that of God; and as such the external master, guide and anchor of his being.

This new position of Wordsworth's mind is, perhaps, worth illustrating at some length from his poetry, and I will sketch some of its phases. It appeared in the very first Poems he published after his return from France, in the Descriptive Sketches in 1793. In them the natural landscape and those who lived in it were knit together, so that Nature was conceived of as inspiriting Man, and Man as making Nature more sublime and fair. In 1795 he illustrates in the lines written near the yew-tree on Esthwaithe Lake the opposite state of mind—in the case of a man so absorbed in himself as to lose the good of the influences of Nature and to be separated from mankind. In 1798, in the lines written when visiting Tintern Abbey, the union of Man and Nature in his mind is complete.

The beginning of it is a condensation of all that we have gone through with him in the Prelude as to the education and influences of Nature on his life. There he looks back on what he was five years before when Nature was all in all to him, and her forms were " a feeling and a love "

> That had no need of a remoter charm
> By thought supplied, nor any interest
> Unborrowed from the eye.

Now it is different, he loves not Nature less; but mankind and its vast interest is wedded to her; and beyond both and yet in both, in the universe without and the mind within himself, there is an all-pervading Divine spirit. Well-known as they are the lines must be quoted :—

> For I have learned
> To look on nature, not as in the hour
> Of thoughtless youth; but hearing oftentimes
> The still, sad music of humanity,
> Nor harsh nor grating, though of ample power
> To chasten and subdue. And I have felt
> A presence that disturbs me with the joy
> Of elevated thoughts; a sense sublime
> Of something far more deeply interfused,
> Whose dwelling is the light of setting suns,
> And the round ocean and the living air,
> And the blue sky, and in the mind of man :
> A motion and a spirit, that impels
> All thinking things, all objects of all thought,
> And rolls through all things. Therefore am I still
> A lover of the meadows and the woods,
> And mountains; and of all that we behold
> From this green earth; of all the mighty world
> Of eye, and ear,—both what they half create,
> And what perceive; well pleased to recognise
> In nature and the language of the sense,
> The anchor of my purest thoughts, the nurse,
> The guide, the guardian of my heart, and soul
> Of all my moral being.

The same position of mind, only marked with less of joy and more of sober sadness is expressed in the latter part of the Ode on the Intimations of Immortality.

Of the poetic result of this marriage in himself of Nature and his human Mind I have already given an instance in speaking of the Stanzas on the picture of Peele Castle, and explained how the imaginative creation of the Poem was not the result only of an impression received from Nature, or of his own thought, but of the blended might of both embracing to produce a child different from both, but having something of the nature of both. I give another instance now in the most imaginative of his Poems, *Yew Trees.* He walks in the shade of the yews of Borrowdale, those "fraternal Four, joined in one solemn and capacious grove," and there flows into his passive mind from Nature a vivid impression of gloom, of darkness and silence. Then his mind springs into activity, fastens on the impression, knits round it thoughts that are similar but different, thoughts of the sacred groves such as that where the Eumenides were worshipped, of groves where ancient powers were seen by wandering men, of death, of all those solemn moral powers that brood silently over Man. At last, out of both these working together, is born the imaginative Creation, and there rises before his eyes an ideal grove in which the ghostly masters of mankind meet, and sleep, and offer worship to the Destiny that abides above them; while the mountain flood, far, far away, as if from another world, makes music to which they dimly listen. Nothing can be more intense in imagination, nor is there anything more unique in English poetry :—

> But worthier still of note
> Are those fraternal Four of Borrowdale,
> Joined in one solemn and capacious grove ;
> Huge trunks ! and each particular trunk a growth
> Of intertwisted fibres serpentine
> Up-coiling, and inveterately convolved ;
> Nor uninformed with Phantasy, and looks
> That threaten the profane ;—a pillared shade,
> Upon whose grassless floor of red-brown hue,
> By sheddings from the pining umbrage tinged
> Perennially—beneath whose sable roof
> Of boughs, as if for festal purpose, decked
> With unrejoicing berries—ghostly Shapes
> May meet at noontide ; Fear and trembling Hope,
> Silence and Foresight ; Death the Skeleton
> And Time the Shadow ;—there to celebrate,
> As in a natural temple scattered o'er
> With altars undisturbed of mossy stone,
> United worship ; or in mute repose
> To lie, and listen to the mountain flood
> Murmuring from Glaramara's inmost caves.

In this case it was chiefly Thought alone which acted on
the images received, but for the most part in Wordsworth
the natural impressions are met by thoughts connected
with human love, and the creation which ensues in the
Poem is one which is obedient to the sympathies of Man,
and yet not forgetful of gratitude to Nature, so that both
are honoured and exalted. There is a little sonnet written
in later life, and one of his best, which illustrates the
whole method of work, and yet marks how unconsciously
—as it was bound to be—it was followed.

XLVIII.

> Most sweet it is with unuplifted eyes
> To pace the ground, if path be there or none,
> While a fair region round the traveller lies
> Which he forbears again to look upon ;

Pleased rather with some soft ideal scene,
The work of Fancy, or some happy tone
Of meditation, slipping in between
The beauty coming and the beauty gone.
If Thought and Love desert us, from that day
Let us break off all commerce with the Muse :
With Thought and Love companions of our way,
Whate'er the senses take or may refuse,
The mind's internal heaven shall shed her dews
Of inspiration on the humblest lay.

Finally, the last book of the Prelude has this same position of mind towards Nature as its under-thought. It begins by a magnificent description of the ascent of Snowdon by night, at first in mist, and then as a light fell upon the turf, he looked up, and lo! *

The Moon hung naked in a firmament
Of azure without cloud, and at my feet
Rested a silent sea of hoary mist.
A hundred hills their dusky backs upheaved
All over this still ocean ; and beyond,
Far, far beyond, the solid vapours stretched,
In headlands, tongues, and promontory shapes,
Into the main Atlantic, that appeared
To dwindle, and give up his majesty,
Usurped upon far as the sight could reach.

---

* I insert this passage, not that I want it particularly, but because it is one of the finest specimens of Wordsworth's *grand style*. It is as sustained and stately as Milton, and here and there one catches the note of Milton as in the two lines beginning, "Not so the ethereal vault," but it is different from Milton's style in the greater simplicity of diction, in the more feminine and gliding motion of the verse, and in the want, therefore, of the solemn chords of mingled sound and thought with which Milton clashes in again and again in a long passage, making the reader halt to breathe. It differs, also, considered as an illustration, from Milton's manner in this, that Milton uses his illustrations for the purpose of making the thing illustrated more real to the sight, whereas in this, one feels beforehand in reading it, that it is being prepared to serve a moral or intellectual purpose. It is a feeling which somewhat spoils the passage from the artistic point of view.

Not so the ethereal vault ; encroachment none
Was there, nor loss ; only the inferior stars
Had disappeared, or shed a fainter light
In the clear presence of the full-orbed Moon,
Who, from her sovereign elevation, gazed
Upon the billowy ocean, as it lay
All meek and silent, save that through a rift—
Not distant from the shore whereon we stood,
A fixed, abysmal, gloomy, breathing-place—
Mounted the roar of waters, torrents, streams
Innumerable, roaring with one voice !
Heard over earth and sea, and, in that hour,
For so it seemed, felt by the starry heavens.

                              Prelude, book xiv.

Out of this vision of the night, when it was wedded to Thought, he creates the image of a majestic intellect, " what in itself it is and would become." Nature had shadowed forth in the whole scene the emblem of such a mind, with all its functions ; and he saw, through the power of his own soul, the ideal substance the shadow of which lay before him. But the possibility of this inter-action lay in the original harmony which he believed had been established by God between the Mind of man and the outward Universe, whereby things in the one were certain to resemble things in the other.

On these resemblances he dwells, always working, observe, on the same large idea. And the analogy which he makes illustrates another part of his theory,— the distinct and active personality of Nature. She is said to exercise a power over the face of outward things, so that moulded, joined, abstracted and endowed,

          With interchangeable supremacy

they make men feel the life that is behind them.

The power that the highest minds bear with them is " the express resemblance" of this power that Nature exhibits. Their mind works as if it were Nature herself, and in a like manner. They also send forth power from themselves which changes, moulds, abstracts, and endows with life the objects of sense, and the thoughts of others; which creates new existences out of the impressions and thoughts it receives ; the least suggestion enables them to build up great things in Thought and Act ; they are equally willing to receive passively impressions, or to work on them ; and often when God sends to them from Nature a new idea—something, as Wordsworth thinks, created for them—they catch it, or are caught by its "inevitable mastery." It is a ceaseless play, a ceaseless interaction between the world of their mind and that of the universe, and both the worlds are living. The imagination of lower minds—for of course this power of which he speaks is imagination, imagination

> Which, in truth
> Is but another name for absolute power
> And clearest insight, amplitude of mind,
> And Reason in her most exalted mood—

is enthralled by the sensible impressions, and therefore their mind is not wedded to the universe ; but in the loftier souls, the Imagination seizes like a master on the sensible impressions and feels through them the vivid spiritual life in Nature ; and this life united to their own inward life quickens them

> To hold fit converse with the spiritual world
> And with the generations of mankind.

They pass, that is, beyond the bounds of their own mind, and of the outward universe, into a higher world than either, a world which is, as it were, the child of these two parents, but a child greater than either of its parents.

And the result of having attained this higher region is a noble moral life, a life of liberty and blessedness.

> Such minds are truly from the Deity,
> For they are Powers : and hence the highest bliss
> That flesh can know is theirs—the consciousness
> Of Whom they are, habitually infused
> Through every image and through every thought,
> And all affections by communion raised
> From earth to heaven, from human to divine ;
> Hence endless occupation for the Soul,
> Whether discursive or intuitive ;
> Hence cheerfulness for acts of daily life,
> Emotions which best foresight need not fear,
> Most worthy then of trust when most intense.
> Hence, amid ills that vex, and wrongs that crush
> Our hearts—if here the words of Holy Writ
> May with fit reverence be applied—that peace
> Which passeth understanding, that repose
> In moral judgments which from this pure source
> Must come, or will by man be sought in vain.

Book xiv.

But the result is not only a noble moral life, but also a deep religious one. Wordsworth brings out this by returning a little on his past, and asking in reference to the passage just quoted, whether he has in his own life gained this moral freedom. It is a humbler destiny, he answers, that he has pictured. He has had his visitations in the solemn temples of the mountains, from careless youth to conscious manhood; he has been a suffering man and suffered with mankind, but he has never tampered with conscience, never yielded in any public hope to selfish passions, never been enslaved by worldliness, never allowed the tendency

> Of use and custom to bow down the soul
> Under a growing weight of vulgar sense,
> And substitute a universe of death,
> For that which moves with light and life informed,
> Actual, divine, and true.

It was fear and love that had done this—and here he is referring to his boyish time—but only love at last, in which fear was drowned; love by which "subsists all lasting grandeur, without which we are dust;" love such as in early spring all things feel for one another; love such as the lover feels for her who is "his choice of all the world;" love which soars beyond all earthly love, but which contains it, the spiritual love that adoring finds its end in God. Here, where the mediæval Platonists ended, Wordsworth ends. The life he had found in his own mind, the life he has found in the outward universe, mingling together "in love and holy passion," have led him finally to the source of the life of both in God. The delight of earthly passion is pitiable :—

> Unless this love by a still higher love
> Be hallowed, love that breathes not without awe ;
> Love that adores, but on the knees of prayer,
> By heaven inspired ; that frees from chains the soul,
> Lifted, in union with the purest, best,
> Of earth-born passions, on the wings of praise
> Bearing a tribute to the Almighty's Throne.

And then he resumes the whole of this history of his mind. The organ of this spiritual Love is Imagination, and it has been the "feeding source" of his long labour :—

> We have traced the stream
> From the blind cavern whence is faintly heard
> Its natal murmur ; followed it to light
> And open day ; accompanied its course

> Among the ways of Nature, for a time
> Lost sight of it bewildered and engulphed;
> Then given it greeting as it rose once more
> In strength, reflecting from its placid breast
> The works of man and face of human life;
> And lastly, from its progress have we drawn
> Faith in life endless, the sustaining thought
> Of human Being, Eternity, and God.

And he who has reached this point, and has the expressing power of the Poet, is to be the prophet of Nature and of men, to tell them of the Manhood that is greater than Nature;—and the revealer in his own life through the power of God whom he adores within him, of a more beautiful and unworldly time, of a world where the heart of Man may become more free and full of purer thought. This is the duty of the Poet—this ought to be the Poet's life. Two passages contain it, one at the end of the Prelude; the other at the end of the Preface to the Excursion. I throw them both together, and close my lecture with them :—

> Prophets of Nature, we to them will speak
> A lasting inspiration, sanctified
> By reason, blest by faith : what we have loved,
> Others will love, and we will teach them how ;
> Instruct them how the mind of man becomes
> A thousand times more beautiful than the earth
> On which he dwells, above this frame of things
> (Which 'mid all revolution in the hopes
> And fears of men, doth still remain unchanged)
> In beauty exalted, as it is itself
> Of quality and fabric more divine.

>   And if with this
> I mix more lowly matter ; with the thing
> Contemplated, describe the Mind and Man
> Contemplating ; and who, and what he was,

The transitory Being that beheld
This Vision ; when and where, and how he lived ;—
Be not this labour useless.   If such theme
May sort with highest objects, then—dread Power !
Whose gracious favour is the primal source
Of all illumination—may my Life
Express the image of a better time,
More wise desires, and simpler manners :—nurse
My Heart in genuine freedom :—all pure thoughts
Be with me ;—so shall thy unfailing love
Guide, and support, and cheer me to the end !"

LECTURE XIII.

IT was natural to Wordsworth, self-removed, as he was, from the crowd of men and from the more everyday interests of the world, that much of his religion should cluster round two things; one of which was the larger interests and vocation of the whole of mankind, and the ideas which push forward or backward the growth of Man; and the other,—the interests and affections and duties that belong to the natural relations of parents and children, brothers and sisters, friend and friend, wife and husband. The former I have already treated of, showing how this secluded man threw himself with ardour into the general struggle of Man for liberty and right, and even in his later conservatism, preserved his vivid interest in human doings. The latter, however, I did not touch on, and my subject this afternoon is the religious thoughts which Wordsworth collected round the days and life of childhood, and, in connexion with this, his view of Immortality.

And first, whatever may have been his stated creed, he laid aside as Poet the severer doctrine of Original Sin, which stains the child with evil from its birth, and brings it into the world as the child of the devil. He compares his infant daughter who makes her "sinless progress," through a world

> By sorrow darkened and by care disturbed,

to the moon "that through gathered clouds moves un-touched in silver purity,"

> Fair are ye both, and both are free from stain.

And instead of being far away from God, the child is nearer to Him than the man; its first faint smiles, of which we cannot tell the cause, are to Wordsworth—

> Tranquil assurances that Heaven supports
> The feeble motions of thy life, and cheers
> Thy loneliness.

And this is supported by the well-known Ode in which we find the isolated Platonic doctrine of reminiscence, which Wordsworth partly modified by Christianity. To understand that Ode, to understand hundreds of allusions in Wordsworth's Poems, it is necessary to have some clear idea of this doctrine, a doctrine seriously held by Plato throughout a great part, if not the whole, of his philosophic life. Its proof rested on the truth of his doctrine of abstract Ideas. These had an eternal existence; justice, temperance, knowledge, love, truth, and the other things of God are real exist-ences, and are the glorious and blessed sights of Heaven, and the divine life of the Gods is in beholding them; they visit them day by day, and draw life and power from their contemplation. Now the soul of each man before it comes on earth has lived in the train of the Gods, and gone up with them to look upon the vision of absolute truth, gazing with the Gods on that divine landscape of abstract ideas which make up Eternal Being. But it has only looked on it imperfectly; glancing at it, as it were, over a hill; seeing it for a moment, and then departing. At some time or other then it comes to earth in human shape, and there its nature is threefold. It is rational, sensual, and moral or spiritual. Then comes in the doctrine of reminiscence. For the whole of after existence is spent in regaining by a series of recollections, and through a continual struggle, the glorious vision which has been lost—the vision of absolute ideas; and the regaining of it will be entrance into true being. Of these ideas, the only one that has any visible form on earth is Beauty. Now, whenever we see earthly beauty, the memory of the heavenly comes back, faintly, but enough to excite the soul; and the germ of the wings the soul once possessed and lost, begins at the sight to push itself forth. It is then that the struggle begins. The sensual soul, which Plato images as a large, misshapen horse, of a dark colour, beholding beauty, rushes blindly to enjoy it, and sees only and desires only the earthliness of beauty. But the spiritual soul, imaged as a white and immortal steed, looks beyond the earthly beauty to the heavenly that it images—and the intense struggle between the two is only settled with difficulty, in those who truly aspire, by the continued dragging back and subduing of the black horse by the rational soul, who sides with the white horse and is the charioteer. At last, after many efforts, the sensual soul is wholly brought under sway, and the vision of true beauty is reached, and with it the vision of the other noble ideas of wisdom, temperance, justice, and the rest. It takes ten thousand years, Plato thinks, before the soul can regain the imperial Palace whence it came.

But it is not only the inward sensual desires that dim the light, and hold back the true soul from attaining ideas, but the world of the senses also, the material world, hampers its efforts and confines it. The only world in which the soul can truly live, is the world of ideas; and the immortal steed is depressed and languishes in a sensible unreal world which has no harmony with it. But the effort ends at last. Again and again the vision of the eternal world, of the ancient glory, flashes before the soul, and recalls the pre-existent life: at each time the soul either falls away from it or draws nearer to it; and finally in those who do not continue falling, the wings the soul had once are entirely reformed, and it rises to abide among the Gods, and daily to see the divine landscape of ideas, and to live by the sight of it. The soul re-enters eternal life.

Hence, the doctrine of pre-existence, and that of reminiscence, are in Plato connected with the doctrine of Immortality as a necessary fulfilment of the two former. We have been once in union with absolute life; we recall in many lives here on earth that past, and grow gradually into union with it; and at last having recalled it all through effort and conquest of the animal nature, we resume it again for ever.

This is the philosophic doctrine a portion of which Wordsworth modified after his own fashion in the "Ode on the intimations of Immortality from recollections of early childhood." He draws from it the conclusion, a conclusion Plato would not have drawn, that the child is nearer to God and to the vision of glory and loveliness than the man. Plato, on the contrary, would have made the grown philosopher more conscious of it than the child. But Wordsworth was really nothing of a Platonist; he only liked these ideas of pre-existence and reminiscence, and made his own thought out of them. Coming in childhood fresh from God, all the world seemed to his soul—since the heavenly light still lingered in it—

> Apparelled in celestial light,
> The glory and the brightness of a dream.

But now, as man he can see this glory no longer; yet in the season of May, when the heavens laugh and the earth adorns herself with joy, he recovers something of the recollections of childhood, he remembers at least that there was a visionary gleam, a glory and a dream that now are fled. And he explains it thus by the main ideas of the Platonic opinion :

> Our birth is but a sleep and a forgetting:
> The Soul that rises with us, our life's Star,
>   Hath had elsewhere its setting,
>   And cometh from afar :
>   Not in entire forgetfulness,
>   And not in utter nakedness,
> But trailing clouds of glory do we come
>   From God, who is our home :
> Heaven lies about us in our infancy !

But soon the sensible world begins to do its work and drags us away from the vision of beauty and life. The growing boy feels the shades of the prison-house closing round him—the youth travels further from it, but is still attended by it:

> At length the Man perceives it die away,
> And fade into the light of common day.

Even Earth herself, the kindly mother, bringing her natural pleasures of sense and affection, of human ties, and with no unworthy aim, lures the child away from, and makes the man forget

> the glories he had known
> And that imperial Palace whence he came.

This, you will see, may be called modified Platonism. The next remarkable passage, however, is not Platonism, and indeed, as expressed, it runs close to nonsense. We can only catch the main idea among expressions of the child as the best Philosopher, the Eye among the blind, that deaf and silent reads the eternal deep, and is haunted for ever by the eternal mind, the mighty Prophet, the Seer blest—over whom his Immortality broods like the Day, a master o'er a slave—expressions which taken separately have scarcely any recognizable meaning. By taking them altogether, we feel rather than see that Wordsworth intended to say, that the child, having lately come from a perfect existence, in which he saw truth directly, and was at home with God, retains, unknown to us, that vision—and because he does, is the best philosopher, since he sees at once that which we through philosophy are endeavouring to reach; is the mighty prophet, because in his actions and speech, he tells unconsciously the truths he sees, but the sight of which we have lost; is more closely haunted by God, more near to the immortal Life, more purely and brightly free, because he half shares in the pre-existent life and glory out of which he has come.

The child is not conscious of this vision. He does not know that he sees God; that he is, as he speaks, revealing the truths of the world in which he half lives; that his common thoughts and feelings have their beauty from his directer sight of the glory he has left: that the glory and beauty which he sees in the world of nature is the reflection of the glory and beauty he saw in another life—that he himself carries with him some of that celestial light. He knows nothing of it. But we, looking back on our childhood, or looking at childhood itself, from an age out which has faded the light we had, remember the light of this vision in our own childhood, and recognise its results and quality in children. We know that what we then felt and now see in children, was and is divine, know it from the bitter contrast, for

> The things which we have seen we now can see no more.

We are conscious that they were, because we have lost them.

Many of the slighter Poems of Wordsworth have this thought as their root. He is thinking of it when he describes the characteristics of a child of three years old, and dwells upon her utter gladness, her self-sufficingness, on the unexpectedness of her words and actions. For she has companions, he would say, that we wot not of. She is living in a world that we cannot see, and acts from impulses derived from it of which we know nothing. Here are the lines:

> Even so, this happy Creature of herself
> Is all-sufficient; solitude to her

> Is blithe society—who fills the air
> With gladness and involuntary songs.
> Light are her sallies as the tripping fawn's
> Forth-startled from the fern where she lay couched :
> Unthought of, unexpected, as the stir
> Of the soft breeze ruffling the meadow-flowers ;
> Or from before it chasing wantonly
> The many-coloured images imprest
> Upon the bosom of a placid lake.

His sister is thinking of the same, when she speaks of
the child who is unconscious of the limits of our thoughts
of time and space :

> Who, worn out with the mystery
> Of time and distance, night and day,
> The bonds of our humanity.

Wordsworth is thinking of the same in his little Poems
of " We are Seven," and in the " Anecdote for Fathers."
The child in the first has no idea of any severance between
earth and heaven ; her dead brother and sister are still a
part of the family ; death is nothing to her knowledge ;
and she speaks in saying—We are seven—one of those
" truths which we are toiling all our lives to find," and
the recollection of which as felt by us when a child—is an
intimation of our Immortality. In the second Poem,
Wordsworth questions his little son, as to the reason he
should like one place more than another, and drives the
boy at last into finding a reason in the existence of a
weather-cock in one place and not in the other. The
boy had no real reason to give, and the father felt that
he had forced the child to say what was untrue. But
in the saying of it, he, unconsciously, made Wordsworth
conscious of the wrong he had done. He felt that he was
reproved, as it were, by the God in the child ; and the

Poem, which is a poor one, and only interesting from our being able to refer it to the same thought that prompted the great Ode, closes thus :

> O dearest, dearest boy, my heart
> For better love would seldom yearn,
> Could I but teach the hundredth part
> Of what from thee I learn.

No lovelier expression of that thought exists than in the last lines of the sonnet composed by the seaside :

> Dear child! dear girl! that walkest with me here,
> If thou appear untouched by solemn thought,
> Thy nature is not therefore less divine :
> Thou liest in Abraham's bosom all the year,
> And worship'st at the Temple's inner shrine,
> God being with thee when we know it not.

Still more strongly does the same thought appear in the little Poem to Hartley Coleridge, then six years old. The first ten lines are steeped in the philosophy of the Ode :

> O thou ! whose fancies from afar are brought,
> Who of thy words dost make a mock apparel,
> And fittest to unutterable thought
> The breeze-like motion and the self-born carol;
> Thou faery voyager! that dost float
> In such clear water that thy boat
> May rather seem
> To brood on air than on an earthly stream;
> Suspended in a stream as clear as sky,
> Where earth and heaven do make one imagery;
> O blessed vision ! happy child !
> Thou art so exquisitely wild,
> I think of thee with many fears
> For what may be thy lot in future years.

And once more, in speaking of Presentiments, he falls back also on this thought, and says :

The tear whose source I could not guess,
The deep sigh that seemed fatherless,
Were mine in early days.

As the boy grows, this innocent unconscious life in the
eternal is more and more invaded by the outward life of
which he becomes directly conscious. His games, his
father's love, the outward scenery of nature and of
Human life, all enthral him, and the vision grows dim
and dimmer. The conscious life of Earth replaces the
unconscious life of Heaven.

But he is not left without visitations. Nature takes
up the work, or rather the divine Life in Nature makes
itself felt again and again, and thrills the boy who has
forgotten his immortal life with a vague sense of it. In
the midst of his eager earthly life, he is suddenly checked,
the beauty or the terror or the mystery of nature touching
him for a moment. It is a sudden recalling—a shadowy
recollection of the childish glory; only it is now often
linked with fear, since it has become unknown. For an
instant he feels as if the outward world had no reality,
and is forced to make things real to him by touching them;
it misgives him that things are as they seem; mysterious
feelings of fear beset him in solitude, as if a Presence that
he could not put by were there; he has dreams, instincts
of things greater than he can grasp, that break suddenly
in upon him in the midst of wild enjoyment, and which
make him thrill with excitement, surprise, and dread.
They come to him, he knows not how, brought by

A rainbow, a sunbeam,
A subtle smell that Spring unbinds;
Dead pause abrupt of midnight winds,
An echo, or a dream.

n from nature we have already traced in speak-
'Prelude."* Certain natural impressions caused
n the sense of unknown modes of being. Certain
motions of the sense made him conscious through their
ministration of a world beyond this world, of something
in him which he had lost, and suddenly remembered.
They were, he says, "gleams like the flashing of a
shield;" that lit for an instant the mind with memory
of the ancient glory, and brought with them a touch of
subdued sadness and surprise.

Such is the thought at the root of the lines on the
boy of Winander; such is the thought which gives its
special quality to the Poem on the "Cuckoo," where the
far-off wandering voice of the bird made it the image of a
mystery, and woke a dim sense of mystery; to the Poem
of "Nutting," when in the midst of the exulting destruction that a boy delights in, a dim reproach creeps in
as if he had done harm to living things. It belongs
to many other Poems, where nature is represented as
touching into momentary consciousness of life the
sleeping forms of the ancient life of the soul before it
came on earth, as sometimes in our more common life
some slight event will bring back during the day a dream
we had dreamt, but had wholly forgotten.

These are the things which, whether coming unannounced to the soul itself, or led to it by Nature,
are, when remembered in after years, powerful to put
the mind into a world different from this; to reprove,
exalt, and give light by bringing to our mind our immortal birth; to support us in hours of obscure distress

* See Lectures vi. vii.

by the high thought that we belong to God, and are born to regain the truths that once we had—and they come again and again till even in manhood we get back through the memories of childhood to the imperial palace whence we came.*

There is the noblest expression of all this in the Ode :

> Not for these I raise
> The Song of thanks and praise,
>> But for those obstinate questionings
>> Of sense and outward things,
>> Fallings from us, vanishings ;
>> Blank misgivings of a Creature
> Moving about in worlds not realised,
> High instincts before which our mortal Nature
> Did tremble like a guilty Thing surprised :
>> But for those first affections,
>> Those shadowy recollections,
>> Which, be they what they may,
> Are yet the fountain light of all our day,
> Are yet a master light of all our seeing ;

---

* In my last lecture I touched on this subject, and the passage in the "Prelude," book xii., which I analysed there, ought to be read along with the Ode. I insert one passage here for comparison :
> Oh ! mystery of man, from what a depth
> Proceed thy honours. I am lost, but see
> In simple childhood something of the base
> On which thy greatness stands ; but this I feel,
> That from thyself it comes, that thou must give,
> Else never canst receive. The days gone by
> Return upon me almost from the dawn
> Of life : the hiding-places of man's power
> Open ; I would approach them, but they close.
> I see by glimpses now ; when age comes on,
> May scarcely see at all ; and I would give,
> While yet we may, as far as words can give,
> Substance and life to what I feel, enshrining,
> Such is my hope, the spirit of the Past
> For future restoration.

13

Uphold us, cherish, and have power to make
Our noisy years seem moments in the being
Of the eternal Silence; truths that wake,
     To perish never;
Which neither listlessness, nor mad endeavour,
     Nor Man nor Boy,
Nor all that is at enmity with joy,
Can utterly abolish or destroy!
     Hence in a season of calm weather
     Though inland far we be,
Our Souls have sight of that immortal sea
     Which brought us hither,
     Can in a moment travel thither,
And see the Children sport upon the shore,
And hear the mighty waters rolling evermore.

Such things grow less and less as years go on; as
middle age touches us, it is only the memory that we
have had such visions that keeps us true to our immortal
destiny; as to the visions themselves, they leave us
altogether, and the light is only the light of common day.
Still now and then the vision does arise, and it came to
Wordsworth in 1818, on an "evening of extraordinary
splendour and beauty." He sees the wonderful effulgence
of the sun setting over hills, the silent spectacle of glory
and radiance on the earth below; and he is swept beyond
the earthly beauty to aspire to the heavenly—nay, half of
the beauty is itself of Heaven, out of the heart of the
perfect life.

Thine is the tranquil hour, purpureal Eve!
But long as godlike wish, or hope divine,
Informs my spirit: ne'er can I believe
That this magnificence is wholly thine;
From worlds not quickened by the Sun
A portion of the gift is won.

The mountain ridges seem a golden ladder, on which one
might ascend to heaven; "wings at my shoulders seem to

play "—the very Platonic expression—he calls on drooping
old men to come forth, and see to what fair countries they
are bound; he bids the genii wake the traveller that he
may meet the dower God gives him in such beauty.

Then comes this passage:

> Such hues from their celestial Urn
> Were wont to stream before mine eye,
> Where'er it wandered in the morn
> Of blissful infancy.
> This glimpse of glory, why renewed?
> Nay, rather speak with gratitude;
> For, if a vestige of those gleams
> Survived, 'twas only in my dreams.
> Dread Power! whom peace and calmness serve
> No less than Nature's threatening voice,
> If aught unworthy be my choice,
> From Thee if I would swerve;
> Oh, let thy grace remind me of the light
> Full early lost, and fruitlessly deplored;
> Which, at this moment, on my waking sight,
> Appears to shine by miracle restored,
> My soul, though yet confined to earth,
> Rejoices in a second birth!

Thus, felt in childhood, often recollected, sometimes
renewed in middle age, he prays in another place that
his old age may keep to its latest breath, those visions of
the soul, these dreams of an immortal life; that he may
rejoice, with quickened spirit, in the admonitions of God's
voice given in the quiet of the heart, or suddenly flashing
on him from Nature—till he feel secure of life in God,
and pray the prayer of one whose immortality is sure.

> Breathe through my soul the blessing of Thy grace:
> Glad through a perfect love, a faith sincere,
> Drawn from the wisdom that begins with fear,
> Glad to expand, and, for a season, free
> From finite cares, to rest absorbed in Thee.

This is the growth of the faith in Immortality. Direct vision of the eternal world and life in it, during infancy— recollection of the glories of that vision when the world has hidden it from our eyes ; frequently repeated recol- lections, all leading us back to the heavenly life and accustoming us to trust in it — sudden outbursts of actual vision such as childhood possessed, when moved by some splendid sight or inspired act; rarely coming, but when assisted by the recollections intensely convincing— quiet philosophic faith in the intuitions of the soul that tell of eternal life, so that

> though nothing can bring back the hour
> Of splendour in the grass, of glory in the flower ;
>> We will grieve not, rather find
>> Strength in what remains behind ;
>> In the primal sympathy
>> Which having been must ever be ;
>> In the soothing thoughts that spring
>> Out of human suffering ;
>> In the faith that looks through death,
> In years that bring the philosophic mind.

Then, as the old man looks back, he sees that his wish has been fulfilled ; the same divine remembrance of beauty that made his heart leap up when he beheld a rainbow in the sky is with him still. That which was his as boy, has been his as man, is his, now that he is old. The child has been Father of the man, his days have been " knit each to each in natural piety." The piety is the piety of immortal hopes; the old man's vision of the future life is co- incident with the child's vision of the pre-existent life. Age is not desolate then. The unutterable dewy light of joy is gone, it rests no longer on Man or Nature. But the love which has come of suffering, the long union with the human heart, the sad but hope-lit experience, do not make him love Nature less than when he tripped as lightly as the brooks that fret their channels, but more; he can still enjoy the innocent brightness of a new-born day; the beauty of all things is not less, but more, because touched with the sentiment of mortal sorrow and mortal victory; they take a sober, but not less lively colouring; and the meanest flower that blows, to a heart so trained, leads him beyond itself to live in the eternal, in the land where men weep not for either joy or sorrow, for the thoughts that are there are too deep for tears.

Abiding then in old age we look back to our childhood. We were nearer then to the divine life, and there the soul recognises most clearly its immortal features:

> Ah! why in age
> Do we revert so fondly to the walks
> Of childhood—but that there the Soul discerns
> The dear memorial footsteps unimpaired
> Of her own native vigour; thence can hear
> Reverberations; and a choral song,
> Commingling with the incense that ascends,
> Undaunted, toward the imperishable heavens,
> From her own lonely altar?

We look forward also, that we may see the life to come, the resurrection of that we once possessed; we have not really lost, but gained, by age, if we have been true to the divine gleams that we could not wholly lose. Old age is then great—raised above the thraldom of the passions that beset guilt, the ambitious worldliness which made the light such common day, the very world of sense that made us forget our ancient spiritual Home.

> Rightly it is said
> That Man descends into the Vale of years;
> Yet have I thought that we might also speak,

And not presumptuously, I trust, of Age,
As of a final Eminence ; though bare
In aspect and forbidding, yet a point
On which 'tis not impossible to sit
In awful sovereignty ; a place of power,
A throne, that may be likened unto his,
Who, in some placid day of summer, looks
Down from a mountain-top,—say one of those
High peaks that bound the vale where now we are.
Faint, and diminished to the gazing eye,
Forest and field, and hill and dale appear,
With all the shapes over their surface spread :
But, while the gross and visible frame of things
Relinquishes its hold upon the sense,
Yea almost on the Mind herself, and seems
All unsubstantialized,—how loud the voice
Of waters, with invigorated peal
From the full river in the vale below,
Ascending ?   For on that superior height
Who sits, is disencumbered from the press
Of near obstructions, and is privileged
To breathe in solitude, above the host
Of ever-humming insects, 'mid thin air
That suits not them.   The murmur of the leaves,
Many and idle, visits not his ear ;
This he is freed from, and from thousand notes
(Not less unceasing, not less vain than these,)
By which the finer passages of sense
Are occupied ; and the Soul, that would incline
To listen, is prevented or deterred.

And may it not be hoped, that, placed by age
In like removal, tranquil though severe,
We are not so removed for utter loss ;
But for some favour, suited to our need ?
What more than that the severing should confer
Fresh power to commune with the invisible world,
And hear the mighty stream of tendency
Uttering, for elevation of our thought,
A clear sonorous voice, inaudible
To the vast multitude, whose doom it is
To run the giddy round of vain delight,
Or fret and labour on the Plain below.

                                        Excursion, book ix.

It was in this faith that Wordsworth lived and died. It was in deep belief in God and Immortality, and in a Saviour from sin, that he passed his quiet days, and found peace far from the strifes of men. It was in the calm— alike removed from stormy passion, and from the disturbing lusts of the world—that this faith gave him, that he wrought out and lived the high morality which he has given to us in the " Ode to Duty," in the fine strain of the " Happy Warrior," and in many noble passages in the " Excursion." It was in this faith that he quietly reposed in his domestic life, and by it enhanced all the faithful affection for wife and sister, children and brother, that nowhere in English poetry burns with a lovelier or a purer light. As age grew on, his calm deepened ; he had "the silent thoughts that search for steadfast light; " he wished, and realised the wish, to present to God his life as a " pure oblation of divine tranquillity." Nor was he without joy in the midst of calm ; there was no stagnant water in the deep lake of his heart; such poems as the " Ode to Duty " and others are filled with a resolute and exalted joy ; and there were times when, as the old man prayed, his delight was transfigured :

> I bent before Thy gracious throne,
> And asked for peace on suppliant knee,
> And peace was given— nor peace alone,
> But faith sublimed to ecstasy.

Nor can I better close these lectures upon him than by the sonnet in which he looks back and looks forward in a strain, where clear knowledge of what Man is in himself alone, is mingled with quiet faith in what he is in God.

AFTER-THOUGHT.

I thought of Thee, my partner and my guide,
As being past away.—Vain sympathies!
For, backward, Duddon! as I cast my eyes,
I see what was, and is, and will abide ;
Still glides the Stream, and shall for ever glide ;
The Form remains, the Function never dies ;
While we, the brave, the mighty, and the wise,
We Men, who in our morn of youth defied
The elements, must vanish ;—be it so !
Enough, if something from our hands have power
To live, and act, and serve the future hour ;
And if, as toward the silent tomb we go,
Through love, through hope, and faith's transcendent dower,
We feel that we are greater than we know.

LECTURE XIV.

—•—

ROBERT BURNS.

WHEN speaking at the beginning of these lectures of theology in the earlier poets of the Natural School, in Cowper and Crabbe who preceded the great outbreak of song, I omitted Robert Burns. I now fill up that gap, which was left for a sufficiently good reason—that though the influences which came on England at that time did have their result upon Burns, they had far less result than on others, because he was essentially the creation of his own land, and of another poetic descent than that of England. With regard to the poetry of Nature, he only carried on in a more vivid and tender way, and on precisely the same lines, the same sort of natural description which had been worked by the Scottish poets from the time they began to write. With regard to what I have called, along with others, the poetry of Man, he was less universal and more national than the English poets who followed him. But when we look at his work on this subject, and compare it with that of the English poets who preceded him, or with that of his contemporaries, Cowper and Crabbe, we find in him a peculiar quality which gives him a distinct rank in the history of English poetry, of which I may as well speak in this connection. He restored passion to our poetry. It had not belonged to it since the days of Elizabeth. No one would guess, who began to read our poetic literature shortly after the death of Shakespeare, how rich the veins of nature and emotion had been in our country. He might read through the whole of our poetry, with the exception of a few songs and sonnets, down to Burns, and not find any poetry which could truly be called passionate. So, when the fire broke out again in Burns, it was like a new revelation; men were swept back to the age of Elizabeth, and heard again, though in different chords, the music which had then enchanted the world. And since his time, our poetry has not only been the poetry of Man and of Nature, but also of Passion. And it sprang clean and clear out of the natural soil of a wild heath, not out of a cultivated garden; it was underived from other poets, for Burns read nothing but a collection of English songs; it was unassisted by the general culture of a literary class, for it was born when he was reaping in the fields, and when he held the handles of the plough; it came direct out of a fresh stratum of popular life. It was as if the Muse had said, I am weary of philosophy and satire, weary of faded sentiment, of refined and classic verse, and of stern pictures of misery, and I will have something fresh, at last; and had driven a shaft down through layer after layer of dry clay, till she touched far below, a source of new and hidden waters, that, loosened from their prison, rushed upwards to the surface, and ran away a mountain torrent of clear bright verse, living and life-giving. Burns added passion to the poetry of Nature and Man.

But independent of the poetry that has to do with these two subjects, and the theology of which I shall speak of in this lecture and the following, there is in Burns a poetry of personality. On this, in its religious aspect, I shall speak in my third lecture.

Our subject to-day is the Poetry of Man from a theological point of view, as we find it represented in Burns.

The poetry of Man began distinctly in England with the first coming to the light of the ideas of the Revolution. Before the great singers came we can trace these ideas in English poetry, and I have traced them in Cowper and Crabbe. They appear also in Burns, but in by no means so full a form. They influenced him insensibly; he does not recognise their power. But in one point he was consciously at one with them, in their claim that the poor should be thought of as men; in the placing of Man—apart from all consideration of caste and rank and wealth and race—foremost. How far he was touched by this, and how far it was specially modified in him, we have now to consider, and it is part of our subject, for it either flowed directly from a new and larger idea of God, or was creative of a larger view of Him.

He was born in 1759, and the first edition of his poems was in 1786. His first work and his youth preceded then the outbreak of the Revolution. We cannot therefore say that he was revolutionised, but he was a born revolutionist, in the sense of being ready, when he thought it needed, to take the part of his own class against selfish rank and wealth; and to appeal for his right to do this

to the common duties and rights of man as man. Not
in Cowper, not in Crabbe, not in any of the after Poets,
was the deep cry of the Revolution more clearly heard
than in the whole of the fine song—

> Is there, for honest poverty,
>   That hangs his head, and a' that ?
> The coward slave, we pass him by,
>   We dare be poor for a' that !
>   For a' that, and a' that,
>   Our toils obscure, and a' that ;
>   The rank is but the guinea stamp,
>   The man's the gowd for a' that.

Being thus himself poor, " following his plough along
the mountain side," and having in him, not discontent
with his poverty, but a heart framed to enjoy and love
all beauty, and to feel all that was human, and being
insensibly influenced by the spirit of the time, he
threw into tender and humourous song the sorrows and
affections of his own class, their religion and their
passions, their amusements and their toil, till all the
world laughed and wept with Ayrshire ploughmen. As
in England, so in Scotland, we now find something better
than the distant sentimental view which we found the
Poets took of the poor. Burns did in 1786 the work
which Crabbe began in England in 1783 and Cowper in
1785. Mark the dates—how they all run together—
And I have often wondered in looking at these lines of
Gray's, which Burns put as motto to the " Cottar's Saturday Night "—

> Let not ambition mock their useful toil,
> Their homely joys and destiny obscure ;
> Nor grandeur hear with a disdainful smile
> The short but simple annals of the Poor—

whether he recognized in them the note of distance, and meant to make his own vivid, lifelike description of a poor man's home, a contrast to the fine-gentleman sentiment of Gray.

One would think so from the Preface and the after-dedication to his Poems;—the passages are interesting and bear upon the present question.

"The following trifles are not the production of the Poet who with all the advantages of learned art, and, perhaps, amid the elegances and idlenesses of upper life, looks down for a rural theme, with an eye to Theocritus or Virgil. To the author of this, these, and other celebrated names their countrymen are, at least in their original language, a fountain shut up and a book sealed. Unacquainted with the necessary requisites for commencing poet by rule, he sings the sentiments and manners he felt and saw in himself and his rustic compeers around him, in his and their native language."

And in the Dedication—

"The Poetic Genius of my country found me, as the prophetic bard Elijah did Elisha—at the Plough, and threw her inspiring Mantle over me. She bade me sing the loves, the joys, the rural scenes and rural pleasures of my native tongue: I tuned my wild, artless notes as she inspired."

At home then, among the poor, he gave them his best work, and it was done, as all the highest work is done, with passion.

In the movement of thought and feeling towards the recognition of the poor and working men as sons of God, and as made of one blood with the rich and learned, there was as yet no natural passion. Cowper and Crabbe, though their sympathy with the lower class was deep, spoke for it and of it, not out of it; and naturally there was no personal passion in their work. They led men to feel with the poor, but it was as men feel with the sorrows and joys of a different race. But when Burns came, it was a different business. I have said that he restored passion to our poetry. He brought it now into this movement. He added its fire to the work which Cowper and Crabbe had done, and threw around poor life and rural nature, for the first time for centuries, "the light that never was on sea or land." When he spoke, whether to ostlers at the inns, or to "jewelled duchesses," as Carlyle calls them, or to literary men in Edinburgh, they one and all felt his fire, and believed that rustic hind and milk-maid, field labourer and beggar, were of like passions with themselves, were just as good and just as wicked, and in the same way, as they were themselves. They recognised the truth when it was told with a passion that was born directly out of the life of poverty and labour, and they said,—These, then, are men and women, not shadows any longer : bone of our bone and flesh of our flesh.

The same passion ran through all he said and did. No one felt more keenly than Burns that tingling of the heart, which at its height produces poetry of word and deed. In that which men ordinarily call Love, we are told that his agitation exceeded anything his friend had ever seen; but of that I do not speak. His emotion was as great, though not so disturbing, in all the other spheres of emotion. Who has not felt the intense thrill of passion in the lines on "Mary in Heaven," in "Mary Morison?" and hearken to this, in which he describes that which most pleased him in the Songs of Lapraik—

> There was ae song amang the rest ;
> Aboon them a', it pleased me best,
> That some kind husband had addrest
>   To some sweet wife :
> It thrilled the heartstrings through the breast
>   A' to the life.

And his only wish was not to produce finespun emotion, or to write to please the critics, but to touch the heart.

> Gie me ae spark of Nature's fire,
> That's a' the learning I desire ;
> Then though I drudge thro' dirt and mire,
>   At plough or cart ;
> My Muse, though hamely in attire,
>   May touch the heart.

And so it has done. Even the wildest pieces of mad humour like "Tam o' Shanter" or the "Jolly Beggars" have so much of intense humanity in them, that they move natural emotion, and reconcile us even to coarseness for the moment. We feel that men are kindly, even in their ill : though I must speak afterwards of the bad results of Burns' victory over the ascetic party in Scotland.

But whatever the ill results, this bright, tender, heartfelt representation of the life of the poor, not only brought the rich and comfortable near to the poor and struggling, and placed both on the common platform of humanity : but it also made the poor themselves contented and in love with life, by bringing out the nobility and beauty of the simple human passions, and of the common working life of men. Even in the sharp contrast which he draws in the "Twa Dogs" between the lives of poor and rich, he himself prefers that of the poor, and gives clear reasons for it — reasons which had their

root in no sentimental view of the question. He
was then no mere wild revolutionist; he did not wish
to level all. He preached a crusade against the selfishness of the rich, but he did not wish the poor to become as the rich. Keep to your own life, he said to
them; learn to live it, to live truly and honestly in it—
to recognise in it the dignity of Man, to rejoice in its
hardy independence, in its simple but deep emotions.

Nor was all this without a religious basis. It was
connected in the mind of Burns with the thought of
God as the Father of the Poor, of God as even the
universal Father before whom each man stood, stripped of
wealth, of rank, of outward show—a character alone. And
this God, in the Poet's mind, was Love, and the source of
all Love was in Him. It was impossible then for Burns
to hold the strong Calvinistic view of the reprobation of
the greater part of mankind. He was continually in
antagonism with it, and many and shrewd were the blows
he dealt it. To him, as well as to Shelley and Byron,
we owe much of our freedom from this inconsiderate view
of God, a view which only could have been born in a
society that was rooted in an aristocratic view of the
world, though strange to say, yet explicable enough if one
had time to go into the matter, it has been the favourite
religion of democracy. As to Burns, his deep conception of the universal power of God's love, led him
to pity the Devil and to hope for his redemption, a hope
that many who still believe in the Devil share with him.

> Ye aiblins might—I dinna ken,
> Hae yet a stake.

On the other side, God's love for Man would make Him

indignant with those who oppressed the weak or injured the poor. And the Poems of Burns are full of this indignation. Not all the rage of winds and biting frost are more unkind, he says, than the miseries

That heaven-illumined man on brother man bestows.

All his religion, he says, came from the heart; and it drove him, when he thought of his poor people and their hard lives, and how beautiful they often were with natural feeling; when he thought how much they suffered and how much was due to them, to refer the origin of their good to God, and to leave the righting of their wrongs to God.

He went further, and threw over the lives of the poor the light of God. Every one knows the scene in the " Cottar's Saturday Night;" every one has felt how solemn and patriarchal it is, and how all the charming gossip and pleasant human fun, and modest love which charm us in it are dignified by the worship of God that follows. But that poem must not be taken as representing the religious feeling of Burns; it is purposely made religious; and all we can truly say of Burns is, that whether as regards his own art, or when he speaks of the lives and love of the poor, he was one of those men who at the end of last century claimed for men a universal Father in God, and vindicated the poor as His children. It is not of course stated directly—that would not be the way of a Poet,—but it is a spirit in his work, and it flows through all his graver poems. It affects also distantly all his poetry, and owing to its influence, we find the grace and tenderness of human feeling used to make beautiful that which the world calls common, even that it calls unclean. This is, indeed, the most sacred work of poetry, and it has so strict an analogy with the means Christ chose to use in His teaching, that it forms another point of union between Christianity and poetry. I have often said that if we would understand Christ's words and works, we must approach them as we approach poetry. The Parables that have to do with Man are poems, in which the common lives and sorrows of men are made divine by interpreting them as symbols of God's relation to men. The world can never forget the Shepherd seeking his sheep, the Father's joy over his son lost and found, the blessing given to the children, the life the Saviour lived among the outcasts and strayed of earth, the glory of love which was shed over the fisher's life, the way in which the whole of humble working life was linked to God, the proclamation of the care of the Highest for the shepherd on the hill, for the sower in the field.

And whatever one may have afterwards to say of Burns' religion, the practical result of much of his poetry in his age was to do similar work to that of Christ—to exalt and beautify the life of the poor, to make them feel that they were cared for and known of God.

It was then, in this way, by upholding Manhood as first, and by exalting the poor as men, and by preaching a common brotherhood, that Burns developed the poetry of Man, and was a child of the ideas of the revolution. But there was another human element in his poetry which I must speak of now—his strong nationality. It was connected with theology, and it was unconnected with the revolution. One of the main ideas of the revolution was its rejection

of all nationalities for the sake of mankind. It proclaimed
one country of which all men were citizens, one nation of
which all men were members, of which all men were
patriots, to which all men were bound to offer up their
lives. A man was not, in the first instance, an Englishman, Frenchman, or Italian, he was a man. Its tendency
was then to repress any strong feeling of nationality, and
to substitute for it a strong Humanity. And we have
found that element in the poets in England who were
most influenced by the revolution. We do not find it
in Burns. Nor is it likely that we should; for if love of
Nature is one of the distinguishing elements of all Scottish poetry, love of Scotland is the other, and Burns is
the descendant of the one as well as of the other.

It seems to be doubted both by Burns and Carlyle
that Scotland was fond of herself till Burns arose—by
Burns in lines to W. Simpson which I shall quote afterwards; by Carlyle when he speaks of the remarkable increase of nationality in Scotch literature, and attributes it
chiefly to Burns. Both of them seem to forget, or not to
know, that the poetry of Scotland has never failed to be
national, even after the union of the two crowns, the
time of which they speak. The Lowland poetry began
in Scotland with James I., and took its first inspiration
from Chaucer, whom James had read while a prisoner
in England. But the remarkable thing is, that while
it retained the manner of Chaucer, it kept none of
his spirit. It was not English, nor even mediæval.
It became entirely Scotch in spirit; it employed itself
on Scotch subjects; and whatever form it took up, ballad,
or fable, or pastoral, or allegory, it gave them all a special

Scotch turn.   And one of its characteristics is a devotional patriotism.   Ballad after ballad records it, and when we come to the greater Makers, it is intense.   Dunbar's "Golden Terge" is one instance; Douglas brims over with it; even Lyndsay, before he was carried away from purely poetic work to political, gives himself to glorify his land.   Again, at a time when personification raged in Scottish poetry, one of the most frequent personifications is that of Scotland herself.   She appears as Warden of the Land, in a noble song of Alexander Scot's, full of a manly freedom and patriotism: and it is patriotism whose main desire is not for warlike glory, but for the glory which belongs to a nobly-governed country whose citizens were free from falsehood, flattery, and impurity.   Or, as in Dunbar's "Thistle and Rose," life is given to the Royal Arms, and the animals and flowers sing the glory of the land.   The same strong feeling, and in this short sketch I can give you no idea of its strength, is continued through Ramsay and Ferguson and a number of minor poets, right down to Burns, whose "Vision" and "Scots wha hae wi' Wallace bled" are the legitimate children of this long patriotic passion.   A flood of Scottish prejudice, he says, has been poured along my veins, and I feel it will boil there till the flood-gates shut in eternal rest.

> The roughbur thistle spreading wide
> Amang the bearded bear,
> I turned the weeder clips aside
> An' spared the symbol dear.

In nearly all his poems we find this traditional nationality, and it entirely prevented him from receiving the denationalising idea of the revolution.   All the characteristics

of the past poets belong to him. He keeps himself throughout to Scottish subjects; his scenery is entirely Scottish, his
love of liberty concentrates itself round Scottish struggles;
his muse is wholly untravelled; and while it gains a certain
strength within its sphere from this limitation, it loses
that breadth of view and depth of passion which belong
to the greater poets. He may have, as Carlyle says, a
resonance in his bosom for every note of human feeling—
and he has—but all the human feeling is Scottish. There
is no need to account for this; the reasons are plain in
his position and his life. Nor have we any need to regret
it, for if Burns had been more universal we should have
lost him; he could not have built a loftier rhyme than
his own rustic national one, and he knew that well. When
the Muse of Scotland appeared to him, she bade him sing
his own people; her mantle was adorned with the rivers,
hills, and boroughs of Scotland, and in her face was the
character of Scotland's poets—

> A hair-brained, sentimental trace,
> Was strongly marked in her face;
> A wildly witty, rustic grace
>   Shone full upon her;
> Her eye, e'vn turned on empty space,
>   Beamed keen with Honour.

And the same " wildly witty, rustic grace " that shone
full upon her shines in all his work. For Scotland's
glory and Scotland's beauty

> I kittle up my rustic reed
> It gies me ease.

And nothing can be better or brighter than the lines in
which he expresses this, written to W. Simpson,

Ramsay an' famous Ferguson,
Gied Forth an' Tay a lift aboon ;
Yarrow an' Tweed to monie a tune,
      Owre Scotland rings,
While Irwin, Lugar, Ayr an' Doon,
      Naebody sings.

The Ilissus, Tiber, Thames an' Seine,
Glide sweet in monie a tunefu' line !
But, Willie set your fit to mine,
      An' cock your crest :
We'll gar our streams an' burnies shine
      Up wi' the best.

We'll sing auld Coila's plains and fells,
Her moors red-brown wi' heather bells,
Her banks an' braes, her dens an' dells,
      Where glorious Wallace
Aft bure the gree, as story tells,
      Frae Southron billies.

At Wallace' name, what Scottish blood
But boils up in a spring-tide flood ?
Oft have our fearless fathers strode
      By Wallace' side :
Still pressing onwards, red-wat-shod,
      Or glorious dy'd.

And this profound patriotism had, in that religious country, where religion lies deeper among the peasantry than anywhere else, where the strife of religion has been violent in proportion to the feeling that it was a matter of life and death, its root in God. God was claimed as the source of patriotism ; it was He that made men love their country, he who inspired those who warred for its liberty. I might quote passage after passage from Douglas, from Dunbar, from Sir D. Lyndsay, from the others ; but let Burns himself answer the call—Burns, whose " warmest wish to heaven was sent " for his dear, his native soil.

O Thou ! who poured the patriotic tide
That streamed through Wallace's undaunted heart ,
Who dared to, nobly, stem tyrannic pride,
Or nobly die, the second glorious part,—
The patriot's God, peculiarly thou art,
His friend, inspirer, guardian, and reward—
O never, never, Scotia's realm desert ;
But still the patriot, and the patriot bard,
In bright succession raise, her ornament and guard !

In these days, when we think less of a national and
more of a universal God, it may strike us as limiting and
dividing a great idea to speak of a patriot's God. And,
when we consider well, there is a great disadvantage in
thinking of a God whose peculiar care is England, or
France, or Germany ; indeed, if we do so, in war for example, our idea of God must become wholly confused.
One or other side must be wrong in claiming God as specially theirs. God is the God of mankind ; His equal
love belongs to and falls on all, on the meanest as fully as
on the most cultured races. That is the large conception
which will free us from the national selfishness into which
patriotism degenerates, and increase that international
kindness and communion which are beginning to be a
mark of our time; nay more, bring us slowly up to the
thought which a century hence will, I hope, dominate
politics—national self-sacrifice. The Christian thought of
personal life is to surrender our personal life and its
interests for those among whom we live. The Christian
thought of social life is to surrender our personal interest
for the sake of the well-being of society, not only of our
own country's society, but of human society. The Christian
thought of national life, which has been prominently put
forward by the Comtists, is that each nation, when the

interests of the whole race are concerned in such sacrifice, should give up its national interests for those of all mankind. Till we attain that, and it will necessitate a general confederation of nations, we cannot be called Christian nations, for we are not regulating our national conduct by the Christian rule of life.

Keeping, however, this thought of God clear as the foundation of our life, we are then able—without ill or unreason following from it—to love God as the God of our country also, as the source of a noble patriotism. For we no longer think of God as the God of England in rivalry or contest with other nations, and claim Him as specially ours to the exclusion of others. We say to ourselves, on the contrary—" Our country has a special work to do in the progress of the whole race; work which is fitted to our national character, and which our special gifts enable us to do better than any other nation. It is God who in his education of the whole of mankind has given us that work. Within its sphere, then, and with this object before us, which is first universal, and afterwards national, God is the source of our patriotism." We love our country then in God, when we love it for a higher reason than its own glory—for the reason that it is the instrument of God to do a special work for Man. We support and cherish the peculiar characteristics of England, because these are needful for the growth of mankind. We love and cherish its scenery because that is one of the most formative elements of our national character, and that character is needed for the growth of Man. We are patriots because we are men who believe that the decay or death of England would damage the interests of the whole race, and delay its progress to the great goal whither God is driving it.

And nothing is lost in that idea of the old power and dearness of patriotism. The old conception is taken up into the new, only all the evil of national selfishness is taken out of it. We love our country none the less because we love man more.

14

LECTURE XV.

In my last lecture I spoke of the poetry of Man as found in Burns, and I dwelt especially on the way in which he—in accordance with the new spirit which was stealing into the world—devoted his work to the interests of the poor among whom he lived, not of set purpose like a philanthropist, but because he could not help it like an artist.

It is his natural poetry of which I shall speak to-day, and we can connect it with the previous lecture by the thought that among the joys that God has given to the life of the poor one of the deepest is the beauty of Nature, and the heart to love it; such a heart as Burns himself possessed, who

> " In his glory and his joy
> " Followed the plough along the mountain side."

Things without money or without price, beauty not hid in galleries, but spread abroad a feast of delight on every mountain-side and stream-fed meadow—this was God's gift to the poor.   And strange to say, Burns seems to think, and he should know something about it, that the poor were better able than the rich and cultured to enjoy the

loveliness of the world. That certainly would not be true
of England now; for there are few things we have so
attentively cultivated as the love of Nature. But it may
have been true in his days that

> The Laverock shuns the palace gay,
> And o'er the cottage sings ;
> For Nature smiles as sweet, I ween,
> To shepherds as to Kings.

Wordsworth, too, takes up the same thought ; he himself
is formed by Nature, step by step ; it never seems to occur
to him that his companions—dalesmen, shepherds, ped-
lers, even the little children—can be otherwise than
lovers of Nature, and able to enjoy its beauty; and
we must take his witness as true, for he lived among
them all his life. But this is certainly not the case
further south, and the lower one goes in England, the
less one finds of it, except in the upper classes, among
whom it has now become almost instinctive.

We have, then, this curious problem at the very outset
of our lecture—that the poor of the north-western part
of England on the border, and of the west border of
Scotland, are lovers of Nature, while the poor of midland
and southern England are not. I do not say that I can
solve that problem; I cannot—but I can make a few
conjectures about it, and it will lead me to speak of the
Nature poetry of Scotland, a poetry so distinct from that
of England that it is necessary to say something about it
before we touch on it in Burns.

The higher appreciation of Nature among the men of
the west border may partly be owing to the grandeur or
wildness of the scenery they live amongst. The imagina-

tion cannot help being awakened and impressed by deso-
lation. Fear is easily stirred in boyhood by the storm on
the moor, or the majesty of mountain loneliness, and fear
awakes imagination. Afterwards, when with manhood
comes courage, fear passes into a sense of the sublime,
and terror has its beauty, since it stirs emotion. But
when perception of the sublime exists, perception of the
beautiful in the peace of nature soon follows : the one
throws the perceiver into the arms of the other. That
may be one explanation, but it is not a sufficient one.
It does not account for this love of Nature among the
dwellers in the quiet scenery of Ayr and Lanark.

Therefore I cannot help conjecturing that a great deal of
the intense perception of Nature's beauty which we find in
early Scottish poetry—especially the wild love of colour—
the descriptions of Gawin Douglas blaze like an Oriental
monarch—may be due to some far-off admixture of Celtic
blood. All the Scotch poets of early date possess it, and
it seems to spring out of nothing. There is no cause for
it in the influence which Chaucer and his school had on
poetry in Scotland, for it does not exist among them ;
nor in the French, for there it does not exist at this early
time of which I speak, except, indeed, where one gets a
touch of Celtic influence. In the absence of any real
cause that I can absolutely point to, I am forced to conjecture that this love of nature was a legacy left by the
Celtic blood among the English of the Lowlands. The old
Kingdom of Strathclyde ran up from our present Wales to
the Clyde, taking in the half of the Lowlands and the
more western parts of Northern England. The Celtic
Poets had this intimate desire to look at Nature, this

passion for colour, this wish to glorify the woods and streams, which is so remarkable in Douglas and the rest. They take, as the Scottish Poets do, isolated natural objects—a rock, a tree, a glade—fall in love with them, and bring them with one magical touch into the domain of Fairyland. Their early literature, their romances, their songs are full of this. There is nothing of it in early English poetry. A few distant echoes of it are heard in Shakespeare, but scarcely any true notes of it in England, till Keats and Shelley and Tennyson. In Scotland, we find it at once, not at all in its perfection, but sufficiently distinct to sever Scotch poetry from all others of the time, and to make it of a different race from English.

Now my conjecture is, that this Celtic element of natural love of the beauty of the world, this special power of seeing Nature, and delight in observing her—which came so early to Scotland, and so late to England—crept in from Strathclyde, mingled in the blood of the English of the Lowlands, and left behind it, when the Celtic race died away, its peculiar note in the Lowland mind. Any way, this is true, that Scotland has always been a land where Poets loved Nature, and that she first sent that love down to England.

The original impulse of the Lowland poetry came, as we have seen, from Chaucer through James the First. We might then expect that its natural description, with which we have now to do, would retain some of the peculiarities of Chaucer's landscape. That is not the case. The intense nationality of the Scotch of which I have already spoken, seized on this element in poetry, and at once and for ever put aside the conventional landscape of Chaucer. The Scottish poets could not realize smooth and soft meadows and fair gardens, and trees standing so many feet apart. There was nothing of the kind in Scotland. Their own scenery forced itself on their notice, and they loved it well. In all the poems, the trees, rocks, rivers, and valleys, are distinctly Scotch; the sun rises in Scotland, the months and seasons as described by Douglas have the character of his own country. We may say that the law which bids a poet describe what lies before him, and write with his eye on the object, in distinction from that which insists on the landscape being always made up of certain stock properties, is due to the Scottish Poets. In England it did not *prevail* till Cowper's time—in Scotland, it was carried out, owing to the love of her people for their own country, before the seventeenth century. It is a curious anticipation by many years of the love of Nature for her own sake which was first rooted in our literature by Wordsworth.

With regard to the description of nature itself, it is absolutely unique at the time. It is perfectly amazing to find, in the sixteenth century, in Scotland, elaborate natural description full of close touches of reality, over-laden with colour, minute, enthusiastic, at a time when nothing of the kind existed, or had existed in England. Here and there it is touched by the convention of Chaucer, as in the use of Latin names for the sun—a survival which we find in Burns—but the feeling for Nature of Douglas and Dunbar, and their natural description, are not only unlike anything that had ever been in England, they remain unlike anything which prevailed in England down to the very end of the eighteenth century. The only man in whom we miss this minute, observant, patient effort to represent Nature as she is, is Drummond—and he was not of the Scottish line—he was Elizabethanized. The whole thing is a curious literary problem, and one of the conclusions to be drawn from it, is this—that we owe our special natural poetry to an impulse received from Scotland. It is not too much to say that the first touches of love of Nature in Pope's time which we find in Gay were due to the influence on him of his friend Ramsay's poems. Neither is it strange to find that he who broke away from the tea-tray landscape of Pope, and was the first poet in England who painted Nature directly, was Thomson, a Scotchman, who came to London with the MS. of his "Winter" in his pocket. He started the impulse which ended in the natural poetry of Wordsworth, Shelley, Keats, and Tennyson, but he drew himself the impulse from a long line of Scottish ancestors who had loved and described Nature.

This is the ancestry of the natural poetry of Burns. If we except the extraordinary love of colour which is one of the characteristic marks of the early Scotch poets, he has the same intense love of Nature and accuracy of description that they possessed. In two things, however, he differs from a man like Douglas. First, his range is not so wide. There was nothing Douglas saw which he did not describe—I might even say catalogue, for the things are put down one after another without any power of artistic combination—but there are only certain things which strike Burns. In fact they come in so often and are so nearly always the same, that a certain amount of conventionality prevails in his natural descriptions. It is the ordinary Lowland scenery on the borders of the

hills ; milk-white thorns, corn-fields, running rivers under
birchen shade, the singing of birds, sheep wandering
on the hills, heather and its flowers, streams in spate,
and certain conditions of the sea—with a special love
for spring and winter—winter being always a favourite
of the Scottish poets. He does not get far beyond this
range, and it is, as I said, narrow. But within the
range, it is exquisitely true and tender, the sentiment of
it is perfect, it is never exaggerated, nothing is forced or
over-dwelt on ; it is the natural and swift reproduction in
words of the landscape, and all that is said sounds sweetly
and smells sweetly to the sense.

Secondly, his natural description arises out of a deep
and natural love of Nature, but it is never alone as that
of Douglas was, never without the element of humanity.
In a delightful passage, when the genius of Scotland's
muse speaks to him in vision, Burns expresses his early
passion for natural beauty.

> I saw thee seek the sounding shore,
> Delighted with the dashing roar ;
> Or when the North his fleecy store
>   Drove through the sky,
> I saw grim Nature's visage hoar
>   Strike thy young eye.
>
> Or when the deep green-mantled earth
> Warm cherished every flow'ret's birth,
> And joy and music pouring forth
>   In every grove,
> I saw thee eye the gen'ral mirth
>   With boundless love.

Nature, too, was bound up with his art : it was she who
gave it half its fire, she who thrilled him often with so

much emotion that he broke into poetry, she who was
mingled up with all his love and sorrow in humanity.

> The Muse nae Poet ever found her,
> 'Till by himsel' he learned to wander
> Adown some trotting burn's meander
> An' no think lang:
> O sweet to stray and pensive ponder
> A heartfelt song—

and there is not a song of his which has not its back-
ground of tender landscape.   But strong as this love of
Nature was in Burns, it never wholly absorbed him.   He
could not, like Wordsworth or Shelley or Keats, sit down
in a wood or on a hill-side and describe what he saw, for
the love of it alone, without a thought of humanity, without a thought of self, absolutely lost in love of the world.
His natural descriptions are always the background for
human figures, for human love or sorrow or mirth.   Man
is always first in Burns; and he either wholly subordinates
Nature to humanity, or he uses it as illustrative of human
life.   I take the lines to the " Lass of Ballochmyle."

> 'Twas even, the dewy fields were green :
> On every blade the pearlis hung,
> The zephyrs wantoned round the bean
> And bore its fragrant scents along.
> In every glen the mavis sang,
> All Nature listening seemed the while,
> Except where greenwood echoes rang
> Amang the braes of Ballochmyle—
> With careless step I onward strayed,
> My heart rejoiced in Nature's joy.

That is complete enough.   Wordsworth would have left
it there, Burns cannot—over the braes he brings a
maiden—

Perfection whispered, passing by,
Behold the lass of Ballochmyle.

It is the same in the two well-known poems of " Mary in
Heaven," and the " Banks of Doon,"—his landscape is
always, not for itself, but for the human feeling with
which he links it ; and where the feeling is most deep, the
landscape is most lovely.

This humanization of landscape is the transition step
between a poetry like Pope's which has Man only as its
subject and rejects Nature, and such poetry as much of
Wordsworth's, in which Nature assumes the first place.
It was made in England by such men as Gray and
Collins, in whose work, if you remember, nature is moralized for man's sake, while it is described with a certain
affection.   Burns, who carefully read Gray, represents in
Scotland such a stand-point, only that it is there not in
progress to a future, but in retrogression from a past poetry
of Nature ; and also, the landscape is not moralized by
Burns, but made passionate with love.

He mingled Man and Nature together, and in doing so
he transfers the depth of his personal affections to natural
objects, and speaks of them with often a sudden tenderness, an exquisite mournfulness of pity, or a quick sympathy with their joy.   His address to the daisy makes one
feel for it as if it were a beautiful child too rudely treated.

Wee, modest crimson-tipped flower,
Thou's met me in an evil hour,
For I maun crush amang the stoure
Thy slender stem.
To spare thee now is past my power,
Thou bonie gem.

But even here he cannot, as Wordsworth does, leave the

daisy and its fate alone. He is driven to compare it with helpless maid and luckless Bard—and finally with himself—

> Ev'n thou who mournst the Daisy's fate,
> That fate is thine—no distant date ;
> Stern Ruin's ploughshare drives, elate,
>   Full on thy bloom,
> Till crushed beneath the furrow's weight
>   Shall be thy doom.

The same quick, simple tenderness went to animals. One sees how Burns loved birds in almost every song. He was a hater of field sports ; and even when in driving his plough he turned up the field mouse's nest, he could not bear the sorrow he was causing; he enters into all the pain and wants of the little thing as if it were a child, till he feels that the mouse is his companion and that he has harmed a fellow-creature.

> I'm truly sorry Man's dominion
> Has broken Nature's social union,
> An' justifies the ill opinion,
>   Which makes thee startle,
> At me, thy poor, earth-born companion,
>   An' fellow mortal !

But here, again, he cannot help, like Gray, moralizing, nor in the end getting back to himself.

> But, Mousie, thou art no thy lane,
> In proving foresight may be vain :
> The best laid schemes o' mice an' men
>   Gang aft a-gley,
> An' lea'e us nought but grief an' pain,
>   For promised joy.
>
> Still thou art blest, compared wi' me,
> The present only toucheth thee.
> But, Och ! I backward cast my e'e
>   On prospects drear !
> An' forward, tho' I can na see,
>   I guess an' fear.

Take one more example, which combines this tenderness
of pathos towards the animal creation with one or two of
his vivid natural touches of storm.

> I thought me on the ourie cattle,
> Or silly sheep, wha bide this brattle
>   Of wintry war,
> Or through the drift, deep-lairing sprattle,
>   Beneath a scaur.
>
> Ilk happing bird, wee helpless thing,
> That in the merry months of spring
> Delighted me to hear thee sing,
>   What comes o' thee?
> Where wilt thou cower thy chittering wing
>   And close thy ee?

As to the theology in all this love of nature, there is
not much of it. Burns had no special philosophy any
more than Keats about the relation of God to nature.
He adopted the old simple view of God as the Creator
and sustainer of the universe that the stern religion of
Scotland had taught his fathers. But the poet's love of
all things was so strong in him that he added to that
idea the thought of God as the lover of the universe he
had made and supported. And the love that God had for
the universe was reflected in the breast of Burns, and so
wrought that when he was most full of it, he drew nearest
to God. It was a love which had no wild tempest of passion
in it, which did not strive or cry in his heart. In it he did
not " feel his pulse's maddening play," nor was he hurled
blindly into wrong. Therefore, all the depth of his
nature found in it peace which had no fierce reaction;
and an uplifting of heart which was freed from over-
driven excitement, and pure. It was when nature was
most softly fair, or when it was sublime that Burns drew

nearest to God. He has recorded this himself in a kind of preface to one of his poems.

" There is scarcely any earthly object gives me more— I do not know if I should call it pleasure—but something which exalts me, something which raptures me—than to walk in the sheltered side of a wood or high plantation in a cloudy winter day, and hear the stormy wind howling among the trees, and raving over the plain. It is my best season for devotion: my mind is wrapt up in a kind of enthusiasm to Him, who in the pompous language of the Hebrew bard, ' walks on the wings of the wind.' "

In such a sentence we see Burns lifted for one moment into that imaginative but dark piety which the Covenanter had, and which was largely derived from the solemn and terrible aspects of the mountains and storms he often lived among. But such piety will often be as gloomy and cruel as the climate, and link to itself a superstition passionate and dark with fear in inferior men, stern and unrelenting in stronger men. From this Burns was freed by the tenderness of his heart, which made him, when he was devotional, love and not fear God; and the terror and gloom of nature—never very great in the Lowlands—did not make him stern to others, nor alas! stern to himself. His love of Nature then did not lead him to that practical love of God which shows itself in doing for love's sake what is right.

It is the case of many : love of Nature often goes with a character gifted or sometimes cursed with an intense power of sympathy which shrinks from putting itself in action ; with strong passions which are not controlled by will; with a joyousness and a power of sorrow which carry the man beyond himself into a region where neither piety nor morality exists, and where he becomes of the same temper as Ariel or Puck, so that if either a call of duty then comes, or a temptation, he will be likely to ignore the first, or fall into the latter. In such a state there is no conscience. We see and feel, and no more; we do not think of acting. This was especially the case with. Burns.

Has then the love of Nature no religious power? Is it better to be without it? I cannot think so. Those who do not feel it, who see and love no beauty, may be moral, but they will never reach the nobler enthusiasms of religion : their religion itself will be without the loveliness and tenderness which attract the soul, and their theology more intellectual than spiritual in its statements. Moreover Ruskin is quite right when he says, " that supposing all circumstances otherwise the same with respect to two individuals, the one who loves Nature most will always be found to have more faith in God than the other." For far more fully than in erring man, are certain grand qualities of God revealed in Nature, righteousness, order, justice, peace, omnipotence, beneficence, judgment. It is strange, I think, how much this knowledge of God through His works, and its natural influence in producing faith, has been neglected in religious teaching, when one remembers that the whole of the Old Testament is full of it. All the Hebrew Poets were profound lovers of Nature, but of Nature seen as the revelation of God's character. When God wishes to convince Job of his unalterable goodness and justice, He makes the whole of Nature and its wonders pass before him. He gives him no theological or pious teaching, but out of the whirlwind asks, Hast thou considered, &c., &c. Through the whole range of the poets who speak in the Psalms, the same spirit is felt. The hundredth and fourth Psalm is almost a kosmos, but it begins with the source and power of all—with God. The angels are God's messengers to direct the forces of Nature. Nature herself is the image of God, his possession and his voice. A hundred texts occur to us. The sea is His and He made it, and the strength of the hills is His also. His righteousness is like the great mountains, His judgments as the deep. In wisdom did He make His manifold works, and He himself rejoices in them. The heavens declare His justice, and His glory; and listen to this, Ps. lxv. v. 5—13.

By terrible things in righteousness wilt thou answer us, O God of our salvation; who art the confidence of all the ends of the earth, and of them that are afar off upon the sea:

Which by his strength setteth fast the mountains; being girded with power:

Which stilleth the noise of the seas, the noise of their waves, and the tumult of the people.

They also that dwell in the uttermost parts are afraid at thy tokens: thou makest the outgoings of the morning and evening to rejoice.

Thou visitest the earth and watered it; thou greatly enrichest it with the river of God, which is full of water: thou preparest them corn, when thou hast so provided for it.

Thou waterest the ridges thereof abundantly: thou settlest the furrows thereof; thou makest it soft with showers; thou blessest the springing thereof.

Thou crownest the year with thy goodness; and thy paths drop fatness.

They drop upon the pastures of the wilderness; and the little hills rejoice on every side.

The pastures are clothed with flocks; the valleys also are covered over with corn; they shout for joy, they also sing.

No one wants to take away the work of Science, the result of which among cultivated men is by deepening the observation of Nature to increase the love of it; but we want to add to it this old Hebrew notion of a Divine Life and Character within it; and this ought to be the work of the Poets, whose business it is to give vitality to things. For if we are left to contemplate a dead world, as much as modern science leaves us to do, the true love of Nature—that which exalts and makes tender—will slowly die away; we cannot long give affection to that which we conceive as lifeless. If we would love Nature well, we must find Life in it: and when we find its Life in finding God pervading it, then love of Nature leads to faith in God.

It is true, little of this is found in the New Testament. The Apostles were so overwhelmed with their special practical work, and so overtaken with the multiplicity of it, that it is no wonder we find nothing of their life with Nature, or of Nature as revealing God. But that does not say that it did not exist in them; and it probably did, if they were influenced deeply by the teaching of Christ. For there alone in the New Testament is this love of Nature seen as leading to love of God, is Nature used as revealing God. He himself, as I have often said, has made plain in his life how dear to Him was the beauty of the world. He loved to wander by the lake, among the corn, and on the grassy hills. He marked the aspects of the sky, the growth of trees, and the beauty of flowers. He loved animals, and drew some of his love-liest teaching from their ways. When weary, he sought the hill-top by night; when uplifted by strong communion, the higher ridges of Hermon ; when exceeding sorrowful, the lonely olive grove.

And his teaching lays the whole of Nature under contribution. He makes Nature a parable of which God in His relations to man is an interpretation. The ways of the sun and wind and rain, of the grass and flowers, of the cornfield, the fig-tree and the vine, were all taken up into the religion that He taught. He bid us seek tho Heavenly Father, not only in the words and life in which He manifested God, but in the book of the common things of earth and air. And he who walks with Christ through the world may feel that the love of Nature is religious.

Still more connected with a moral life, and with one which prepares the soul for God, are the same tenderness and love when they are felt for animals. I have already said that no Poet ever more deeply felt the sorrows of created things than Burns, nor stronger anger against their slaughter for sport. The "Wounded Hare" will live in men's memories when hares are no longer shot for sport. To him horses, dogs, birds, the dwellers on the moors and in the grass were friends. When Mailie died

> He lost a friend and neebor dear
> In Mailie dead.

That is the feeling which marks civilization. The savage must slay for life and life's support ; the half-civilized man carries out the practice of the savage without his excuse ; and it is the characteristic of that class of ours, which one of our own day has called the barbarian class, to find amusement in slaying. It is of course a remnant of barbarism, and it is obliged to be kept up by laws which bear hard on the poor, for the sake of the sport of the rich. Before an advancing civilization such laws as the game laws, and such barbarisms as keeping whole tracts of country desert for the sake of game, must perish.

There is no doubt in my mind, that however amusing and however manly such sports may be, they are hardening to the heart; and they set men apart from the nobler thoughts and tenderer feelings of life, not altogether, but up to a certain point. They are cruel, and the indulgence of cruelty, however it may be condoned by society, barbarizes it. And so far as it is cruel and accustoms to cruelty, it separates men from God and from love; and that it is unconscious cruelty and is not felt as such by the conscience, does not make the matter better, but worse. One of the things then that our Christianity has to get rid of, is the destruction of life for the sake of sport; of all sports which bring with them needless suffering of animals and needless irritation of men. The whole thing is a part of that aristocratic element which lingers still among us, but is passing to its fall.

Every Poet then, who like Burns, increases that larger tenderness of the heart which not only loves men, but hates to give pain to the lower animals, is, so far at least, religious in his poetry. And nearly all our later Poets have done this sacred work, and have made it a part of their theology. Their device has been the device of Coleridge.

> He prayeth well, who loveth well
> Both man and bird and beast.

LECTURE XVI.

I HAVE spent two Sunday afternoons in speaking of
the poetry of Man and of Nature and of the theology in
them, as represented in the work of Burns. Our subject
to-day is concerned with some aspects of his life so far as
they bear on the personal religion that appears in his
poetry, and with his relation as a Poet to a special form
of theology.

We have seen how well and manfully, when he was
young, he accepted his place as a poor man, and how he
honoured Poverty by song. But his poverty did not
guard him against the temptations which beset his artist
nature. He had but little power of Will when his passions were excited, and whether it was love, or fame, or
the pleasures of the table, he was swept away by all alike.
The natural result of this course of life, combined with
want of Will, was that he never set himself to any
ordered music, never adopted or pursued any end with
any perseverance. These elements in his character were
developed into unfortunate prominence by his visit to
Edinburgh. He was taken out of his natural atmosphere,
and though he kept his independence, and retained his
free nature, his life was spoilt by the change. His frank

ness and audacious personality made him unwelcome to those who had lionized him at first, and he was gradually dropped. And when he was put aside he did not like it, and he could never breathe easily again the air of humble life. It was a severe trial. A few weeks before he was flying from his country, an exile and in despair, and now he was at the summit of the wave of Society, his name in every mouth. A few weeks later and the whole pageant had dissolved. He was back again in a small country place, discharging the most unpoetical of offices. He took the glory and the fall with equal good temper and manliness, though they both intensified his errors. He was not dazzled at Edinburgh into believing that his fortune was made. He knew that he was too bold and rough to win patronage, and he went home to fulfil his duties as an exciseman, the only place that Society could find to employ the genius of Burns. It was like Society; and yet, though we are indignant, it would be unfair to lay all the blame of the Poet's life on the neglect of Society. If Burns had been a little nobler in character, with some self-restraint, some purposefulness in life, he might have been happy and written his poems, as an exciseman. But he could not; passions, appetites, and irregular excitement carried far beyond what he could bear, soon ruined his life. He had gained a taste for fame, and he was continually invaded by persons who led him away from his work. His fashionable life produced results which brought him to an early death. It stimulated the fatal qualities of his nature; it spoilt the unity of his life by fixing one end of its axis among the rich and another among the poor, and it threw him into the worst company—the

company of the lionizers of genius, who seek it to be amused
and then mock at the source of their amusement. It was,
no doubt, his own fault that he perished; but it would have
been well, if the big people had let him alone, or at least,
if they who flattered him had done something better for
him than set him to catch smugglers. It is all well
summed up in Carlyle's " Lectures on Heroes; " in a
delightful passage, which I remember being told by one
who heard it, was closed exactly as it is in the book—
Carlyle pronouncing with inimitable meaning in his voice
the last word " But"—and then rapidly passing behind
the curtain of the platform.

" Richter says, in the island of Sumatra there is a kind
of Light-chafers—large fireflies—which people stick on
spits and illuminate the ways with at night. Persons
of condition can thus travel with a pleasant radiance,
which they much admire. Great honour to the fire-flies!
But —— ! "

I do not think I ever see fine and fashionable people
" taking up " a poor artist, or making a show in their
drawing-rooms of a struggling genius—and trying, in
their blind, barbarian way, to help him on,—especially
when they demand that the artist should submit his individuality to their caprices—without a desire to say to
him— For God's sake, bear any poverty rather than yield
to this. They do not mean badly, but they have no
intelligence to mean better; and their tender mercies will
kill your powers. You may not be Samson, but it is
bitter to make sport for the Philistines. It degrades the
intellect and corrodes the heart.

There were two things, then, in his life which spoiled

him. Want of aim was one; and unrestrained passion was the other; and both characterize one type of the artist, the second or rather the third-rate type. In the highest artist, the aim of his life is clear, and he never fails to see it and to labour for it. His passion also, which he must possess, is always in his power. He may choose to indulge it, but he does so purposely, and he can check it when he will with ease; but he rarely chooses to indulge it to the prejudice of his art, whatever that art may be. For the sake of his art, he wills to be temperate and he is; and while enjoying all things to the very top of enjoyment, he is always capable of staying his hand at the point where enjoyment threatens to pass into satiety.

Burns had neither of these qualities. "The great misfortune of my life," he says, "was to want an aim:" and bitterly he regrets it in hours when solemn thought was uppermost. The note he strikes at the end of his "Address to the Field Mouse" is still more plainly heard in the "Ode to Despondency,"—

> Happy, ye sons of busy life,
> Who, equal to the bustling strife,
> No other view regard!
> E'en when the wished end's deny'd,
> Yet while the busy means are ply'd,
> They bring their own reward:
> Whilst I, a hope-abandoned wight,
> Unfitted with an aim,
> Meet every sad returning night
> And joyless morn the same.

At other times—and how characteristic this is of such a nature—he accepts his aimlessness as a good thing, or at least, as something which cannot be helped, and is to

be made the best of. He is in good spirits, his mood is
happy, and he contrasts his thoughtless and wild enjoyment with the miserable state of those that live by rule,
whose hearts are never touched by impulse :—

> For me, an aim I never fash ;
>   I rhyme for fun.
>
> *   *   *   *   *
>
> I'll wander on, wi' tentless heed
> How never-halting moments speed,
> Till fate shall snap the brittle thread,
>   Then, all unknown,
> I'll lay me with th' inglorious dead,
>   Forgot and gone !
> But why o' death begin a tale ?
> Just now we're living, sound an' hale ;
> Then top and maintop crowd the sail,
>   Heave Care o'er side !
> And large, before Enjoyment's gale,
>   Let's tak the tide.
>
> *   *   *   *   *
>
> An anxious e'e I never throws
> Behint my lug, or by my nose ;
> I jouk beneath Misfortune's blows
>   As weel's I may ;
> Sworn foe to Sorrow, Care, and Prose,
>   I rhyme away.

And then he turns upon those whose life he half despises,
and at times half regrets :—

> O, ye douce folk, that live by rule,
> Grave, tideless-blooded, calm, and cool.
> Compared wi' you—O fool ! fool ! fool !
>   How much unlike ;
> Your hearts are just a standing pool,
>   Your lives a dyke !

I have no special fondness for over-purpose in life, for
living by rule. The common advice—find one aim, and
pursue it to the exclusion of all others, is good worldly

advice, but that is not always the best. He who allows
everything else to be absorbed in the pursuit of one
aim will probably succeed in his aim, and be called by
the world the most prudent and intelligent of men.
He may be prudent, but he will scarcely be intelligent.
For he will become a man of only one thought, and all
those parts of his nature which he cannot bring into
activity round his special thought, will become dead for
want of use. He will not, and he cannot grow. It is
better to be like Burns than to be one of that type.

But if the aim you propose to yourself be one of
those which, because they are ideal, seek their food from
every quarter, and claim as helpers the powers of heart,
spirit, and brain ; if it allow not only of enjoyment
and growth through variety of interests, but also of
wise passiveness and healthy idleness ; and yet is itself
so pure and high as to prevent passiveness from producing sloth, and activity from degenerating into a
disease—then to have a clear aim is absolutely right,
and man, in fact, cannot achieve greatness in life, or
worthiness within, unless he have it. But if he has such
an aim, its very essential difference is, that it sets its
possessor free from the slavery of over labour ; that it
takes him out of the class of the " douce folk who live by
rule." And the great artist possesses it : Burns did not.

The other lesson of the life of Burns, is that of the
evil of unrestrained passion. I do not use the word in
the sense of the passion of love, though that was the
special frailty of Burns ; but of all deep emotion, whether
arising from appetite, or sense, or the vision of ideas. In
this large sense, it is not passion itself which is harmful ;

nay, as I have often said, nothing can be done well without emotion; nothing perfectly without intense emotion. The cold-hearted folk, however practical, have no powerful influence on the world. And in all art, it is absolutely necessary. "Put your passion into it," says Keats; and he gives in that phrase the first principle of art. We have already seen that because Burns possessed this quality, he poured new life blood into English poetry. And all that was best in the man and his poetry came out of it:—his spirit of universal kindness, his indignation at wrong, his inability to cringe, his insight into nature, his love of animals, his vivid entrance into, and his glorifying of common life, his deep religious feeling towards Him whose very self was Love—nay, we owe to it even the goodness in his badness, the touch of wild self-sacrifice, of a higher love than the sensuous love in his sins, which did not redeem them, but made them more capable of pardon, more open to repentance than those sins of self which do not shock society. Nor was he unaware of this himself, and he has said it with his own special force :—

> I saw thy pulse's maddening play
> Wild send thee Pleasure's devious way,
> Misled by Fancy's meteor ray,
>   By Passion driven :
> But yet the light that led astray
>   Was light from Heaven.

You see, he does not deceive himself, for Burns had one of the noblest qualities a man can possess—entire sincerity with himself; it never occurred to him to be untrue. Though the light of Heaven was in the affection, yet, through his own fault of will, it led him astray.

15

There was no will towards Right strong enough to check the rushing tide of enjoyment. Impulse and its gratification took the moment and became its master. Whether it was the pleasure of society, or the appetite for drink, or the passion of love, or the fire of indignation, it was all the same ; he was swept away into their extreme : and of course became in turn the prey of dark despondency, of torturing remorse, of religious gloom, of the evils of over-indulged satire.

He ran the course so many run. Having no restraint of self, he sank into satiety, and the misery of satiety seeks a new excitement or new phases of the old—till excitement becomes the only food of life. But there is a limit to excitements. The time comes when either no more exist or we have exhausted all our powers of enjoyment. Then come the tyranny and the punishment. We again seek the old excitement, driven by its lash, but when we drain the cup which once was pleasure, it is pain. The "crime of sense is avenged by sense that wears with time." It is that very torture which the mediæval poets invented for the avaricious—molten gold poured down their throats ; our enjoyments have become red-hot and burn our life away ; nor, worst of all, can we get rid of them —we must drink them though we abhor them.

Enjoyment is a necessity of life, and its morning air. It is equally vain and wicked to lessen or decry it, for we have not half enough of it. But it is a shameful thing when men, not ruling it with temperance, degrade it in the eyes of others by making it equivalent to satiety. Enjoy then ; but keep the beauty of enjoyment by self-restraint in it; and then I venture to say—though there are those so utterly base as to restrain themselves in vicious enjoyment that they may keep the pleasures of sin longer—that your enjoyments will on the whole keep pure, that there will not be much in them which will offend the eye of God, that they will serve your growth, and give you power to do all your work in a stronger and finer manner.

Again, wanting all will in passion, Burns wanted, when under its dominion, the sense of right and wrong. In the hour of excited feeling he was willing to let everything go—Law, Honour, Conscience, and Religion. Nothing remained but his passion; and it was right, and everything that stood in its way, wrong. It made its own wrong and right, and as usual the two became inextricably mixed together—for apart from the moral question, it is the oddest thing in all such states of feeling that there is often really a touch of right in the wrongness, and a shade of wrong in the rightness that we feel.

But it is not a good thing when the conscience gets puzzled; and when it gets altogether confounded, as it sometimes does, and goes, wearied out, to sleep, and leaves passion to have its own way—not only is much sin done, but this also happens—all the charm and good of passionate feeling dies or begins to die.

> I wave the quantum of the sin,
> The hazard of concealing,
> But och ! it hardens a' within,
> And petrifies the feeling.

There is no enduringness in passion of any kind when

it deliberately drugs the conscience. For the conscience wakes out of its heavy sleep when the day of excitement has passed by, and wakes up so angry that it lets in remorse, and remorse is an ill companion. It does not heal, it so mauls the soul that the memory of the excitement becomes poisonous. And it finally ends by bringing on the reckless indulgence which is hated while it is going on, and which adds, when exhaustion comes, another bitter element to the curse of satiety. The glory and delight of true passion are destroyed, and the man ends as Burns ended, in a ruined and wasted life. "The wind bloweth over him and he is gone, and the place of him knoweth him no more." This is the lesson of the life of Burns. He knew it himself. He puts it at the close of the epitaph he wrote for himself.

> Reader, attend !—whether thy soul
> Soars fancy's flights beyond the pole,
> Or darkling grubs this earthly hole,
>   In low pursuit :
> Know—prudent, cautious, self-control
>   Is wisdom's root.

Yes ! and enjoyment's root also; though I should take exception to the words "prudent" and "cautious." For no life can be perfect which is overmastered by either prudence or caution.

Again, the special theological turn which some of his poems took, arose out of this unbridled passionateness. For their strong opposition to Calvinism was more the result of anger at the penance the kirk imposed on him for open sin than of any religious zeal. He seized on the patent objections to the doctrines of reprobation, effectual calling and the rest, and used them as stalking horses for his avenging satire; and the bitter feud which existed on these doctrinal subjects between MacGill and Dalrymple, the two ministers of the town of Ayr, supplied him with all the opportunity he wanted. His first satirical poem, " The Holy Tulzie " (quarrel), ridiculed a quarrel between two ministers, Moodie and Russel, on " effectual calling," and delighted the opponents of Calvinism. It was followed by " Holy Willie's Prayer," the most ferocious blow that was ever dealt at the ugly side of Calvinism—over ferocious, as usual with Burns, to do any really good work against it; and so full of coarseness and wild irreverence that it only shows how high religious rancour ran among the clergy when these elements in it were condoned by one side for the sake of the occasion it gave them against their enemies.

It is true that Burns, in his wiser moments, would always have been a foe to the extreme Calvinistic doctrines, on the ground that he felt, being a lover of all things himself, that they made God into a Demon of Selfishness. His heart, like Shelley's, hated and denied that dreadful theology. But he never saw the good or the poetry which underlie its ideas, and his attack on it was just as much, if not more, caused by the natural reaction of the Bohemian nature against the ascetic type of Calvinism. Of that type he found two forms: one the stern, righteous asceticism, which condemned all gaiety as unworthy of an immortal soul; which secluded the religious man wholly from all worldly things as in themselves profane; which chastised with the utmost severity of word and deed all sin, and especially the sins of passion; and which lived up to this standard truthfully;—the other the sham asceticism—a type Calvinism is sure to produce by its unnatural strictness—the crime of men who, wearing the mask of a stern religion, in secret indulged in all kinds of wickedness, and then fell back on their election by God to eternal life to free them from fear, and to enable them to sin at their ease.

Against the first Burns proclaimed the doctrine of a more liberal religion, and claimed the right of enjoyment; and so far he was right. But he could no more put limits to the statement of this than he could put limits to his own practice of it, and the statement went so far as to condone immorality of every kind. Conviviality was glorified, drunkenness was exalted into an excellence, illicit love was made poetical, and in the delight of the reaction from the over-strictness of Calvinism, which the poems of Burns encouraged, the whole tone of morality in Scotland was lowered; and in nothing more than in the frightful impulse given to a hospitality which insisted on the canonization of drunkenness, and made the pleasures of the table the true impulse of art and song. We trace this even in the works of a man like Wilson, whose "Noctes" are deformed by it.

Whatever thanks then we may owe to Burns for his exposure of the ghastly side of Calvinism, must be largely modified by the evil he did in the way he exposed it. It is a bad thing to expel an evil opinion by an evil practice, and though it sounds like a paradox, it is not so uncommon.

Against the second, that is, the sham asceticism which was a cloak of sin, the indignation of Burns was righteous.

We cannot but rejoice at the way in which he flayed alive William Fisher, the Holy Willie of the Poem, a leading elder, " a great pretender to sanctity, austere of speech," and rigid in observance. He died drunk in a ditch, and his life was as immoral as his death was vile. But the besetting sin of want of self-restraint is as visible here as in the former case. Burns was overmastered by his impulse to satire as he was by his impulse to indulge appetite. In attacking hypocrisy, he was swept away to impute hypocrisy to nearly all who lived a strict life or were severe in speech or manners. In condemning uncharitableness he became himself uncharitable.

A free life which loses love to the unloving, is on the point of drifting into that temper in which liberty is made the servant of uncharitableness; and that freedom is not freedom which is bound to be abusive. Burns often had no mercy on unmercifulness, and it often wants it as much as frailty. Nothing can be better than his address to the unco guid or rigidly righteous; these lines that I read are steeped in the spirit of Christianity,—

> Then gently scan your brother Man,
>   Still gentler sister Woman ;
> Though they may gang a kennin wrang,
>   To step aside is human :
> One point must still be greatly dark,
>   The moving *Why* they do it ;
> And just as lamely can ye mark,
>   How far perhaps they rue it.
>
> Who made the heart, 'tis He alone
>   Decidedly can try us,
> He knows each chord its various tone,
>   Each spring its various bias :

Then at the balance let's be mute,
  We never can adjust it;
What's *done* we partly may compute,
  But know not what's *resisted*.

But he forgot, and indeed it is the hardest thing Charity has to remember, that the unco guid are often as much the victims of circumstances as the weakly sinful. They are born, many of them, with as much of the milk of human kindness in them as others, but their education—their sect and its restrictions, the severity of their parents, the whole atmosphere of gloom and terror which their religion gives them to breathe—have crushed all tenderness and mercy out of them, and when they come to be men and women, they have stones for hearts. And they are intensely disagreeable and often shamefully cruel. But, if they are not hypocrites, they are worthy of infinite pity: for their evil may partly be not their fault, and if they wish to escape from it, nothing can be more difficult. The anger they arouse in men, the way they are naturally left alone, fixes them in their moroseness and seems to excuse it. Their sin is bound upon them; if they strive to break through it, they are met by a disbelief only too well earned, and they are soured the more. It is their punishment, but it is, if we think charitably, a very pitiful thing. Our work on them should not be that of abuse, but of effort to pierce through the rock to where the springs of human kindness lie in them. We should meet half way any effort they may make, forgive at once and say—" To-day I will abide at thine house;" so shall we perhaps, with Christ, save a soul by love.

But Burns became still more wrong when he made the evil lives of persons who seemed to be religious into a kind of excuse for his own evil. "At least he made no boast," we may say, and we trace the spirit of this excuse in his poetry, "he did not conceal his wrong doing, nor use religion as a garment to cover sin." But this is the worst of sophisms. That others are very bad, worse than we, does not make our badness one whit the less bad; and that we are sincere in the midst of our sin, while others are insincere in theirs, proves, it is true, that our character is higher, and that we have more chance of repentance, but it does not make our sinfulness less.

Nor, indeed, did Burns often make such an excuse for himself. It was only when he was irritated and in opposition. He was at root true, and he never flinched from self blame. But he had no force to make self-blame into active repentance, and he went on sinning and being sorry, and sinning again, to the end of the chapter—

> To right or left, eternal swervin'
> He zigzagged on.—

Knowing the right, he could not consistently do it; and the misery of that was deep and was one of the things which killed him. You may remember his epistle to Andrew Aiken, a noble piece of good advice, the last two verses of which are worth quoting. The first shows how well he knew his own wrong and the right he wanted, while nothing can be more pathetic than the quiet despair of the last two lines, "Video meliora, deteriora sequor,"—

When ranting round in pleasure's ring,
  Religion may be blinded ;
Or if she gie a random sting,
  It may be little minded ;
But when in life we're tempest driven,
  A conscience but a canker—
A correspondence fixed wi' Heaven
  Is sure a noble anchor !

Adieu, dear, amiable youth !
  Your heart can ne'er be wanting !
May prudence, fortitude, and truth
  Erect your brow undaunting !
In ploughman phrase, "God send you speed,"
  Still daily to grow wiser ;
And may ye better reck the rede
  Than ever did th' Adviser.

His was not the temperament which drifts into irreligion. His sinfulness and his consciousness of it, which never became less bitter, kept him always from infidelity. He was always, like the Prodigal Son, coming to himself and saying—"I will arise and go to my Father," —but he never got more than half-way in this world. Even if he had been a philosopher as well as a Poet, the need of his nature for sympathy and for some one to lean on, would have always prevented him from Atheism. His fear and his love alike made him confess a God; but the God he confessed was never brought near enough to his heart and life to have over him the influence of a person whom he knew loved him well enough to die for him. I see no trace in Burns's poetry that Christ had any meaning to him; I see nothing but a fine Theism. God was the unknown, Almighty Cause of all his hope and fear, his judge, the author of his conscience; the giver to him of passions wild and strong,

to whom he appealed for mercy since He was all-good;
who could not act from cruelty or wrath, on whom
with all his sins he threw himself for pity—

> Where human weakness has come short,
>   Or frailty stept aside,
> Do thou, All Good ! for such thou art,
>   In shades of darkness hide.
> Where with intention I have erred,
>   No other plea I have,
> But, thou art good, and Goodness still
>   Delighteth to forgive.

It might have given Burns strength to conquer his errors
if he could have felt for Christ the same kind of personal
love which he felt for Man and Nature. What he wanted
is what most of us who have anything of his temperament want, a higher motive of love. The sins which
arise from the weakness that passion engenders cannot be
overcome by struggling with them; they are too strong
for us. But when we have a higher love for a perfectly
good and loving person who is our divine Friend,
than we have for any one on earth, then that love
enables us to conquer. A heavenly passion only subdues the evil that is in earthly passion. But Burns
could not get that. The Christ presented to him had, ac-
cording to the teaching of that time and country, nothing
in the world to do with him. He had not loved him, nor
died for him, did not care about him: the Christian
ministers of Ayrshire blotted out Christ for Burns,
and threw him back unhelped upon himself. He had no
refuge but Theism, and Theism was not enough for him,
though it may be enough for some. So he died, still
weak, still self-victimized, still longing for good, and still

unable to realize it; and the tenderest and wisest thing
we can say of his life in this world is in part of his own
epitaph :—

> Is there a man whose judgment clear,
> Can others teach the course to steer,
> Yet runs, himself, life's mad career,
>   Wild as the wave :
> Here pause—and, through the starting tear,
>   Survey this grave.
>
> The poor Inhabitant below
> Was quick to learn and wise to know,
> And keenly felt the friendly glow,
>   And softer flame :
> But thoughtless follies laid him low,
>   And stained his name.

And the noblest thing we can say of him in the future
we may say in the words of Wordsworth—words which
concentrate much of what I have said as to the good and
evil results of his life and work on mankind—words
which finally leave the shattered life and wasted soul
in the arms where Burns would, at last, gladly nestle
and be at peace,—

> Enough of sorrow, wreck, and blight;
> Think rather of those moments bright
> When to the consciousness of right
>   His course was true,
> When Wisdom prospered in his sight
>   And virtue grew.
>
> *   *   *   *   *
>
> Through busiest street and loneliest glen
> Are felt the flashes of his pen ;
> He rules mid winter snows, and when
>   Bees fill their hives ;
> Deep in the general heart of men
>   His power survives.

What need of fields in some far clime
Where Heroes, Sages, bards sublime,
And all that fetched the flowing rhyme
  From genuine springs,
Shall dwell together till old Time
  Folds up his wings?

Sweet Mercy! to the gates of Heaven
This Minstrel lead, his sins forgiven;
The rueful conflict, the heart riven
  With vain endeavour,
And memory of Earth's bitter leaven,
  Effaced for ever.

But why to Him confine the prayer,
When kindred thoughts and yearnings bear
On the frail heart the purest share
  With all that live?
The best of what we do and are,
  Just God, forgive!

THE END.

CHRIST IN MODERN LIFE.

SERMONS PREACHED IN ST. JAMES CHAPEL, LONDON.

By Rev. STOPFORD A. BROOKE, M. A.,

Honorary Chaplain-in-Ordinary to the Queen.

I volume, 12mo. Cloth. . . . . . . Price, $2.00.

D. APPLETON & CO., Publishers,

549 & 551 BROADWAY, NEW YORK.

PRIMARY TRUTHS OF RELIGION.

By Right Rev. THOMAS M. CLARK, D. D., LL. D.,

BISHOP OF RHODE ISLAND.

1 vol., 12mo.   Price, $1.00.

From the *Alligemeine Literarsche Zeitung*, Berlin:

" We find in this book of the Bishop of Rhode Island a contribution to Christian apologetics of great interest and value. The book discusses, in five parts, the problems of Theism, the fundamental principles of morals, revelation, inspiration, and Christianity. The great questions pertaining to these several heads Bishop Clark has most satisfactorily solved with a genuine philosophical spirit, and on the basis of comprehensive studies. The work gives evidence throughout of the author's familiarity with the fundamental problems of the philosophy of religion. The Bishop is, without doubt, an eloquent and original thinker; and his work, which, in its logical development, is acute, and clear, and precise, will enchain the interest of the readers for whom it has been written. As a short but exhaustive book for doubters, we greet this production of one of the most distinguished members of the American Episcopate, and wish for it an abiding success."

From the *English Churchman and Clerical Journal*, London:

" Bishop Clark has published this pithy treatise to meet the unsettled state of mind of his own countrymen in relation to the ' fundamental principles of faith and morals.' The language is admirably lucid and clear, and the meaning of the writer is never buried under profound and technical phraseology, too often used in such works. Clergymen will find it excellently fitted for teaching to thoughtful working-men in their parishes."

* From the *Church Opinion*, London:

" Bishop Clark's work is invaluable, as it is not written in a style above the capabilities of the general public, but, in words easy to be understood, refutes the doctrines of Positivism."

From a review in the *Literary World*, London:

" We welcome this book from the pen of an American Bishop. Dr. Clark has done well in this volume on 'The Primary Truths of Religion.' With clearness, conciseness, logical force, breadth of tone, wise discrimination, convincing statement, he deals with fundamental facts. Indeed, the whole work is one which may be put into the hand of any thoughtful, sincere unbeliever in the great truths with which it deals. Its candor will awaken admiration, and its reasoning lead to faith."

From the *New York Express :*

" The author of this valuable little work is a distinguished Bishop of the Protestant Episcopal Church, and has conferred a benefit on his co-religionists and on earnest Christians generally, by the production of this estimable hand-book of Orthodoxy. Avoiding dogmatic theology, he clearly and with great eloquence presents the scriptural and historical evidences in favor of revealed religion, meeting the cavils of objectors with calm and well-digested arguments that will claim attention from even the most confirmed skeptics. The chapters on the evidences of the great truths of Christianity are especially worthy of commendation. Indeed, the whole work will prove an acceptable addition to the controversial religious literature of the day."

From the Boston *Transcript :*

" This clear and candid treatise is not dogmatic, but entirely true to its title. The writer, in a plain and lucid style, addresses himself to the unsettled condition of mind which prevails so extensively in regard to the doctrines that underlie all our 'Systems of Divinity.' His answers to fundamental questions are given in a catholic spirit that recognizes the fact that doubt is not sinful in itself, and there is no little skepticism which is to be treated with sympathetic and rational consideration."

From *The Living Church :*

" The book of the Bishop of Rhode Island is timely. It is of a kind which the church needs. It is fair, honest, and open. It does not sneer at what it does not understand. It addresses itself in simple and honest terms to honest and thoughtful men. It is calm and judicial. It states opposing views with great fairness; it takes up a position which must command respect, and it states it in terms which are moderate, and show appreciation of the force of opposing views."

New York: D. APPLETON & CO., Publishers, 549 & 551 Broadway.

A thoughtful and valuable contribution to the best religious literature
of the day.

RELIGION AND SCIENCE.

A Series of Sunday Lectures on the Relation of Natural and Revealed
Religion, or the Truths revealed in Nature and Scripture.

By JOSEPH LE CONTE,

PROFESSOR OF GEOLOGY AND NATURAL HISTORY IN THE UNIVERSITY OF CALIFORNIA.

12mo, cloth.   Price, $1.50.

OPINIONS OF THE PRESS.

" This work is chiefly remarkable as a conscientious effort to reconcile
the revelations of Science with those of Scripture, and will be very useful to teachers of the different Sunday-schools."—*Detroit Union.*

"It will be seen, by this *résumé* of the topics, that Prof. Le Conte
grapples with some of the gravest questions which agitate the thinking
world.   He treats of them all with dignity and fairness, and in a manner so clear, persuasive, and eloquent, as to engage the undivided attention of the reader.   We commend the book cordially to the regard
of all who are interested in whatever pertains to the discussion of these
grave questions, and especially to those who desire to examine closely
the strong foundations on which the Christian faith is reared."—*Boston
Journal.*

" A reverent student of Nature and religion is the best-qualified man
to instruct others in their harmony.   The author at first intended his
work for a Bible-class, but, as it grew under his hands, it seemed well to
give it form in a neat volume.   The lectures are from a decidedly religious stand-point, and as such present a new method of treatment."
—*Philadelphia Age.*

"This volume is made up of lectures delivered to his pupils, and is
written with much clearness of thought and unusual clearness of expression, although the author's English is not always above reproach.
It is partly a treatise on natural theology and partly a defense of the
Bible against the assaults of modern science.   In the latter aspect the
author's method is an eminently wise one.   He accepts whatever science has proved, and he also accepts the divine origin of the Bible.
Where the two seem to conflict he prefers to await the reconciliation,
which is inevitable if both are true, rather than to waste time and words
in inventing ingenious and doubtful theories to force them into seeming
accord.   Both as a theologian and a man of science, Prof. Le Conte's
opinions are entitled to respectful attention, and there are few who will
not recognize his book as a thoughtful and valuable contribution to the
best religious literature of the day."—*New York World.*

D. APPLETON & CO., Publishers, 549 & 551 Broadway, N. Y.

THE EXPANSE OF HEAVEN;

A Series of Essays on the Wonders of the Firmament.

By R. A. PROCTOR, B. A.

1 vol., 12mo. Cloth. . . . . . Price, $2.00.

"It is Mr. Proctor's good fortune that not only is he one of the greatest of living astronomers, but that he has a power of imparting knowledge that is not equaled by any living astronomer. His style is as lucid as the light with which he deals so largely, and the plainest of readers can go along with him with entire ease, and comprehend all that he says on the grandest subject ever discussed by mortal intelligence. Most scientific writers either cannot or will not so use the pen as to make themselves understood by the many; not so with Mr. Proctor: he both can and does so write as to command the attention of the million, and this too without in the least derogating from the real dignity of his sublime theme. Few of us can study astronomy, because that implies a concentrated devotion to an inexhaustible matter, but we all can read astronomical works to our great advantage if astronomers who write will but write plainly; and in that way, without having the slightest claim to be spoken of as "scientists," we can acquire no ordinary amount of knowledge concerning things that are of the loftiest nature, and the effect of which must be to elevate the mind. Such a book as 'The Expanse of Heaven' cannot fail to be of immense use in forwarding the work of education even when it is read only for amusement, so forcible is the impression it makes on the mind from the importance of the subjects treated of, while the manner of treatment is so good."—*Boston Traveller.*

"Since the appearance of Ennis's book on 'The Origin of the Stars,' we have not read a more attractive work on astronomy than this. It is learned enough to be instructive, and light enough to be very entertaining."—*Alta California.*

"It reads like a work of fiction, so smooth and consecutive is it; but it inspires the worthiest thoughts and the highest aspirations."—*Boston Commonwealth.*

"Perfectly adapted to their purposes, namely, to awaken a love for science, and at the same time to convey, in a pleasant manner, some elementary facts."—*Church Herald.*

"This is not a technically scientific work, but an expression of a true scholar's conception of the vastness and grandeur of the heavens. There is no dry detail, but blended with the scholar's discoveries are the poet's thoughts, and a true recognition of the Almighty's power."—*Troy Times.*

D. APPLETON & CO., Publishers,

549 & 551 BROADWAY, N. Y.

FRENCH HOME-LIFE.

Reprinted from Blackwood's Magazine.

SECOND EDITION.

One Volume, 12mo.   Cloth, $1.50.

CONTENTS :

Servants—Children—Furniture—Food—Manners—Language—
Dress—Marriage.

"This is a work of singular knowledge, written by a man possessing rare powers of observation and social tact. That the writer has resided long in France, the most superficial glance into the book will make clear ; for, whatever the passing traveler can do, he cannot attain to such result of clear picture, vivid contrast, and firm hold on general causes as we have here. The chief value of the work—apart from its graceful, lively style—is that, together with the familiarity which long residence gives, we have all the freshness of an outside beholder. This makes it simply delightful reading both to those who know and those who do not know French life."—*British Quarterly Review.*

"The present book of essays, which might in justice be called a guide-book to the French mind, will tell the reader all that he ought to know by this time, and certainly does not know, about French ways. Less amusing than M. Taine's work on England, it is deeper and in the main truer. The writer, indeed, does not aim at being amusing; he seeks to give philosophical analyses of the customs which constitute home-life on the other side of the Channel, and he quite succeeds."—*Pall Mall Gazette.*

"'French Home-Life' is so rich in suggestive remarks and interesting details, it is so full of the knowledge derived from practical experience, that the reviewer is tempted, as the reader probably will be, to linger over its pages. A book like this is fruitful of thought and comment, and the kindly spirit that pervades it is worthy of all praise."—*Spectator.*

"This is a book which will help to dispel the remains of a very unfair and antiquated prejudice, and we therefore welcome it with sincere pleasure."—*Morning Advertiser.*

"He dissipates a variety of delusions which are too general in England, and it is to be hoped that his book will persuade us to take more charitable views of our friends across the Channel, in enlightening us as to their real natures and actual habits."—*Times.*

"A clearer, a truer, and in many instances a better idea of the people of France as a people, in their manners and habits as they live, than has hitherto been commonly and ignorantly entertained in this country."—*Morning Post.*

"Nous en avons assez dit pour faire comprendre tout l'attrait que présente un pareil livre. En le lisant les Anglais apprennent à mieux nous juger; nous apprendrons, nous, à mieux nous connaître."—*Journal de Paris.*

New York: D. APPLETON & CO.

WILKES, SHERIDAN, FOX.

The Opposition under George the Third.

By W. F. RAE.

8vo.   Cloth. . . . . Price, $2.00.

A Splendid Work, Gorgeously Illustrated.

MILITARY AND RELIGIOUS LIFE

IN

THE MIDDLE AGES,

AND AT THE

Period of the Renaissance.

By PAUL LACROIX.

Illustrated with Fourteen Chromo-lithographic Prints, by F. Kellerhoven, Régamey, and L. Allard, and upward of Four Hundred Engravings on Wood. One Volume Imperial Octavo. Half Morocco, $12.00; Half Calf, and Half Morocco Extra, $15.00; Calf, $18.00.

"Lately we published the 'Manners, Customs, and Dress, during the Middle Ages,' a necessary sequel to 'The Arts of the Middle Ages.' To understand this important period of our history, we must, as was pointed out at the time, go back to the very source of art, and study society itself—the life of our forefathers. The volume of 'Manners and Customs' initiated our readers into all the secrets of Civil Life; the present work treats of the Military and Religious Life of the same period. It is superfluous to say any thing about the chromo-lithographs and engravings contained in this volume. They have been selected with the same view that dictated the publication of those appearing in the two previous volumes—a desire to produce a living image of the past. Each volume forms a collection of archæological treasures, got together after the most laborious research; they are attractive to the eye, full of interest and instruction, and we feel that our readers will have in them a complete museum, such as has not hitherto been within their reach."—*Extract from Preface.*

D. APPLETON & CO., Publishers,

549 & 551 BROADWAY, N. Y.

INTERNATIONAL SCIENTIFIC SERIES.

NOW READY.

No. 1. FORMS OF WATER, in Clouds, Rain, Rivers, Ice, and Glaciers. By Prof. JOHN TYNDALL, LL. D., F. R. S. 1 vol. Cloth. Price, $1.50.

No. 2. PHYSICS AND POLITICS; or, Thoughts on the Application of the Principles of "Natural Selection" and "Inheritance" to Political Society. By WALTER BAGEHOT, Esq., author of "The English Constitution." 1 vol. Cloth. Price, $1.50.

No. 3. FOODS. By EDWARD SMITH, M. D., LL. B., F. R. S. 1 vol. Cloth. Price, $1.75.

No. 4. MIND AND BODY. The Theories of their Relation. By ALEX. BAIN, LL. D., Professor of Logic in the University of Aberdeen. 1 vol., 12mo. Cloth. Price, $1.50.

No. 5. THE STUDY OF SOCIOLOGY. By HERBERT SPENCER. Price, $1.50.

No. 6. THE NEW CHEMISTRY. By Prof. JOSIAH P. COOKE, Jr., of Harvard University. 1 vol., 12mo. Cloth. Price, $2.00.

No. 7. THE CONSERVATION OF ENERGY. By Prof. BALFOUR STEWART, LL. D., F. R. S. 1 vol., 12mo. Cloth. Price, $1.50.

No. 8. ANIMAL LOCOMOTION; or, Walking, Swimming, and Flying, with a Dissertation on Aëronautics. By J. BELL PETTIGREW, M. D., F. R. S., F. R. S. E., F. R. C. P. E. 1 vol., 12mo. Fully illustrated. Price, $1.75.

No. 9. RESPONSIBILITY IN MENTAL DISEASE. By HENRY MAUDSLEY, M. D. 1 vol., 12mo. Cloth. Price, $1.50.

No. 10. THE SCIENCE OF LAW. By Prof. SHELDON AMOS. 1 vol., 12mo. Cloth. Price, $1.75.

No. 11. ANIMAL MECHANISM. A Treatise on Terrestrial and Aërial Locomotion. By E. J. MAREY. With 117 Illustrations. Price, $1.75.

No. 12. THE HISTORY OF THE CONFLICT BETWEEN RELIGION AND SCIENCE. By JOHN WM. DRAPER, M. D., author of "The Intellectual Development of Europe." (*In press.*)

No. 13. THE CHEMISTRY OF LIGHT AND PHOTOGRAPHY. By Prof. VOGEL, Polytechnic Academy of Berlin. (*In press.*)

No. 14. ON PARASITES IN THE ANIMAL KINGDOM. By Mons. VAN. BENEDEN. (*In press.*)

No. 15. THE THEORY OF DESCENT AND DARWINISM. By Prof. OSCAR SCHMIDT, Strasburg University. (*In press.*)

Other eminent authors, as WALLACE, HELMHOLTZ, PARKS, MILNE-EDWARDS, and HAECKEL, have given strong encouragement that they will also take part in the enterprise.

D. APPLETON & CO., PUBLISHERS, 549 & 551 Broadway, N. Y.

International Scientific Series.

D. APPLETON & CO. have the pleasure of announcing that they have made arrangements for publishing, and have recently commenced the issue of, a SERIES OF POPULAR MONOGRAPHS, or small works, under the above title, which will embody the results of recent inquiry in the most interesting departments of advancing science.

The character and scope of this series will be best indicated by a reference to the names and subjects included in the subjoined list, from which it will be seen that the coöperation of the most distinguished professors in England, Germany, France, and the United States, has been secured, and negotiations are pending for contributions from other eminent scientific writers.

The works will be issued in New York, London, Paris, Leipsic, Milan, and St. Petersburg.

The INTERNATIONAL SCIENTIFIC SERIES is entirely an American project, and was originated and organized by Dr. E. L. Youmans, who spent the greater part of a year in Europe, arranging with authors and publishers. The forthcoming volumes are as follows:

Prof. LOMMEL (University of Erlangen), *Optics.* (In press.)

Rev. M. J. BERKELEY, M. A., F. L. S., and M. COOKE, M. A., LL. D., *Fungi; their Nature, Influences, and Uses.* (In press.)

Prof. W. KINGDON CLIFFORD, M. A., *The First Principles of the Exact Sciences explained to the non-mathematical.*

Prof. T. H. HUXLEY, LL. D., F. R. S., *Bodily Motion and Consciousness.*

Dr. W. B. CARPENTER, LL. D., F. R. S., *The Physical Geography of the Sea.*

Prof. WILLIAM ODLING, F. R. S., *The Old Chemistry viewed from the New Standpoint.*

W. LAUDER LINDSAY, M. D., F. R. S. E., *Mind in the Lower Animals.*

Sir JOHN LUBBOCK, Bart., F. R. S., *The Antiquity of Man.*

Prof. W. T. THISELTON DYER, B. A., B. Sc., *Form and Habit in Flowering Plants.*

Mr. J. N. LOCKYER, F. R. S., *Spectrum Analysis.*

Prof. MICHAEL FOSTER, M. D., *Protoplasm and the Cell Theory.*

Prof. W. STANLEY JEVONS, *Money: and the Mechanism of Exchange.*

H. CHARLTON BASTIAN, M. D., F. R. S., *The Brain as an Organ of Mind.*

Prof. A. C. RAMSAY, LL. D., F. R. S., *Earth Sculpture: Hills, Valleys, Mountains, Plains, Rivers, Lakes; how they were produced, and how they have been destroyed.*

Prof. RUDOLPH VIRCHOW (Berlin University), *Morbid Physiological Action.*

Prof. CLAUDE BERNARD, *Physical and Metaphysical Phenomena of Life.*

Prof. H. SAINTE-CLAIRE DEVILLE, *An Introduction to General Chemistry.*

Prof. WURTZ, *Atoms and the Atomic Theory.*

Prof. DE QUATREFAGES, *The Negro Races.*

Prof. LACAZE-DUTHIERS, *Zoology since Cuvier.*

Prof. BERTHELOT, *Chemical Synthesis.*

Prof. J. ROSENTHAL, *General Physiology of Muscles and Nerves.*

Prof. JAMES D. DANA, M. A., LL. D., *On Cephalization; or, Head-Characters in the Gradation and Progress of Life.*

Prof. S. W. JOHNSON, M. A., *On the Nutrition of Plants.*

Prof. AUSTIN FLINT, Jr., M. D., *The Nervous System and its Relation to the Bodily Functions.*

Prof. W. D. WHITNEY, *Modern Linguistic Science.*

Prof. C. A. YOUNG, Ph. D. (of Dartmouth College), *The Sun.*

Prof. BERNSTEIN (University of Halle), *Physiology of the Senses.*

Prof. FERDINAND COHN (Breslau University), *Thallophytes (Algæ, Lichens, Fungi).*

Prof. HERMANN (University of Zurich), *Respiration.*

Prof. LEUCKART (University of Leipsic), *Outlines of Animal Organization.*

Prof. LIEBREICH (University of Berlin), *Outlines of Toxicology.*

Prof. KUNDT (University of Strasburg), *On Sound.*

Prof. REES (University of Erlangen), *On Parasitic Plants.*

Prof. STEINTHAL (University of Berlin), *Outlines of the Science of Language.*

E. ALGLAVE (Professor of Constitutional and Administrative Law at Douai, and of Political Economy at Lille), *The Primitive Elements of Political Constitutions.*

P. LORAIN (Professor of Medicine, Paris), *Modern Epidemics.*

Prof. SCHÜTZENBERGER (Director of the Chemical Laboratory at the Sorbonne), *On Fermentations.*

Mons. DEBRAY, *Precious Metals.*

Redwood Library

SELECTIONS FROM THE RULES

1. Three volumes may be taken at a time and only three on one share. Two unbound numbers of a monthly and three numbers of a weekly publication are counted as a volume.

2. Books other than 7-day and 14-day ones may be kept out 28 days. **Books cannot be renewed or transferred.**

3. Books overdue are subject to a fine of one cent a day for fourteen days, **and five cents a day for each day thereafter.**

4. Neglect to pay the fine will debar from the use of the Library.

5. No book is to be lent out of the house of the person to whom it is charged.

6. Any person who shall soil (deface) or damage or lose a book belonging to the Library shall be liable to such fine as the Directors may impose; or shall pay the value of the book or of the set, if it be a part of a set, as the Directors may elect. All scribbling or any marking or writing whatever, folding or turning down the leaves, as well as cutting or tearing any matter from a book belonging to the Library, will be considered defacement and damage.